JOHN QUINCY ADAMS

The Critical Years:

1785-1794

John Quincy Adams

The Critical Years:

1785-1794

by

ROBERT A. EAST

BOOKMAN ASSOCIATES, INC.

NEW YORK 3

E
377
.E2

Library of Congress Catalog Card Number: 62-15530

Manufactured in the United States of America

TYPOGRAPHY BY ELECTRA COMPOSITION CORP.

To

Elsie and Frank

When John Quincy Adams spoke of a "critical period" in his commencement address at Harvard College in July, 1787, he justified later historians in their use of the phrase. The young graduate said that the problems facing America in this critical period demanded public faith, and he argued that a country's greatness is related to the maintenance of its credit.

That young Adams was undergoing a critical period of his own in these years may be seen in his private history. It is a story of trial and error and controversy in the life of a young man on his way to greatness. Only a few months after making his nationalistic commencement address he became opposed to the federal plan for national reform itself. (When reminded of this long afterwards, he was to label it a lesson in humiliation.) Several years later his controversial newspaper writings on the "rights of man" were to help precipitate political factions on a nation-wide scale. Other of his early writings supported a distinctively American viewpoint on the turbulent subject of foreign affairs.

In that portion of his life herein reviewed, personal and public problems were frequently related. Many of his experiences reflected problems of American society of that day, and sometimes his attitudes on public issues were a reflection of his private concerns. Definitions of purpose became clarified for both himself and his country only in the face of difficulties.

Our story takes up John Quincy Adams' career after he returned from Europe in 1785 as a youth of eighteen. We follow him through nine years until at the age of twenty-seven he was sent to Holland in 1794 on a diplomatic mission by President Washington. Periods of long residence abroad thus preceded and followed his residence as a young man in America. His experiences at home, however, returned him to Europe as a publicly recognized man.

The years under review are those of John Quincy's education at Harvard, of his study of law in Newburyport and early practice in Boston, and of his emergence as a notable contributor to the American press. They are years also marked by illness, by frequent depression of spirits, and by a love affair, by the writing of romantic poetry as well as of political prose, and by clubbing and roistering and attending the theater. A most revealing circumstance was the abandonment of his "literary" journal in the last six years, for this had been a deeply cherished project begun shortly before his return from Europe. Out of his confusion he found self-expression in taking those courageous stands on public affairs which were to characterize him for the rest of his life.

These were unusually difficult years also because he was in the process of becoming great under the most difficult of circumstances—being the son of a great man, and of a great mother, too. The ideas of the father were loyally supported by the son to the point that his own are sometimes almost indistinguishable. He had inherited the whole American Revolutionary ardor of John and Abigail Adams, but also their conservative code of political and personal behavior.

How well John Quincy Adams fared under this double burden in early manhood the reader may judge for himself. In the story of the nine years which follows, however, let the scars as well as the triumphs be noted. His critical period of life furnishes examples of both.

Let it be acknowledged also that it was his incredible industry and honesty in recording his thoughts and experiences—and of his descendants in preserving the records—which make this story possible.

This study, begun over a decade ago, has been variously encouraged. Once, when browsing in a bookstore (also a favorite pastime of young John Quincy Adams), I found a copy of the *Letters of Mrs. Adams* bearing the name of my old teacher, Evarts Boutell Greene. This I took to be a good omen. The release of the microfilm of the Adams family papers was an inestimable scholarly boon. The work itself was lightened by the interest of my friends. The manuscript was read in whole or part by R. Leith Skinner, M.D., of Greenwich, New York; by my son-in-law, James E. Mooney of Worcester, Massachusetts; by Reinhard Luthin of New York City, eminent biographer of Abraham Lincoln; and by Professor Joseph Dorfman, distinguished economic historian of Columbia University.

To my good friend and colleague, Professor Irving Raymond of Brooklyn College, and to his wife, Henrietta Dana Skinner Raymond, I am deeply indebted for critical reading and skilled literary assistance.

Among other colleagues at Brooklyn College, John Hope Franklin kindly read the manuscript; Morris Roberts furnished literary criticism; and Hans Trefousse and the late Solomon Frank Bloom gave steady encouragement.

The reader will please understand, however, that none of these good people is to be held responsible for any errors in this work. I claim full responsibility for these, myself.

Permission to quote from the microfilm of the Adams Papers was given through the courtesy of Mr. L. H. Butterfield for the Adams Manuscript Trust. Use of the microfilm was made possible through the facilities of the Columbia University School of Library Service, and the courtesy of its curator, Miss Darthula Wilcox.

The journal of Alice Tucker was read through the kindness of Mr. Gordon Hutchins of Punkatasset Farm, Concord, Massachusetts.

The historical repositories I have been privileged to use include the libraries of Brooklyn College and of Columbia

University; the New York Public Library and the New York Historical Society; the American Antiquarian Society of Worcester, the Massachusetts Historical Society of Boston, and the Public Library of Newburyport, Massachusetts.

Publication of this volume was assisted by a grant from the American Council of Learned Societies.

As I said on a similar occasion many years ago, I am above all indebted to my wife, Elizabeth Paddock East, in preparing this work. The words are an inadequate expression of gratitude to her, as is the dedication to our children.

New York City   Robert A. East
April, 1962

TABLE OF CONTENTS

There was, in truth, in J. Q. Adams,
a great deal of human nature.
—CHARLES FRANCIS ADAMS, JR.

CHAPTER ONE

RETURN TO BRAINTREE

"Such sentiments as a young
American ought to entertain"

A reader of the New York *Independent Journal* of July
20, 1785, would have found many references to the recent
American Revolution along with the usual news items of
human interest. In addition to being informed of the hang-
ing of a notorious counterfeiter, and of a husband who repu-
diated all debts contracted by a wife who had "eloped" from
his bed and board, the reader might have observed that the
American Congress was meeting in the city. He could have
considered an offer of "CASH" for certain of its depressed securities. He would have learned that debtors of a dissolved
war-contracting firm had to make payment immediately to
Alexander Hamilton, attorney-at-law, or be sued. An ob-
servant reader could hardly have failed to mark another
name made prominent by the Revolution, although in a
very different connection:

And on Sunday arrived his most Christian Majesty's Packet, Le
Courier de l'Amerique, in fifty-six days from l'Orient, com-
manded by Fournier, in whom came passenger, the son of the
Hon. John Adams, Esq., Minister Plenipotentiary from the
United States of America, to the United Netherlands.

The reference was of course to John Quincy Adams, a
young man who had just turned his eighteenth birthday
aboard ship. Originally he had come from the country town
of Braintree on the Massachusetts South Shore. In 1779 at

15

the age of twelve, together with a younger brother, he had
reluctantly accompanied his father on a diplomatic mission
to Europe for a second time. An earlier voyage to France
had only recently ended and the boy had wanted to stay
home to prepare for Harvard. He had been persuaded to
sail again by his mother, although she had long ago warned
him that "the great theatre of the world" upon which he
was entering so young was full of "temptations and vice." [1]

Wonderful indeed was the maternal influence exercised by
Abigail Adams! She would have preferred that her eldest
son find an ocean grave than become an immoral or grace-
less child, but had exhorted him to remember that these
were the times "when a genius would wish to live." [2] The
thought applied equally to herself. This eloquent daughter
of a country minister and his well-born Quincy wife in
eastern Massachusetts, had become the very embodiment of
the heroic matron in the American Revolution. She was the
adored and adoring wife of John Adams, a sturdy farmer's
son of the region who had gone to Harvard and become a
lawyer, a learned patriot, and the model for her sons.

John Quincy Adams had spent six romantic years in Europe—his brother became homesick and soon returned—as
a companion to his father and as a clerk for the American
envoy, Francis Dana. He had studied languages, politics,
and stage performances all the way from Cape Finisterre to
St. Petersburg and London, and studied also at the University of Leyden and under private tutors. The returning
youth was a prodigy of culture and learning, somewhat awkward in his Latin and in need of much more work in Greek
and perhaps mathematics.[3] Even more was he a prodigy in
morality, with which his parents had assiduously taught him
to identify patriotism.[4]

The young man had become uneasily aware of the ques-
tionable effects of long foreign residence, even though his
mother and sister had joined the family abroad after the

war. He had become more familiar with French than with his own language.[5] A foppish grandson of Dr. Franklin's seemed to him to have become more like a Frenchman than an American. It had been shocking to hear lovely, young Mrs. Bingham of Philadelphia say, "J'aime beaucoup mieux l'Europe que l'Amerique," although he charitably attributed this to the fact that her husband had grown rich from war-time privateering, and presumably for that reason was enjoying Europe to an exceptional degree.[6]

The decision to return to America had been John Quincy's own, although it should be noted also that his parents were sceptical about the state of morals at foreign universities. He looked forward with some dread to the long years and new experiences of "formal" study, first at Harvard where he hoped to enter the Junior class and then to the years preparing for the practice of law. Yet he was sure that in America, with a share of common sense, he could eventually make his own living and thus be *independent* and *free.*" [7] He already had a high respect for the economic verities, and was no doubt fully aware of the family feeling about the sacrifices made by his father in public service.

His was a courageous act for a youth, even for one who had for several years been fully conscious of having entered into manhood.[8] He confessed to himself that he was ambitious, although he hoped that his subject was laudable." [9] Dana had already noted that the young man seemed to feel "a certain superiority about himself." It is worth recording that the young man tended to neglect such criticism at the time! [10]

This opinionated but sensitive youth resembled his mother in features, but he had learned to strike a pose like his bellicose father—head cocked, one eye half-closed, his right hand in his pocket. He was fully aware of the responsibility of being his father's son, even though he was not naturally endowed with all the latter's strength. In person he was not elegant, being in this respect like his father, rather short and plump; but he was used to having his hair fashionably groomed and carried a sword like any European gentleman, a custom laid aside soon after his return.[11] Indeed, his manners must have been somewhat formal and European. When writing his mother, he had learned to address her very properly as "Dear Madam." Only years later did he regularly say "Dear Mother," the salutation that she preferred.[12] He was nevertheless coming home with high hopes for an American cultural renaissance in which he intended to participate. Litterature was already a passion with him and he had recently begun to keep an elaborate journal.[13]

Whatever of courage and self-importance John Quincy Adams brought back from Europe was going to be very important for his survival in America. He was about to be exposed to all the enervating influences of the native land he had never wanted to leave. First in a series of shocks was the heat of American summer, such as he had not known for years and towards which he showed some of his mother's nervous sensitivity.[14] There was also to be a steady challenge to his self-esteem, which a few years later was to come near causing tragedy. Within a year the appearance of this young cosmopolite was so changed that in addition to loss of weight, his dirty linen and long fingernails aroused mirth and compassion in a female cousin when she saw him at college.[15] Finally, this habitual companion of older people was about to be exposed to the company of numerous young persons, with all the problems of passion and of "sensibility" which this implied. In the struggle between sense and sensibility, John Quincy Adams was to be saved only by pride and prejudice in that corrosive American society for which he so ardently yearned.

The "tedious" voyage of eight weeks on *Le Courier* which John Quincy took in 1785 would seem to have been a perfect time for nostalgic reflection, as he bade farewell to a

brilliant European society. If this was so, there is no evidence of it in his meticulous journal. On the contrary, it is
full of observations of weather and trade winds of the south-
ern route from l'Orient, of considerations whether a lightning chain at the masthead was large enough to be any good,
and, above all, of judgments on the character of his ship-
mates. The most sentimental observation on the entire voyage is that recorded on July 4, in which he apostrophized
his native land. "I wished very much to arrive in America
before this day, which is the greatest day in the year for
every true American, the anniversary of our Independence.
May heaven preserve it. . . ." He concluded with a quatrain
of patriotic verse.[16]

Earlier in the voyage he had committed himself to a stranger form of patriotic expression, the more revealing because
it showed him in his precocious role of moralizer. One of
the ship's officers was an egotistic Frenchman whom young
Adams suspected of having lost all tender feelings because
of the life he had led, and who moreover had made the
shocking statement that he cared not what would happen
to the whole universe, once he was dead. What was even
worse, he had during the war married an American girl.
John Quincy gravely reflected, "It does not give me pleasure
to see my Countrywomen form such connections but as he
will never settle in America, the harm is not great." [17] One
might almost conclude from this that he considered it preferable for a sailor to have a girl in every port, than to have
him permanently contaminating America through marital
fidelity! In any case, an almost unbelievably idealized concept of America emerges from his odd reflection.

It would be entirely wrong to conclude, however, that the
returning native was a naïve young man, ill-equipped to
recognize the raw character of men and affairs in the turbulent republic which was sighted on July 16 above the Jersey
heights of the Neversink River. Idealization of country did

not blind him to faults which he was sure existed in America as elsewhere; and he had not been long ashore when he was writing of a distinguished visitor that she probably was leaving the country with a lower opinion of American virtues than she had held on her arrival.[18]

Nor was he simply a moral prig. His youthful journals, for all of their maxim-book character, are enlivened with flashes of dry humor, and however straitlaced his private reflections, his egoism did not detract from his sense of humanity or love of the society of his fellow men. It is noteworthy that while in New York City, he occasionally went back to *Le Courier* so long as the packet remained in port to dine with the captain and ship's officers. He also tried to assist one of his less desirable fellow passengers, a quarrelsome and eccentric person of dirty appearance and mysterious habits, when the latter's trunk was seized by the customs officials. He had originally observed that this poor fellow had a "good heart." But when he found that his rather simple attempt at influence had failed in clearing the subject, he merely recorded, with obvious approval, that "in this country the laws are supreme to everything." [19] Apparently this had not been his experience with the European customs.

After two busy, warm weeks in New York, occasionally enlivened by a swim in the North River, young Adams wrote his father, newly established in London as minister to Great Britain, that "in this place I hear nothing but politics." [20] This was unquestionably true in one sense, although it left out of account the remarkable social life of a quite nonpolitical sort that he was also beginning to enjoy, despite some difficulty he was having in adjusting to the manners of Americans. As in the fable of "The Miller, His Son, and Their Ass," he said that he was finding it difficult to please; he had to avoid exciting people's derision by showing too much formality, or giving offense by showing too little.[21]

Politics could not have been avoided even if John Quincy

had so desired since he had brought despatches to many important persons, including John Jay, the Secretary of Foreign Affairs, with whom he at once renewed his boyhood acquaintance in Europe.[22] There were also old friends of his father among the officials and members of the Congress, especially the Massachusetts and Virginia delegates, with whom he now became acquainted. Among these were the affable Rufus King, and young James Monroe who apparently developed a real liking for him.[23] Mr. Jay invited him to stay at his home, but Richard Henry Lee of Virginia, the President of the Congress, was so insistent on his taking an "apartment" at his house that he felt constrained to settle there. He sometimes attended the President's formal dinners with as many as twenty-five men of affairs present.

Politics were indeed in the air. There were rumors of economic and political crises and talk of the "universally considered" necessity that the states give commercial power to Congress. However, it is interesting to note that President Lee himself vigorously opposed this, one reason being his hope that such persons as John Adams could get favorable concessions abroad, even on the difficult subject of pre-war debts.[24] Men like Secretary of Congress Thomson, who was many years John Quincy's senior, drank tea with him or took evening strolls on "the batteries," no doubt to listen to his youthful but informed accounts of European affairs, or stories of his much admired Jefferson and of Dr. Franklin. A congressman from Virginia urged him to study law in the South under the celebrated Chancellor Wythe. This would be good for the Union. General Henry Knox at his lovely home outside the city was "vastly polite." It was all very flattering and politically very interesting, and helped to delay his departure for Boston.

There were other interesting distractions, however, in the affairs of polite society, especially those involving young American ladies. Young Adams now entered upon a brief social career which he obviously enjoyed wholeheartedly, although New Yorkers in their manners seemed to him to resemble Europeans too much.[25] He entered upon a continuous round of tea drinking and entertainment which furnished exceptional opportunities for the study of the female character, that most fascinating of intellectual pursuits. It was the beginning of what was to be his principal avocation in the years ahead—the enjoyment of feminine company invariably followed by devastating analysis. The critical study of his fellow beings was not new to him, of course, but its possibilities in the female department were now vastly extended. One obstacle to admiration was the painful fact that almost all of the "finest girls" in and about New York had been pro-British during the war.[26] His "New York" journal is enlivened with his opinions of the young ladies he met, some of whom were "very fine," "amiable in character," or "perfect beauties"; but more often "great talkers," "too much the coquette," or "too affected" for his taste.

His interest in the fair sex did not cease even at church. When at service in St. Paul's Chapel, while he always carefully noted the text, he also carefully noted the young ladies and their beaux. On an overnight trip to Jamaica, Long Island, he met the interesting female relatives of Colonel William Smith, a former aide-de-camp of Washington. The Colonel had recently joined the Adamses in London as secretary to the American legation and presently was to be the successful suitor of sister Nabby Adams. Of the Colonel's own four or five young sisters, only Sally was really handsome in John Quincy's opinion. He was to become better acquainted with this attractive girl in the future. Indeed, she eventually married his brother Charles.

Back in the city he sometimes found it difficult to escape from President Lee's "musical evenings," as he sought younger and more attractive company.[27] One group, with whom he sometimes met at a private home of an evening,

featured a young lady who sang with particular grace, even
if not in a clear, strong voice. She sang a song of her own
composition, "One fond kiss before we part," with the accompaniment of a harpsichord played by the most skilled of the
ladies in town. What John Quincy particularly admired was
that the soloist performed without requiring to be urged "as
some Ladies do." At the end of the second performance, "she
sung so prettily that when I returned home, instead of continuing my Satirical lines, I immediately began upon the
most insipid style of panegyric; but a few days will cure
me," he laconically added. True enough, he soon began to
lose enthusiasm for the singer and to find that she was not
free from that affectation which he had found some ladies
mistook for grace. He does not tell us whether the oft-
repeated song had begun to pall.

One evening another young miss, who had a sweetness in
her countenance which he said he preferred to beauty,
showed him a catalogue of satirical verses on the belles of
the city, entitled "A Receipt for a Wife." He did not think
it witty, but was again moved to become "poetaster" and to
try his own hand at something similar. The results were
rather mixed. Although he could see that he had "no talent
at all at versifying," he wryly confessed to a partiality for
his own efforts, probably fair and honest self-criticism. It is
possible that the "Receipt" also gave him the idea for his
own celebrated poem, "A Vision," which he was to compose
several years later.[28] His deep interest in satire was partly
due to the agreement he and sister Nabby had made before
he left England to keep each other informed in their letters
about the "characters" they encountered.[29] Indeed, John
Quincy was to do this so exhaustively as far as young American ladies were concerned that eventually his sister was
moved to protest against his strictures. He was too prone to
make quick judgments about people, she said.[30]

His lament was fast becoming, "When shall I see a beauty

without any conceit?" [31] But he was riding for a fall. A certain young lady, bearing one of the great family names of colonial New York, seemed at first meeting to be a great talker who actually said very little. Such superficiality, he graciously acknowledged, must necessarily be pardoned in a lady. Two weeks later he found himself liking her somewhat better, and even walked with her on "the Mall" in Broadway. The next day when he took tea at her home he endeavored to excuse himself for not having waited on her before, but was merely told for his pains that he would have done better to have made no apology at all! Several days later he made a cutting remark about the young lady in his journal, which was no doubt a sop to his wounded vanity.

It was now well into August and high time for John Quincy Adams to leave the pleasures of New York and to set out for Yankee land and home. Since he had arrived in the country too late to make the Harvard Commencement in July, there had been little need for haste. It was possible to take a packet to Providence, but friends advised him to make the trip overland so as to form an opinion of the country and to make useful acquaintances. He also had many letters to deliver in Connecticut, especially those of Colonel David Humphreys, a native son in France. John Quincy traveled in company with a young friend, Le Ray de Chaumont, who had also just arrived from Europe. The young Frenchman had carried a petition to Congress from the merchants of France and had a letter from John Adams introducing him in Boston. He and John Quincy must have had similarly sophisticated tastes since they recently had been reading *Aesop's Fables* in French together.[32] Chaumont had a two horse chaise while Adams had bought a rather expensive horse for Chaumont's servant to ride. It turned out to be an unreliable beast that had a tendency to fall down, but after a second start the two friends finally got off on August 13. John Quincy's horse continued to stumble and refused to work in the chaise, while Chaumont's horses frequently got galled. Since the weather was abominably hot and the roads invariably poor, in these respects it was a bad trip.[33] John Quincy found the weather especially trying.

The route followed was the main road through Stamford, New Haven, Hartford, and Springfield to Boston, with occasional stops between towns or, more accurately, cities, since many Connecticut towns were getting incorporated as they prepared to cope with new problems of the post-war era. Some of these places were of the greatest interest to the young ex-expatriate. New Haven, of course, had a college to visit, headed by the "curious" Dr. Stiles. He was very polite but called to mind Jefferson's characterization that he was an example of the deepest learning without a spark of genius. There were other distinguished men to be met en route. Notable was the eminent Colonel Jeremiah Wadsworth of Hartford who had made a large fortune as agent for the French forces during the Revolution, and to whom John Quincy had already delivered in New York some business information on behalf of the Marquis de la Fayette. Wadsworth, who invited the young travelers to dine, lived in a "very elegant manner." [34] In Hartford, also, there was an old fellow scholar and boyhood traveler, Jesse Deane, the son of the apostate Silas. John Quincy stoutly averred that he would have been ashamed to miss him.

On Sundays, no doubt, the young travelers found ample evidence that Connecticut deserved its national reputation for psalm singing. On the other hand, in one place at least, changed times had brought to the "land of steady habits" no less than a dancing master, and formal balls at which a visitor might see a few genteel ladies who were "favoured by nature." [35]

The most thrilling experience of the entire trip was the discovery of a literary renaissance centered in Hartford. There John Quincy went into a bookseller's shop—this had been a favorite practice of his in Europe—and purchased a new publication he had heard was of high caliber, *The Conquest of Canaan*. This ponderous epic poem of America had been written by a Connecticut man, the Reverend Mr. Timothy Dwight. The affable Colonel Wadsworth also made him a present of *M'Fingal,* a comical, poetic treatment of Revolutionary Toryism by the celebrated local, Mr. John Trumbull. This gentleman had once been a law student of John Adams *pere,* who was the model of the patriot in the poem. After Trumbull received a letter from John Quincy, he sat in conversation with him for two hours, in the course of which they discovered a mutual lack of partiality for Voltaire.

Young Adams considered these poems extremely important, the "two pieces in which American's have endeavour'd most to soar as high as European bards." [36] *M'Fingal,* he had heard, was generally agreed to be equal if not superior to Butler's *Hudibras*. Of the other no criticism had as yet appeared, doubtless owing to its recent publication. In the course of the following winter in snowbound Haverhill, Massachusetts, John Quincy was to devote many a social evening to reading aloud *The Conquest of Canaan* to assembled company, and to spend long hours analyzing its contents for the dubious benefit of his journal. These works, he was sure, were glorious achievements, a justification of American culture, if admittedly open to some criticism. They were a source of great pride to the returning American who had plenty of ink in his own blood.

The trip was now approaching its grand climax as Yankee land unfolded with its blunt-mannered but familiar people.[37] Springfield was reached and passed, despite even poorer roads; and on August 25, by dint of an early start they made the final forty-two miles to Boston, arriving at lodgings on State Street at nine o'clock that night. John Quincy recalled that this last day of his trip was St. Louis's Day in France, a time of a very un-American sort of celebration. The next day was one of the happiest he had ever known. He met friends of his childhood and some of his dearest relatives, including his younger brother Charles who had sailed with him to Europe so long ago. No one without his experience, he recorded, could conceive how much pleasure there was "in returning to our Country after an absence of 6 years, especially when it was left at the time of life that I did, when I went last to Europe." [38] How much interest his countrymen, other than his relatives, took in his return is unfortunately not clear. At least one Boston paper had copied the news of his arrival in New York, but another had rather obviously ignored it.[39]

Braintree, seven miles distant on the South Shore, was the ultimate goal, but first he delivered a letter from the enterprising Marquis de la Fayette to Mr. Samuel Breck, another prosperous war-time agent of the French forces in America. This presumably was on the same business that the Marquis had addressed to Colonel Wadsworth—a joint-stock scheme for organizing the American whale oil trade with France.[40] Then he took off in the chaise on the gala last leg of the journey, accompanied by Chaumont and the French consul, first visiting gouty Governor Hancock at Dorchester, Lieutenant Governor Cushing and his lady, and then Mr. and Mrs. James Swan, the latter gentleman still another business agent of France. From there John Quincy went on alone, first to the Warrens at Milton and then to see his "honoured Grandmamma" at Uncle Adams' house. (For some reason he recorded that he was sure that she greeted him as warmly as anyone else.) Finally he arrived at his Aunt and Uncle Cranch's in Braintree. There he was introduced to their roomer, Mr. Tyler, a young local lawyer.

Alas for the irony in human affairs! Had John Quincy Adams only known, he would have hailed this last acquaintance as the real answer to the literary part of his American Odyssey. Royall Tyler was to become more successful in demonstrating the literary glories of his native land than all of the pretentious Connecticut Wits together. He was to be the author only two years later of "The Contrast," a dramatic satire on British manners and the first genuinely popular work by an American playwright. The irony was all the greater since John Quincy was to see a good deal of Mr. Tyler in the busy month that followed, for this congenial neighbor was the favored suitor of sister Nabby Adams—or at least had been until Nabby had been whisked off to Europe by her parents the year before. John Quincy even innocently read bits of her letters aloud for Tyler's benefit, despite the sad truth that the "engagement" had already been terminated on a unilateral basis in London where Nabby was being exposed to the dangerous charms of Colonel Smith. However, this news had not yet been received in Braintree.

> Why should our thoughts to distant countries roam
> When each refinement may be found at home?

the indignant Tylor was to ask in "The Contrast." Nabby's problem of having her parents interfere with her love life foreshadowed the romantic difficulties of John Quincy Adams himself a few years later.[41]

The long trip was now over. The Braintree home of John Quincy's yeoman ancestors and of much of his boyhood had been reached at last. The next day being Sunday, he dutifully fell into old habits and attended Mr. Wiberd's familiar meetings in the North Precinct Church, both morning and afternoon. The effeminate old bachelor preacher was to get hold of him as soon as possible to ask a host of questions, mostly concerning the women of the countries he had visited, because, as he sarcastically said, he always asked about the best things first.[42] There were surprisingly few new faces in the congregation except, of course, for the youngsters. His cousin, Billy Cranch, who was his own age and already at Harvard, he found greatly altered, but was told that he, too, had changed as much. Finally in late afternoon, accompanied by the attentive Mr. Tyler, he went to see his old home on the farm at the foot of Penn's Hill. It looked so lonely and empty that he could not bear to stay long; but he characteristically paid a visit to the library which he found in fairly good order. The memory of the place moved him to write a nostalgic letter to his mother, although she had told him several times that she wanted no sentimentality in his letters from America.[43]

His own conduct and modesty throughout this trying period greatly pleased his Aunt Mary Cranch, who was charmed with his appearance. She was sure that he had been "formed for a Statesman," like his father. But his manner must have been a bit overwhelming, for Aunt Mary rather oddly added that his keen "penetration" into character was so amazing that she was glad she had nothing to hide! So at least she wrote his mother. His excessive curiosity was to be noted by another relative.[44]

On returning to Boston the next day, the young "statesman" became more acutely aware than perhaps he had been of the commercial problems disturbing his fellow countrymen. He learned the horrid news of the business failure of Mr. Samuel Otis, another war-time contractor and the son-in-law of Uncle Isaac Smith, with whom he had dined only two days before. He gloomily reflected that it would not be long before every merchant in Boston would fail, for they seemed to be breaking, one after the other.

The days immediately following must have been equally depressing. Next morning John Quincy attended the State Supreme Court and heard Chief Justice Cushing—he was as dignified, he said, as Lord Mansfield in England—charge the grand jury in a case involving post-war neglect of public education exhibited by so many towns. Then he took the trip to Cambridge where he laconically noted that brother Charles had acquired "additional importance" since entering Harvard. The next day was devoted to exploring the college, where he found the library good but not really excellent. He did admire some very fine portraits by Mr. Copley, Boston's famous expatriate artist whom he had met in England.

At last came the all important interview with dignified President Willard, to whom John Quincy bore a letter from his father who had been in correspondence about him. After a perfunctory examination in cetrain classical works with which he was not well acquainted—he later rather resentfully said that he had not read "certain" books—the President advised him to return in the spring and then offer for the Junior Sophister class. So that phase of his trip ended in a certain personal deflation, despite the opinion of one of his relatives that Harvard should have felt honored to have had him apply there! [45]

Lighter spirits soon reasserted themselves. While driving one of his female cousins to Braintree soon afterwards, John Quincy sang strange songs and indulged in such antics that she was sure that people thought him a "crazy creature." [46] Back in Boston the day after his rejection at Cambridge, together with friend Chaumont and the inevitable French consul, he attended the Concert Hall where a "forenoon" ball was held from one to three in the afternoon, and where "all the beauties of Boston seemed to be assembled" in "one bright Constellation." So he could not have been too dejected. His final activity with Chaumont, who was now preparing to leave, was to play a game of billiards.

Soon it was time for sophisticated if somewhat deflated John Quincy Adams to leave also. He had to take a trip of about thirty miles to the little town of Haverhill in northern Massachusetts to arrange with Reverend Uncle Shaw for several months of tutoring preparatory to offering again at Harvard. In the course of making that journey he passed through Concord and Lexington, and was moved to deep patriotic reflection, that these little known places had been rendered forever memorable by the blood of the first martyrs in "the

glorious cause of American Liberty." The tribute was accompanied by a learned observation which no doubt was natural
for a traveler to make, that posterity would revere this spot
more than the Dutch did the place where Egmont and Hoorn
had been martyred. This was, he studiously recorded, at
Brussels.[47]

When John Quincy had been about to leave France in
April, his father had written Cousin Samuel Adams about the
prospects of the long-absent youth. Sam would recall how he
once had led the child about Boston Common teaching him
to hate the British troops and to applaud the town militia:
John Adams had expressed the hope that his son would again
be instructed by the kind of political company that would
"inspire him with such sentiments as a young American
ought to entertain." [48] From the record of the long journey
home which John Quincy Adams had now completed, it
seems fitting to conclude that such feelings had never left
him; that he was a very paragon of Americanism, one in
whom foreign experience, despite its cultural impact, had
merely sharpened national consciousness.

CHAPTER TWO

WINTER IN HAVERHILL

"I have not to reproach
myself with Vice"

The winter of 1785 in Haverhill was a setting worthy of
Whittier's youth. If the residents of Reverend Mr. John
Shaw's home were never exactly "snowbound," they did experience a season of remarkable vicissitudes of weather, beginning with the great rains of October when the Merrimac
rose even higher than during the freshet of '45. There followed freakish snowstorms with intermittent thaws and the
savage onslaughts of the coldest weather ever known.[1] Young
John Quincy Adams was afraid one day in early December
that the cold had ruined his horse, and a month later he was
wishing for a thermometer such as he once had in St. Petersburg so that he could compare the local temperature with
that in Russia. Such weather, and especially the heavy snow
which he dreaded because of its "dull lifeless sameness," [2]
could hardly have added to a peace of mind already disturbed
for a number of reasons.

There were other aspects of the residence of the Reverend
Mr. Shaw which would also have appealed to Whittier. It
was a religious household, primarily of happy people, but
with its full share of human drama that year, both without
and within. The minister's wife, Elizabeth, a younger sister
of Abigail Adams, was to be remembered years later by her
nephew as worthy of canonization. She was withal a romantic
and spirited creature if what critics said was true—and apparently even saints can have critics—that she preferred white

bread to brown at tea! [3] However, the Reverend John Shaw
of the First Parish Church could not have afforded his slender
wife [4] many such luxuries even if he would, being in a profession so abominably paid that he eked out a living only
with the aid of boarders and students. Among these was
young John Quincy Adams himself from October, 1785, to
March of the following year. Mr. Shaw is said to have been a
minister of the Calvinist system, his preaching evangelical.[5]
His wife's nephew thought his preaching satisfactory if not
really admirable.[6] Some of the townspeople, however, refused
to come to meeting when Mr. Shaw was in the pulpit, an old
custom on the part of the religiously disgruntled. Such ill-
will hurt the good man deeply.

The Reverend Mr. Shaw, for all of his goodness, was in
personal affairs "no chicken," as Fielding might have said—
and John Quincy knew his Fielding well enough to have
identified the reference.[7] Shaw told John Quincy bluntly that
he was presumptuous for his age, when his student in the
classics wanted to argue about matters of theology. Indeed, he
"thought it a little strange, that at 19 a youth should make
such positive decisions, in opposition, to persons much older
. . . ." [8] He criticized young Adams' "uncharitable" way of
thinking because he challenged the ideas of persons who had
made a lifetime study of theology. [9] In the first instance John
Quincy was contrite, acknowledging his reputation for being
obstinate, dogmatic, and pedantic; but on the second occasion
he was more belligerent than ever. He wanted to know why
any authority, simply because of age, should persuade him
that black was the color of white, although he admitted that
he judged colors "only as they strike my senses." [10] This qualification was probably a concession to the teaching of John
Locke, for in recent weeks he had been puzzling over the
Essay Concerning Human Understanding, a work he knew
would be required when he applied to the upper Junior class
at Harvard.

The gist of the dispute lay in young Adams' contention that the self is the ultimate motive for all human actions. He refused to accept the idea of everlasting torment for actions beyond human control, or any notion that to him suggested an imperfect deity. Small wonder that he irked his Calvinist uncle! He had gone so far in his private thoughts as to conclude that a liberal attitude in religious matters could not be expected from a pulpit; and that while the clergy criticized the "palpable absurdities of the Romish church"—he himself had been at pains to remark them in Europe—"they fall into others equally ridiculous and the never failing source of texts from Scripture is continually produced." [11] Part of the difficulty, he was persuaded, came from unscholarly translations, a thought prompted by a recent discussion he had had of Channing's *Universal Salvation*—with one of his uncle's critical neighbors.

More suggestive than the actual subject of the dispute was the date of its eruption. It came towards the end of John Quincy's tutoring period, after four months at the Shaw residence. It revealed an irritability and restlessness that had steadily been growing upon him, producing strong opinions on many subjects. Trying personal experiences both at home and in the town were no doubt contributing factors.

In this connection it should be remembered that John Quincy had been steadily engaged in a "cramming" program of study, primarily in reviewing his knowledge of the classics in the hope of being admitted to Harvard with advanced standing in the spring. This program had begun with a month of work in Greek grammar, a study which he utterly detested. He then read the New Testament in Greek except the Gospel of Mark from which he anticipated no trouble; also Homer's *Iliad* and the *Cyropedia* of Xenophon, the latter a "crabbed piece of work" with which he wrestled for two months. Latin review was fortunately more enjoyable—the *Ecologues* of Virgil, the *Odes* and *Satires* of Horace, and then

several plays of Terrence. These at least appealed to his poetic instincts. They also gave him a wonderful opportunity
for moralizing on the subject of ancient compared with modern times. In this contrast he favored the modern, primarily
because of its superiority in religion. During the last three
months of the program he devoted Saturday afternoons to
reading Watts' *Logick,* with its baffling study of syllogisms,
and to the work of the "Pyrhonistic" Mr. Locke. This was
more or less the assigned reading already undertaken by the
Junior class at Harvard.[12]

All this preparation was done in what must have been a
rather crowded house, and one likely to have been either
overheated or freezing cold. In addition to his aunt and uncle
and presumably their children, his youngest brother Tommy
was living there. One and sometimes two female boarders
were also present. In his chamber overlooking what would
have been the village green in summertime,[13] John Quincy
attempted to keep a rigorous schedule of about ten hours of
study a day, but found this almost impossible. It was hard to
get started early by reason of household noise. He then fell
into the habit of rising late, between eight and nine o'clock
—perhaps also a result of European influence—and hence accomplished less in the morning than at night. When he conscientiously tried to do with fewer hours of sleep, he found
that it could not be done.[14]

Though this carefully ruled household normally retired
after prayers at nine o'clock in the evening, John Quincy
customarily worked at his desk until midnight or one A.M.,
concluding his day by making entries in his journal or writing letters. Once he "burnt his fingers, stubbed his toes" and
retired at two o'clock. Probably flickering candles dimly lit
the chilly room. His friends became deeply concerned over
his health.[15]

By the first week of January his eyes had become so sore
that one day he could neither read nor write except, presum-

ably, to make a journal entry to that effect. The soreness was
an early warning of a weakness in his eyes from which he was
to suffer over the years, an ailment perhaps reflecting an intense emotional strain he was undergoing, or perhaps caused
by an inheritance on the maternal side.[16] With such a routine
of work he had not unnaturally lost weight after arriving in
Haverhill.[17] By the middle of January he was looking forward eagerly to the end of his period of tutoring, although
for other reasons than his studies.

All this might have made "Jack" a very dull boy, indeed,
had it not been for a social life somehow sandwiched in between study hours albeit on a reduced scale from what he
had previously known. On Sunday evenings it was customary
for country ministers to have company. Occasionally John
Quincy read poetry aloud of an evening to the ladies. Among
the selections was Dwight's *Conquest of Canaan,* the patriotic
epic he was digesting for his journal. From the journal itself
he once read aloud his critical comments upon the follies of
young ladies! He also sang French songs for their amusement.[18] Then there were local residents who invited the
neighbors for tea and sometimes even for whist, although
John Quincy himself had turned against cards as too wasteful
of time for men, if not for ladies. The Whites, who had a
three storied mansion on Water Street, with whom his cousin,
Eliza Cranch, was visiting, were the most prominent and hospitable of the local gentry. A number of younger people in
the neighborhood also had an occasional romp of an evening,
playing "cross questions," "drop the handkerchief," and other
games.[19]

Above all there were opportunities for conversation with
neighbors and with visitors coming from the nearby commercial towns of Newburyport and Salem. Although these
talks were often insipid, there were more serious discussions
on religious subjects, or dreadful complaints about the "decay of trade" and the dangers of paper money. On at least one
occasion, John Quincy expressed scepticism about such "com-

monplace" economic observations, in light of what he thought
was the absence of any real distress. Despite the "groaning"
of the merchants he had heard it "whispered" that times were
actually getting better.[20] But as has been suggested, he was
becoming argumentative on many topics. Tommy said to him
one day, "I think, Brother, you seem to differ most always
from everyone else in company." [21]

One source of change and comfort to the opinionated
young scholar was the occasional company of his cousin, Mr.
John Thaxter. This fledgling lawyer of Haverhill had been
a tutor of his youth while Thaxter was studying law with
John Adams. He had also been a companion of John Quincy's
on the trip to Europe in 1779. Thaxter must have been a
pleasant source of reminiscence, but at the present time he
was of special interest. Despite his continual debating of the
wisdom of marriage and the silly deportment of lovers, Thaxter was reported to have become attached to the "beauty" of
the town.

Once or twice there were sleighing parties. Then, after the
first of the year, assemblies for dancing, which scandalized the
Baptist preacher and various other good folk. In the eyes of
cosmopolitan young Adams these critics were simply envious
persons who disliked seeing others amuse themselves. Employing specious excuses, such persons, he thought, merely
wished to meddle in the affairs of other people, "which mankind in general are too prone to." [22] Dark hours for dark
deeds, seemed to sum up the suspicions of the narrow-minded.
Unfortunately for the cause of the dance some of the participants lacked "prudence." A few days after one assembly, during which a "misfortune befel one of the Ladies," a "scandalous Advertisement" was found one morning fastened on a
signpost, causing more disagreeableness. At the next assembly
John Quincy himself did not dance all evening.[23] Perhaps it
was another manifestation of his growing uneasiness and discontent.

It had been unfortunately true from the very beginning of

his Haverhill residence that John Quincy had occasionally shown signs of depressed spirits—a new experience to him, he said.[24] This was, after all, the first period of rest he had known since his return to America only three months before. Such spirits were perhaps a natural reaction for a sophisticated youth who after six years of foreign travel had been entombed in a little New England town. His stay had also been disturbed from the first by his interest in the pardonable but dangerous study of female character, no longer based on casual meetings wtih a variety of young ladies such as he had briefly known in New York,[25] but on daily association with an attractive household companion. Finally, soon after arriving in Haverhill he had witnessed a local tragedy arising out of mental illness, a subject that always fascinated him but which also helped to put him in a darkened mood.[26]

One of the first beauties he had met in Haverhill was the daughter of a prominent neighbor, a young person who the previous winter had "distress'd her Parents" by being seized with "a melancholy." The girl had recovered in the spring, and while she still showed symptoms of her disorder by a great curiosity as well as by absent-mindedness, she now exhibited an unusual flow of spirits.[27] This paradox aroused John Quincy's deepest interest and sympathy—quite unnecessarily it would seem since the girl was soon to enter upon what apparently turned out to be a very respectable married career. It evoked from him a theory of mental health:

When a scale is weigh'd down on one side, it is extremely difficult to lighten it immediately just as much as is necessary to make the balance just; the danger is that the other side should in its turn weigh down.[28]

"To make the balance just." It was an ideal that young John Quincy was also trying to set for himself, with indifferent success in Haverhill. A balance between passion and reason was to be a most desirable guide for his own immediate future. Within three weeks he was admitting to himself "a degree of Melancholy which may be owing to my having been so much confined these three or four days, but I rather imagine proceeds from another cause. When our Reason is at variance with our heart, the mind cannot be in a pleasing state." [29]

This was a new aspect to melancholy. Meantime a most depressing event happened almost before his eyes. One evening at a neighbor's there was present a lady who because of illness had for two or three months "been deprived of her Reason." This must have made for rather strange company— but no stranger than the aftermath. About half an hour after the lady had left with her husband, the latter rushed back to say that she had disappeared from home. It was feared that she had "gone to the river" since she had attempted this twice before. The whole neighborhood was aroused to find her, but to no avail until the next day when, indeed, it was too late, for the lady had finally succeeded in drowning herself.[30]

Such shocking news affected people in different ways, although in the Puritan world the idea of death itself was almost gloomily venerated. (No lest zestful person than Abigail Adams herself frequently acknowledged that preparation for death is the chief business of life.[31]) Some persons in Haverhill resignedly said that the tragedy merely demonstrated God's inscrutable wisdom. John Quincy himself tried to philosophize away the lady's loss of reason on the grounds that it might at least make other people sensible of their own; but even he confessed the next day that his spirits had never been so depressed. The suicide cast a pall over the whole neighborhood, even postponing the advent of dancing assemblies.

Occasionally there were other local tragedies such as the accidental death of a young friend of Tommy's. But the worst of all emotional suffering was a disturbance raised by the presence of a lady boarder, a miss of seventeen named Nancy who had lost her parents and had been residing with the Shaws for a year. While still abroad John Quincy had heard from

his sister about this girl, and the first time he met her he was
strangely affected. "She appears to have something peculiar
in her character," he thought, and he was wild to know what
she wrote about him a few days later to his cousin Lucy
Cranch in Braintree. Her critical faculties also made an immediately favorable impression when she scored off a neighboring minister, no less, for not paying enough attention to
his wife! John Quincy ordinarily qualified any admiration he
might have for such outspokenness, especially in religious
matters—that is, in other people than himself—and especially
on the part of young ladies. But in this case he gave whole-
hearted assent, agreeing that the minister's looks alone were
enough to "chill one on a hot day," and that he acted more
like a Dutchman than an American.[33] Here was an international touch, reflecting the broadening influence of his recent
travels!

At times there were two female boarders at the Shaws, who
interspersed their residence with visits to neighbors. The
elder was his cousin Eliza Cranch. At twenty-one she was not
exactly a beauty but a very sweet girl of vivacious imagination which, happily, she had not indulged in reading "un-
meaning novels or unmoral plays." Now John Quincy knew
all about these diversions and agreed with the best opinion
of the day that they were the principal cause of the loss of
female virtue. Cousin Eliza had come from Braintree primarily to visit Peggy White, who had a new harpsichord
which they intended to study together. By accident or design
her visit coincided almost exactly with that of John Quincy.
He regarded her almost as a sister; she kept not only an admiring but a very sharp eye upon him. Indeed, it was Cousin
Eliza who had immediately sent out the alarm to Aunt Abigail in London that Nancy's presence in the Shaw household
created a "dangerous situation" for Cousin John. The female
Cranches seem to have made it their special duty to keep

their cousin Adamses from entanglements in love. However, Eliza herself had several unfortunate affairs, including one even at Haverhill.

Undeniably disturbing was charming Nancy. She, too, was not exactly a beauty, but she had "one of the most expressive Countenances, I have ever seen; her shape is uncommonly fine and her eye seems to have magic in it." This girl was simply "bewitching." She also had a kind heart, he was sure, only one insensible of the pain she caused when she led her admirers on by declaring that her heart was free. She had been in company in Boston too young, and had obviously known too much admiration. Like Eliza she read a good deal but unfortunately "not with so much advantage, as she would, had she not been drawn so young into the stream of Dissipation." It was a common fault in the upbringing of young ladies in America, John Quincy said, a situation not tolerated in Europe.[35]

Such then was the kind of girl who deeply affected this Puritanical young cosmopolite—a sprightly, attractive co-quette who not only read novels but had been exposed to the "dissipated" society of Boston! She probably also was a bru-nette since he was not attracted by blondes—at least not at this time.

Within a month of his residence at Haverhill, that is to say the month of the detested review in Greek grammar, poor John Quincy found himself in a state of emotional turmoil in which he wrestled with himself manfully.

I have heretofore more than once, been obliged to exert all my Resolution to keep myself free from a Passion, which I could not indulge, and which would have made me miserable had I not overcome it. I have escaped till now more perhaps owing to my good Fortune, than to my own firmness, and now again I am put to a trial. I have still more Reason, than I ever had, to ex-press my feelings; but I am also persuaded that I never was in greater danger.[36]

Such a disclosure of passion would seem to afford but one possible interpretation of the difficulties being experienced by this tormented youth. However, a simple explanation would be misleading. Words like "passion" and "dissipation" have overtones for the modern reader which were not necessarily true for the eighteenth century. They also suggest that the diarist was for all of his conscientiousness not only inclined to be romantic but even melodramatic. One suspects that he sometimes entertained himself with thrilling words; but that is not the principal point. John Quincy concluded the above statement about his passionate situation with what at first seems a puzzling remark. In fact it is illuminating. "One Circumstance there is which gives me hope; and if it takes place, will put an end to my danger & my fears." What danger was he really talking about?

The probable answer is that his salvation would lie either in Nancy's soon leaving the Shaw's, or in the eventuality of one of her beaux making her a formal proposal. Certainly the "danger" that young Adams had in mind was that he himself might be so moved. In other words, the real danger was a hasty declaration of marriage—truly a threat to a young man situated like himself. Let us remember that to a moral person like John Quincy Adams, the eighteenth century expression "passion" was synonymous with the idea of marriage. Hence a conflict of "reason" or "prudence" with the heart meant a struggle to keep open a career which might be spoiled by a hasty or otherwise undesirable alliance.

He had already drummed this kind of caution into himself, a caution based on worldly observation and one deeply cherished by the Age of Reason. Only a month before he had attended the wedding of a Boston lady with a British officer, a match foolishly approved by the lady's Anglophile father. Not only was there a lack of money but the participants had known each other for only three months. Such a match he had reflected at the time was "too often the emblem of a sudden passion." [37] So it was with the most evident relief that he presently heard the news that Nancy was going to visit a bereaved neighbor's family—it was the family of the recent suicide which had affected Nancy deeply. He could not conceal from himself that this news gave him pain, yet he wished that she would stay away as long as he himself remained in Haverhill. He had been reminded by someone that very evening of the misfortune under which a youth must labor who does not subdue "the tender passion." But he added, "I needed not the caution." He almost worked up a tirade on the subject, and concluded:

May it be my lot, at least for the years to come, never to have my heart exclusively possessed by any individual of the other sex. A man courting appears to me at any time of life, much below his natural dignity; but in a youth it is exceedingly absurd and ridiculous.[38]

Some of this sounds as if it had come directly from the mouth of the ubiquitous Mr. Thaxter. But whatever the source, a crisis had plainly been reached and passed. By December 6 he was in much better spirits, hoping that the gloom which had oppressed his mind for some weeks was by now entirely dispelled. He was sure that he now had nothing to fear "from a Quarter, which has given me a great deal of anxiety." When two days later he encountered Nancy at a neighbor's he thought he had never seen her "coquet it" quite so much, and critically began to wonder if he had not overrated the girl. He loftily resolved to avoid showing her either affection or resentment, as "passions that prejudice the mind."

Unfortunately, Nancy returned home a week later. Soon John Quincy was again lamenting the shortcomings of young ladies who were interested in "high flown Romance" and in reading novels and plays instead of history, especially that of their own country. But he clung grimly to his aloofness. Although he admitted to his mother on December 28 that the Shaws' female boarder had many amiable qualities—could Madam Adams have made a pointed inquiry from London? —he assured her that she need have no fear for her "young Hercules." [40] On New Year's Eve he reflected gravely on past events, particularly asking himself if he had been sufficiently improving his use of time. He recorded with evident self-satisfaction that however errors may sometimes have misled him, in this as in preceding years, "I have not to reproach myself with Vice." [2]

The affair might thus seem to have been decisively settled. However, a price remained to be paid—on the installment plan. Later he came to learn that he was being "suspected" and to feel an increasing coldness towards Nancy. The deluge of moral admonitions which his parents had poured upon him as a boy—no doubt very wisely when he was alone in Europe—began to bear slightly bitter fruit in America. This was not the result of his having been "prudent" in conduct, but because to a mind trained like his such decisions always called for elaborate justification, often leading to an exaggeration of issues and to excessive suffering. While he was aware of the danger of falling from affection into critical resentment, it is doubtful if he was as yet fully aware of the price he would have to pay for making decisions based on both worldly and moral reasons.

Early in January he began to feel confirmed in a painful opinion and to think himself to be in an intolerable situation, "to be suspected and spied, and guarded, all from a chimera arising in a person's brain." His alarmed relatives were undertaking precautionary measures! He gave them credit for having good intentions but compared their strange activities to giving a well man a dose of physic. The truth is that Aunt Eliza had recently discovered a poem John Quincy had written to "Delia" and immediately had jumped to the

conclusion that he was seriously interested in Nancy. If Aunt
Eliza had read the satire carefully it is difficult to see how she
could have made such a mistake. But from that moment she
had kept John Quincy under the "closest observation." As a
result of such officiousness he was soon being made to retire
an hour later than usual, besides experiencing the vexation
of being "suspected." [42] He was only too thankful that his
residence was rapidly coming to an end. It was the day after
making this observation that he lambasted critics of dancing
and all people who were prone to meddle in the affairs of
others.

Fortunately for his peace of mind, Nancy again left the
household a week later to board with a neighboring family.
One can only guess at the reason. Young John Quincy again
drew a deep breath of relief, and immediately proceeded to
dissect the poor girl's character.

Her going away has given me pleasure, with respect to myself;
as she was the Cause of many disagreeable little circumstances
to me. There was a time, when I was sensible of being more
attached to Her, than I would wish to be; to any young Lady
to whom I was not in any way related; but it was of very short
duration; indeed her character is such, as acquires a person's
affection, much easier than she preserves it. [43]

He sagely concluded that Nancy would have to acquire
prudence. When he saw her again one night at dinner, he
reflected that he had never known a young lady of whom he
had thought so differently at different times. Two weeks later
he was debating the question whether it is possible to love
and despise a person of the opposite sex at one and the same
time, and concluded that it is often so. But real love, he
thought, is a very different thing from fleeting affection for a
coquette whose character is so contemptible because it is
founded on vanity. It must have been about this time that he
told his Aunt Eliza a cock-and-bull story, reassuring her on

his inability to be interested in Nancy because he had once been smitten abroad by a young lady who, he claimed, resembled Cousin Eliza.

When John Quincy met Nancy for the last time before he left Haverhill—he was later to meet and even to call on her several times but always punctiliously—he found her very formal. In turn he made a cool entry in his journal. "I was not displeased at it, and returned it as much as I could, where a person will not be upon terms of friendly intimacy, I wish never to be behind hand with him [sic] in Ceremony." [45] So now, the blame was all hers.

By ironic coincidence on the following day the last Sunday sermon he heard preached in Haverhill was on a text from "Solomon's Song." The properties of the "dove" were shown to coincide with those of the church of Christ, and "some good practical observations drawn." At the afternoon lecture on the same subject, the visiting preacher, who spoke without notes and with little previous study, became extremely vociferous and took to "screaming" whenever he became "embarrassed." What effect all this had on the properties of the "dove" the diarist does not record. He was now much more concerned with the behavior of the preacher. Perhaps a similar observation might have been made of his own recent embarrassment over his own "Solomon's Song."

Time was now flying. News had come that certain lectures at Harvard were to be given earlier than expected. John Quincy Adams packed his trunk, paid a few visits, mounted horse at seven A.M. on March 14 and arrived in Cambridge a little after sunset, a journey of over thirty miles. The next day he was examined before President Willard, four tutors, three professors, and the librarian. This presumably was the entire Harvard faculty if friendly Dr. Waterhouse was present.[4] John Quincy construed some lines of Horace and Homer, parsing words wrongly in each author. There followed questions on Watts' *Logick* and, of course, a consider-

able number on Locke's *Understanding,* "very few of which
I was able to answer." Questions were also asked about the
shape of the earth and similar matters, "some of which I
answered, & others not." There followed an inquiry whether
he had studied Euclid and arithmetic, and then the grand
finale—turning a piece of English prose into Latin.

Perhaps there was a humorist on the board of examiners,
although this would have been out of character for staid President Willard.[47] The selection to be translated somehow exactly fitted the case of this sophisticated young moralist who
had learned to play cards and dance, who had seen innumer-
able operas and plays abroad, and who enjoyed reading Fielding and Sterne. It might also have been written for a young
man who had only recently been defending the giving of
"assemblies" in Haverhill!

There cannot certainly be an higher ridicule than to give an air
of Importance, to Amusements, if they are in themselves contemptible & void of taste. But if they are the object and care of
the judicious and polite and really deserve that distinction, the
conduct of them is certainly of consequence.

Whether humorously intended or not, the assignment was
soberly and no doubt correctly translated. Fifteen minutes
later, following consultation, President Willard said, "You
are admitted, Adams," and told him to report to the college
steward. After furnishing bonds, which were arranged for by
Dr. Cotton Tufts of Hingham, a distant connection and more
or less a business agent for the Adamses, John Quincy was
assigned a room on the third floor of Hollis Hall. He then
tried to settle down to the work of the upper Junior class.
This was impossible to do at once because on the very first
evening the Sophomore class had a "high-go." Some of its
members got drunk, and sallied out and broke the windows
of three of the tutors before staggering back to their chambers. "Such are the great achievements of many of the sons

of Harvard, such the delights of many of the students here,"
observed the newly admitted Junior. For all of this, John
Quincy Adams had finally entered upon that portion of his
career which he was always to remember as the best thing
that ever happened to him.

What kind of a person was this opinionated young man
who had experienced the breadth of Europe as well as the
narrowness of a small New England town? Who could arrogantly dispute with his elders in theology and yet rise above
the charms of a village coquette? How did he relate his ideas
about men and society to the process of education, which he
was now about to enjoy on a formal scale for almost the first
time in his life?

Some of these questions John Quincy himself tried to answer several months after entering Harvard, in a somewhat
confused address before a literary society he had been invited
to join.[48] As might have been expected he attacked the idea
that education is in any way connected with happiness in the
ordinary sense. In a "perfect state of nature" he thought that
man would be even happier for never having heard of New-
ton. (His father had apparently felt the same way when he
had tried to teach him calculus!) Both happiness and unhappiness seemed to him to be local matters, irrespective of government or civilization. He had seen "more sprightliness,
more cheerfulness and contentment" in one of the "most despotic monarchies on Earth" than in any other place. Presumably he referred to France, since his boyhood letters from
Russia would scarcely suggest that country. People there
knew nothing at all of freedom and so could not possibly miss
it, he said.

He thought that there was no accounting for tastes in happiness among various peoples. The Indians of North America, he observed, took pleasure in torturing prisoners. Those
in the West Indies enjoyed themselves by lying under trees.
In the Far East where men were of naturally "warm" consti-

tutions, the height of felicity was found in "being forever buried in the Embraces of perpetual Virgins, without ever finding their Vigour impaired." "May we not therefore conclude, that civilization does not increase the sum of happiness among Men?"

What then is the function of education, according to young John Quincy Adams? Obviously, to raise the status of the individual from his natural and no doubt "happy" condition. Since all men are naturally violent in their passions, education and civilization seek to curb these by appealing to the more exalted virtues, which are based upon duty. Youth, he admonished his fellow students who were no doubt aghast at his world outlook, is the time for the improvement of the heart and the understanding. They should remember above all else that education "inspires the soul with those exalted and divine Sentiments which form the Patriot and the Sage."

So the newly admitted upper Junior at Harvard was not looking for "happiness" at all, but for those qualities that make for a better civilization—patriotism and wisdom. Natural happiness and natural man, *exeunt!* He had passed them by in Haverhill.

CHAPTER THREE

HARVARD COLLEGE

"The passions of the mind"

Having hitherto escaped Cupid's darts, through a little resolution and some good luck, John Quincy Adams expected to be safe for fifteen months at Harvard while he made study his mistress.[1] That natural man and educated man are fundamentally opposed to each other was now an article of faith. He identified education with virtue, and believed in the corollary proposition that man is primarily distinguished from brute creation by the "passions of the mind." [2] Like the great moralist, Dr. Johnson, whom he faintly resembled but only slowly came to venerate, he cared little for bucolic pleasures when he could be with his fellows at beloved Cambridge. He always suffered an unusual amount of "heartburn" when he spent vacations at nearby Braintree,[3] although this may have been partly due to a weak digestive system when confronted with Aunt Mary Cranch's whortleberry puddings and apple "pyes." [4]

From the moment he entered Harvard as a Junior with advanced standing in March, 1786, until his graduation in July of the following year, young Adams was utterly enthralled with the place—except, of course, for having to get up to make six o'clock chapel! [5] While his enthusiasm was not one of unqualified academic admiration, it was a genuine mixture of scholarly and fraternal affection. He took special delight in the companionship of his fellow students, as was perhaps natural for one who had had to pass so much of his life in the company of older persons. He was himself conscious of being several years older than he thought a person should be at college. This situation he blamed on his European travels.[6]

The consciousness of being older—he was aged twenty when a Senior—as well as being traveled and learned, was to raise a serious problem for him at college. He had a feeling of superiority, especially towards his tutors.[7] Although he was far from being alone in his dislike of the latter, a certain arrogance of manner unquestionably characterized young John Quincy Adams. His parents had long tried to correct this although his mother thought it his only fault! Such arrogance had recently cropped up at Haverhill in his opinionated criticism of the theology of his Uncle Reverend Shaw.[8] To persist in such contentiousness could do him infinite harm, his relatives thought. When confronted with family warnings, primarily from his mother via Aunts Shaw and Cranch, he protested that his attitude towards his instructors had always been respectful. To be sure, he recalled how once he had barely been able to keep from laughing while conversing with an "ignorant" tutor; and he was to assert after graduation that his sharply critical opinions had been no secret to the faculty.[9]

Yet John Quincy clearly tried to respond to the admonitions of his mother. She pointed out that it was natural for tutors to be young and inexperienced since "sallaries" were so low. His efforts to control his arrogance achieved considerable success, according to both of his aunts.[10] Indeed, he actually ended his days at Harvard with an uneasy sense of having been reduced in his opinions about himself and his prospects to a level nearer truth.[11] No doubt this was a salutary result in some ways. Unhappily it also suggests that a loss of self-confidence may have been added to the burdens of this introspective youth while acquiring an academic education. It should be remembered that almost all of his education prior to entering Harvard had been by private instruction.

The last and sole quarter of John Quincy's Junior year was devoted to completing those Latin and Greek texts he had been brushing up at Haverhill, together with a series of lectures in natural philosophy, and recitations in Euclid and metaphysics. His Senior year had a much simpler curriculum. There was no study of languages at all, recitations only in metaphysics and mathematics and sometimes in divinity, with occasional public lectures including a repetition of those in natural philosophy.[12] More important requirements for Seniors were the occasional "forensics" on metaphysical and political subjects which were read in the college chapel. Public "exhibitions" which resembled commencement performances were also held there several times a year.

The entire Senior year was obviously designed primarily to train students in the art of public debate and address. Similar opportunities were also given to John Quincy Adams in the preparation of orations and forensics for the meetings of the two literary societies he had been invited to join soon after his arrival: the "A.B." and the Phi Beta Kappa. Except for the mastery of books required for recitations before his tutors, in addition to whatever reading he did on the side, his education in the last year consisted almost entirely of writing and declaiming on controversial subjects. He revelled in the literary and mental exercise this sort of activity entailed, if not always in the execution.

The social features of college life were for John Quincy Adams clearly subordinate to the intellectual, but very desirable diversions from too much study. There were occasional dinners or teas at the home of President Willard and his hospitable wife, or at that of jovial Professor Williams who gave the lectures in natural philosophy and was the father of the agreeable Jenny. The students themselves sometimes served tea at "clubs" in their chambers, and even held dances there of an evening. Since these affairs were strictly stag, one must assume that the boys danced jigs together. Occasionally

John Quincy smoked a pipe as did his father, perhaps for reasons of sociability rather than strict enjoyment. He derived real pleasure from playing the German flute, an instrument he had bought soon after his arrival in Cambridge and on which he had been taking lessons. He had to reassure sister Nabby that his playing did not injure his health.[13] He joined the Handel society at college and also participated in family concerts at Braintree during vacations. There his cousin Eliza Cranch played the pianoforte with a skill no doubt greatly improved as a result of her instruction in Haverhill, while Billy Cranch, a classmate, scraped the fiddle accompaniment.[14]

Nor was "Cupid" entirely foiled by an academic calendar. · During an extraordinary eight weeks' winter vacation, begun in early December because of the heavy snows and a shortage of wood, the students were turned loose on the neighborhood or sent home. John Quincy and his good-natured chum, James Bridge of Pownalborough, Maine, boarded at Professor Wigglesworth's in Cambridge. There they made the acquaintance of the amiable Peggy Wigglesworth and of her eighteen year old cousin, the satirical Catherine Jones,[15] a young lady who alternately attracted and repulsed John Quincy but who was to remain his close acquaintance for several years. There was also an older "young lady," a Miss Ellery of Newport, much more charming in disposition, who was visiting at the nearby home of his old friend and patron, Judge Francis Dana of Cambridge. Although John Quincy was very proud of the work he was able to accomplish during that winter recess—he read Montesquieu, a volume of the *Idler,* and works on chemistry, elocution, and algebra [16]—he was now able to renew his study of the female character. It may be noticed in passing that he had also had at least one letter from his old friend "Delia" in Haverhill,[17] that much maligned young lady acquaintance of the recent past.

All this was not important, however, compared with the

academic purposes of college life. There can be no doubt about John Quincy's devotion. He had scarcely become established at Harvard before his Aunt Mary was reporting to his mother that he did not leave his studies long enough to maintain health. Cousin Eliza Cranch soon afterwards found him in his chambers in a high state of dirt and quite negligent of his person, but apparently very happy. He was so devoted to his work his mother heard that he seldom even went to Boston. A full year had passed at Harvard before he missed a single lecture, a remarkable record considering the indifferent behavior of most of his classmates. But his assiduousness worried his relatives. His frequent ill health, including stomach trouble and spells of dizziness, they attributed to too little exercise.[18]

In addition to conscientiously preparing recitations, John Quincy laboriously transcribed all his lectures and copied into his journal his many orations and forensic debates. It is a wonder that he was able to do anything else but write. Apparently he did not even take time out to admire the view of the Cambridge pastures and distant Boston from his upstairs room in Hollis Hall.[19] At least he never mentioned so doing. However he took notice of practically everything else for his journal, whether it was an occasional drunken student falling down stairs or the "high-goes" of undergraduate celebrants. He himself seems never to have joined the latter. While he usually sympathized with his fellows in their activities, he was no carouser or troublemaker. For one thing, as his mother had warned him, he had to be a model to his two younger brothers both of whom were also at Harvard during his Senior year. Both obviously regarded him with deep respect, good-natured Tommy and charming, irresponsible Charles, although the latter was averse to being "lectured" by his older brother.

In oratory and disputation, John Quincy's activity was really astonishing. As a potential lawyer, he was aware of special need of practice in public speaking, something which remained an ordeal for years. In addition to preparing a speech, one had to learn how to make the voice effective, how to keep from moving one's feet too much, and how to employ related bits of histrionics. His laborious attempts at these affairs may well be imagined. On one occasion at least it was hilarious. He himself told with obvious enjoyment how, soon after his admission as a Junior, on declaiming "All the world's a stage" one night before the entire college in chapel, his description of the learned justice "with fair round belly" caused general laughter.[20] His own plumpness was the cause, perhaps made ludicrous by his manner of declamation. It is no wonder that he was to lose weight before his college career was over.[21]

His college addresses have been termed conventional exercises on time-honored academic subjects and, presumably, of little interest.[22] While it is true that the subjects were seldom new and John Quincy sometimes had to defend points of view of which he did not really approve, his addresses do reveal something of his habits of thought and methods of analysis. Since he invariably made it known in his journal whether or not he approved of the argument he was maintaining, his real attitude is usually clear. Later on he sometimes even repeated these oratorical sentiments when confronted with real problems. By and large, John Quincy's literary efforts throw considerable light on those "passions of the mind" he cherished as an undergraduate.

During his fifteen months at Harvard, which included generous quarterly vacations, he wrote and read a total of seventeen orations and forensic disputations, not counting his commencement address. Seven of these were delivered before the "A.B." society and three before the Phi Beta Kappa. Two were given at the public "exhibitions" and consisted of a forensic and a conference type of debate. The literary society pieces, those written for the "A.B." and the

Phi Beta Kappa, were read in students' chambers or in the quarters of the college Butler who was vice president of PBK. All the others were delivered in the chapel. Of the latter the "exhibitions" were by far the most important. In addition to the College Overseers, relatives of students and other outside visitors could attend these affairs. If the visitors could stand the ordeal they could then write to any fond but absent parents—such as John and Abigail Adams in London—telling them about the impression made by their son.

What did these literary productions reveal about John Quincy Adams' thinking as a college student? Of course he dutifully defended the notion of immortality's being a reasonable idea, although he did so largely on the grounds that it was in line with what had always been the expectation of most peoples.[23] For an individual to realize his highest potentialities, he was sure that one must learn to substitute duty for passion.[24] Even marriage for fortune can be defended against marriage for love, he argued, because the former may result in lasting benefits whereas "lust" can become satiated.[25] An unnatural example of romantic tragedy is that of Desdemona in "improbable" "Othello"; [26] but he also argued that young ladies have the right to be "forward" in making efforts to avoid the terrible fate of becoming "old maids." [27] In overcoming difficulties in life, industry —next to "innocence" the most amiable quality in man—is indispensable even for geniuses; yet persons born without great abilities cannot do "anything" simply by labor.[28] Just as the general character of people is influenced by general physical causes, so the individual's character in sensual matters may be attributed to his physical make-up.[29]

None of these analyses seems particularly startling, unless it is that of the role of poor Desdemona (many years later he was to develop the thesis that she had caused all the trouble by marrying the Moor against her parents' wishes); or John Quincy's concept of the physical "character" of man. More revealing were his ideas on the problems of society, particularly those relating to government and politics.

One of his most persistent convictions was that of the moral character of civilization, for which he considered enlightened religion to be the principal inspiration. It was his belief that there had been good, practical improvement in human affairs since the advent of Christianity. He could not forget the savage butchery of ancient times. In most parts of the earth it also seemed to him that there was progress in human affairs.[30] This young Puritan scholar may never have been a social optimist, but in several of his early speeches at Harvard he expressed some of that confidence so characteristic of the Age of Reason. He must have become particularly well acquainted with that point of view when he had lived in France.

Then in the late summer and fall of 1786 came news of civil disturbances in backcountry Massachusetts. For John Quincy Adams as for so many of his generation, Shays' Rebellion was an intellectual as well as a social shock. (Its effect was so pronounced on his father in London, that he was moved to complete a book on the dangers of popular forces in government that was to plague him the rest of his days.) The rebellion did not, however, turn John Quincy Adams into a reactionary. He continued to be highly suspicious of the "aristocratic" Order of the Cincinnati, whose members had been officers in the Continental Army, and to consider himself a better republican than most of his classmates at Harvard.[31] However, the riots did sharpen his apprehension of the doctrines of egalitarianism and increased his scepticism about popular movements of any kind. They also strengthened his sense of the utility of law and lawyers, which the

rioters and other persons were bitterly attacking as a contrib-
utory cause of the social and economic distress in Massachusetts.

Word of the uprising of hundreds of men against the Court
of Common Pleas in Northampton in early September[32]
had confirmed the fears long held by many persons about
the dangerous direction of domestic affairs. Threats to issue
paper money and to adopt ingenious tender laws had been
increasing in recent months in Massachusetts as elsewhere.[33]
The desperate need for national revenues was at the same
time being unconscionably held up by the refusal of New
York State to accede to a national import. In London, newspaper jibes about the state of American affairs had reduced
John and Abigail Adams to exasperation and despair. John
was extending his property holdings in Braintree as the best
form of security for the troubled times, although beginning
in January, 1787, he began to order additional investments
in American government securities when he learned that
Europeans were secretly buying.[34] The difficulty of collect-
ing taxes in Massachusetts was attributed by cousin Sam
Adams to the insidious influence of old Tories, still trying
to destroy faith in the Revolution. As early as July, 1786 the
outspoken Stephen Higginson, prominent Boston merchant
deeply concerned by New England's lack of foreign markets
and the chaotic state of the public credit, informed John
Adams that domestic matters were fast approaching a crisis.
When it arrived, every man of property and influence would
have to "give the Tide a right direction," he said.[35]

"The devil I am afraid has got among us," wrote Charles
Storer to Abigail Adams on August 15. This former aide of
John Adams in England, an admirer of Nabby and a great
favorite of Abigail's, had recently returned to America and
had become filled with the greatest pessimism because of
the "anarchy" in interior Massachusetts. He had also been
horrified at the recent Harvard Commencement to hear an

open discussion of "delicate" political subjects. There were
some "truths," in his opinion, which were better left concealed.[36]

While such domestic troubles were brewing, and no doubt
for that very reason, the Phi Beta Kappa at Harvard bravely
undertook one warm night in July to debate, "Whether civil
discord is advantageous to society"? This was the occasion
of John Quincy's maiden appearance before the society and
he "had" to speak for the affirmative. Nevertheless he made
an interesting argument. While concurring that civil discord is a "fiend of hell," he held that detestable principles
may sometimes have beneficial results, just as, to reverse the
argument, good intentions may have bad consequences. He
argued that base passion, though regrettably not restrained
by reason, must have been given to man to assist him in
defending his cause.

In other words, controversy can be a good thing. Too much
calm may be the forerunner of danger for nations as well as
for ships. Were it not for continuous opposition, intriguing
men would always have their way. Taking the example of
Rome, John Quincy denied that it had been the strife between the patricians and plebians which had brought on the
evils of political usurpation. Civil discord, if kept within
bounds, could be a useful thing, he asserted.[37]

Obviously, this was a trumped up argument and only narrowly missed violating John Quincy's profound misgivings
on the subject of "passion." Yet when he first heard on September 7 of the uprisings at Northampton, while he immediately condemned the malcontents for being at fault—for
getting into debt and being idle—he philosophized in his
journal rather closely along the lines of his Phi Beta Kappa
address of the previous July. "Such disturbances if properly
managed may be productive of advantages to a Republican
Government, but if they are suffered to gain ground, must
infallibly lead to civil war, with all its horrors." He likened

the disturbances to deadly drugs which if properly tempered can become highly medicinal.

This was the closest that John Quincy Adams ever came to showing any appreciation of Shays' Rebellion. Subsequently he simply condemned it as social anarchy. Nevertheless, in a brilliant flash it revealed how reluctant he was to abandon a point of view, even one based on special pleading; or, perhaps to speak more truly, it showed how reluctant he was to discard his own admirable reasoning. It certainly demonstrated how readily the rationalizing power of the intellect could be confused with true "passions of the mind." There is even a suggestion in his philosophizing of that weakness of which a close friend of the family, General James Warren of Milton, was soon accused. The general, who had been sulking in fancied political neglect, was said to permit his personal views to be rationalized into sympathy for the rebels.[38] The allegation was his political ambition. The most tender-hearted of the Adams' clan had once remarked that Warren's "all or nothing" attitude was worthy of a "Caesar." [39]

From September until the snows of winter the excitement raised by Daniel Shays and Job Shattuck continued. Local developments were fully recorded in John Quincy's journal because the college was used at one time as emergency headquarters for two companies of militia. There were also rumors that the rebels might attack the court in Cambridge. A martial spirit quickly developed around Boston as young gentlemen volunteers formed companies, but John Quincy Adams was not among the college students included. Indeed, he was to reflect gravely the following Fourth of July on the extent to which a martial spirit had in consequence become fixed upon the public. No doubt his European experiences had made him peculiarly aware of such dangers.

If John Quincy had any deeper suspicions about the political implications of Shays' Rebellion at the time, he must have kept them to himself. A year later he was to refer quite frankly to the "monarchical power" in Massachusetts.[40] Certain other persons were not so circumspect. In October, 1786, Benjamin Hichborn, an old-time Whig merchant of Boston, wrote John Adams in hurried secrecy that should the convulsions in Massachusetts continue, there was a determination in the minds of men of greatest influence to change the form of government throughout the continent. Five months later Hichborn referred to popular suspicion about Governor Bowdoin's being a "Frenchman" in league with the "British," but much adored by Stephen Higginson, John Lowell, Theophilus Parsons "and that set." Although Hichborn was sure that Hancock would be re-elected governor, he said that Nathaniel Gorham—a man of dubious political principles—still had expectations.

An even more lengthy and explicit analysis of the situation had been made by Samuel Osgood in November, in connection with the larger problem of federal reform. In case of civil war, he wrote, there was a strong likelihood that men of property would attach themselves to the military element. Many persons were already prepared to risk anything for a change. Osgood thought that British influence emanating from Canada could be traced among the insurgents in Massachusetts, with the design of establishing a monarchical government in America and placing one of George III's sons on the throne.[41]

Meanwhile the Harvard Seniors went on with their debating and the problems raised by the rebellion were reflected in their discussions. At the first college "exhibition" on September 26, John Quincy and Billy Cranch had very juicy "parts" in a forensic, on the relationship between equality and liberty. John Quincy argued that the question was really the desirability of a pure democracy. Declaring that nature has created an inequality among men, he condemned democracy as the most dreadful of tyrannies, and cited the

present state of the country as proof that too great a degree
of equality is prejudicial to liberty. The effect that Shays'
Rebellion had had on his thinking, at least for purposes of
debate, would seem to be self-evident. As to what Cousin
Billy said in reply there is unfortunately no record. However, his mother wrote sister Abigail that both boys had
good compositions although neither had spoken loudly
enough; that four hundred ladies and gentlemen had attended; but that if the boys ever again had parts that neither
she nor Betsy Cranch could stand attending the affair.[42]

A few days earlier, at a Phi Beta Kappa meeting, several
members had read a forensic on "Whether internal tranquility is a proof of prosperity in a Republic"? The Shaysites
were obviously making the Harvard Seniors happy, if no
one else! Two months later, amidst rumors that the insurgents were descending upon Cambridge, John Quincy addressed the "A.B." on the causes of the "present evils" and
gave the usual answers: a decay of public virtue, and a
tendency to luxury and dissipation since the heroic days of
'76. Soon afterwards came the remarkable snows of December and the extraordinary eight weeks winter vacation at
Harvard. By the end of that period the insurgents were
either all captured or dispersed, and new topics for debate
were being sought by the students. For John Quincy a new
interest had in the meantime developed in various young
ladies of the town, as already noted. While this interest did
not take his mind entirely off scholarly matters, it presumably did contribute to a diminution of his interest in the
troubles of the Commonwealth.

The second half of John Quincy's Senior year, which began
with a slow resumption of classes in February, was marked
by several minor intellectual trends on his part. His liking
for the mathematical branches of science had steadily grown
upon him. The series of twenty lectures on natural philosophy given by Professor Williams in the spring, while regret-

tably not new, fitted in with his interest in fluxions, levers, transits of Venus, and shocks from electrical machines. He found astronomy especially fascinating. This was a forecast of a life-long interest in science which was to benefit his country half a century later.

Another newly appreciated interest was ancient history. In the fall he had absorbed the Abbé Millot's *Elements of History,* and more recently had been reading Montesquieu's *History of the Romans.* The subject was now further unfolded in his re-reading the fascinating pages of Gibbon's *Decline and Fall,* of which fortunately he had his own copy. (Such books could only be borrowed from the college library two at a time, every other Friday.) Gibbon he considered a philosopher rather than an historian, and regretted his occasional preference for an epigram to a serious reflection.[43] John Quincy never did like epigrams. Nevertheless, Gibbon was to remain for many years a favorite author to whom he could always turn for solace and inspiration.

The burden of reciting to tutors, which he had always considered a waste of time, was greatly reduced in the latter part of the year when afternoon classes were dropped.[44] Indeed, in the last quarter of the year classes seem to have been disbanded altogether so that Seniors were free to do just about as they pleased, which apparently for most of them was little or nothing. Such also were John Quincy's intentions, as he airily informed his Aunt Mary when he was in Braintree on vacation in April. However when he returned to Cambridge he found immediately that he had to go to work on the commencement oration which he had been selected to deliver. He wrote his father in June that he was just beginning to have an opportunity to look after his health, which had suffered from his constant application for many months.[45]

The general quality of subject matter for forensics and orations in the last two quarters seems to have declined somewhat, at least for the Phi Beta Kappa. The principal discussions in that society were now about young ladies and love. John Quincy himself participated in two of these weighty debates. Perhaps it was a natural aftermath of the long winter recess, for other students as for himself. Several of the class forensics in metaphysics were on more prosaic subjects, such as "capital punishment" and the "effects" of Christianity. At a meeting of the "A.B." society in April, John Quincy also developed the interesting thesis that modern civilization has lost the veneration for music and poetry of olden times.[46] It will be remembered that he had a personal interest in both subjects. He had occasionally engaged in "rhyming" as well as in playing the flute throughout the year.

The really big event in the spring, however, was the public "exhibition" on April 10. Once again John Quincy had a very favorable part, the second time on three occasions and a sign of high academic standing—or of academic favoritism, in some people's eyes. He was assigned the task of defending the profession of law against physic and divinity as being most beneficial to man. This was done by a "conference" method, and he was wishing the whole conference "to the devil" before his preparation ended. Since the legal profession was currently under heavy public attack, his part was doubly important. Putting the law on a par with divinity for discussion was a daring idea in itself. According to his Aunt Mary he was "greatly applauded" on this occasion; and a young lady spectator sweetly averred that in his composition he had displayed the triple qualities of scholarship, candor, and delicacy. John Quincy himself was obviously pleased with what he considered the approbation of the audience. It was the best thing he ever did as an undergraduate and may well have won him his commencement honor.[47]

There was a refreshingly vigorous and hard-hitting tone to this oration, if one makes due allowance for the decorous style of the day. Despite the young author's sense of "delicacy," he scored off the other professions with palpable hits. He pointed out that the lawyer in living on the follies and vices of mankind is not so very different from either physician or preacher. If a lawyer makes a mistake his action is much more clearly apprehended than that of the physician! As society becomes more complex, he argued, only lawyers and the courts can protect the liberties of people. Even under tyrannies this was true, as proved by the Parlements of Paris; whereas the clergy is often an instrument of oppression, this well-traveled young man observed. However the goals of all three professions are equally high: they respectively defend *"health, liberty, innocence."* Any man, he said, can render his profession useful if he unites talents and virtue in his work.[48]

If Reverend Uncle Shaw had come down from Haverhill to attend this "exhibition" he might have gently winced once or twice at his wife's nephew's remarks. Fortunately there is no evidence of his having made the trip. Indeed, Uncle Shaw remains a rather mute and shadowy figure in the records of the Adams family. According to his wife, moreover, John Quincy had acted so agreeably on a trip to Haverhill a few weeks previous as to convince them both that the "only" error they had ever detected in him—here Aunt Eliza agreed in numbers with sister Abigail!—had been entirely removed. This referred of course to the delicate subject of the sophisticated young man's having disputed arrogantly with her husband the year before. She now playfully characterized John Quincy as having a "facetious disposition." He had so happily and freely discussed all his pleasures and amusements with her that she was sure he had nothing he need *"wish"* to hide. This was a reference to his old problem of "Delia" at Haverhill and to his affairs of the heart. Romantic Aunt Eliza was by way of becoming an expert about such matters. Indeed, they had constituted her principal avocation since girlhood.[49]

A similar picture of this much improved young man had

recently also been furnished by his other maternal aunt. Mrs. Cranch assured sister Abigail that John Quincy had acquired the affection of his class as well as the approbation of his teachers, despite his contempt for all dignity based on pomposity. The only reason that his relatives had ever had to worry about him, she said, had been because of his talent for satire. However Abigail's advice and that of Nabby, and no doubt that of his relatives in America, the Cranches and Shaws, had had a beneficial effect.[50] There apparently had been no dearth of good advice!

One of the most delightful bits of evidence of John Quincy's gift for "satire," as well as his attitude towards the college officers, was a poem he wrote in March of his Senior year. It was entitled, "Lines Upon the Late Proceedings of the College Government." It probably got into general circulation; it certainly deserved to. The circumstances related to the behavior of some members of the Junior class who greatly irked by the 'distribution" of parts for an "exhibition" had proceeded to get drunk and to raise cain.[51] John Quincy's sympathies usually lay with such offending students; he had once even argued that it was no crime to get drunk.[52] Members of his own class had quarrelsome reputations also. They not only had strained relations with their tutors but were always disputing with President Willard about academic matters. Soon they were even to be protesting against the class's holding a public commencement.

The poem described the "trial" of the offending Juniors who were faced with the possibility of being dismissed to private study, *i.e.,* "rustication."

> The government of college met,
> And Willard ruled the stern debate.
> The witty Jennison declared
> That he had been completely scared.
> "Last night," says he, "when I came home,
> I heard a noise in Prescott's room,

> I went and listened at the door,
> As I have often done before.
> I found the juniors in a high rout;
> They called the President a tyrant;
> They said as how I was a fool,
> A long-eared ass, a sottish mule,
> Without the smallest grain of spunk;
> So I concluded they were drunk."

After the "testimony" of other tutors and professors, the "trial" concluded with the sage rebuke of President Willard:

> "The rulers, merciful and kind,
> With equal grief and wonder find
> That you should laugh and drink and sing,
> And make with noise the college ring.
> I therefore warn you to beware
> Of drinking more than you can bear.
> Wine an incentive is to riot,
> Destructive of the public quiet.
> Full well your tutors know this truth,
> For sad experience taught their youth.
> Take then this friendly exhortation!
> The next offense is rustication."

The offending youths had been let off with a reprimand!

Despite his undeniable talent for satire, John Quincy Adams was both academically successful and no doubt greatly "improved" as he came to the end of his college career. One would have supposed him to have been quite happy. Unfortunately he was not. For him, as no doubt for so many others, the very thought of leaving college was depressing. It had come to mean so much in his case that he could only lament not having returned from Europe sooner. Ill health also continued to inconvenience him. Gunning and fishing at Braintree during the April vacation had not prevented the usual case of heartburn, and another spell of dizziness soon after his return to college. He was busy in the latter part of

May in preparing his commencement address, but the general tone of college life had sadly declined for all Seniors. Skylarking, carousing, and a lack of routine did not agree with John Quincy Adams, either then or later.[53]

A more subtle and therefore more disturbing problem pertained to his hopes for the future, to his private ambition and anticipation of success in the years ahead. On this score his college experience had given him no real answers. It had even raised serious questions. Because of his everlasting penchant for self-criticism, and the continual admonitions of his family, not even his recent experience as a much applauded public speaker could completely bolster up his ego. And he still had the commencement ordeal ahead.

The first serious doubts about his effectiveness on the platform had arisen after his first "exhibition," the previous September. He had heard some student remark that his forensic was the "meanest" ever delivered in chapel. It had cut him to the quick despite the panegyrical things he had heard from others.[54] He loved that word "panegyrical." Adverse criticism was doubly distressing because he had just been confessing to himself of being very ambitious, but at the same time miserably admitting that he obviously lacked certain qualities necessary for success. He declared, in the words of Hotspur, that if it were a sin to covet honor he was the most offending soul alive; yet he could not convince his associates that his deserts should equal his expectations. If only he could be content with small distinctions, although he confessed that he despised men of that ilk.[55] Such gnawing self-doubts must always have been with him as he wrote and declaimed his way through that Senior year at Harvard. Such devastating self-analysis could not have been a passing reflection.

Something even like a morbid state of mind had revealed itself the following March, when he heard that his old patron of St. Petersburg days, Judge Francis Dana of Cambridge, had been taken with a stroke. Now referring to the judge as a "second father," John Quincy bitterly upbraided himself for once having neglected his admonitions, presumably on the subject of arrogance. All that he could unhappily say in self-defence was that he had finally checked some of the failings to which the judge had long ago called attention.[56] Such self-reproach reinforced the warnings he had been continually receiving from his family. Incidentally, his concern over Judge Dana's condition was deep and lasting. Both he and his brother Charles "watched" for several nights while the judge was critically ill. John Quincy passed his watch in reading "insipid" novels, a type of light literature with which he seems to have kept *en rapport*.

The "exhibition" in April may have been reassuring, but the prospect for commencement raised new doubts. Both young Adams and his gifted classmate, Nathaniel Freeman, had been assigned "English" orations, *i.e.*, not given in Latin, and the choicest parts. While writing his piece, John Quincy's consciousness of "having no talent at rhetorical composition" gave him much anxiety. He particularly dreaded comparison with the formidable Freeman and the "disgrace" that might be reflected upon himself.[57] Unfortunately, time was to prove that his fears, however exaggerated, had an element of truth in them because suspicions of favoritism were to influence some people's judgment at commencement.[58] The prospect was an additional factor in depressing the young graduate who, by all the rules, should have been reasonably happy.

The "passions of the mind" were now threatened with erosion from idleness at Braintree as time dragged on while he waited "dully" for commencement. Unlike his father, he apparently never did any farm work or other heavy physical labor. Part of his time was spent in writing for his journal long character sketches of his classmates, a laboriously analytical task upon which he had been engaged throughout the spring. He read another frivolous novel, also "the Beggar's

Opera," which he disliked, renewed his acquaintance with some young lady friends and went out walking with an agreeable new one. He also became deeply concerned about enabling an impecunious classmate to return for his degree. While dining at the convalescent Judge Dana's one evening, he met the witty and learned lawyer from Newburyport, Theophilus Parsons, with whom arrangements were being made for him to study in the fall. The prospect of this also greatly distressed him. He dreaded returning to the stage of "general society" which he had already met "with disgust" and once quitted in favor of Harvard.[59]

While amusing himself one idle day in July by reading inscriptions in the burying ground at Braintree, he saw and pursued a large snake. It caused him to wonder if it could be the guardian of someone's bones? [60] Yet only a few months earlier he had been addressing a literary gathering at college on the subject of superstition which he had denounced as showing lack of reason! To do this young philosopher justice, however, he had concluded those remarks by candidly admitting that few of us are guiltless in this respect.[61] He had obviously remained aware that there are some kinds of human weakness which stubbornly resist the "passions of the mind." Even the reduction of his conceit as an undergraduate had been accompanied by increased apprehensions about the future, for he was a highly imaginative human being as well as an industrious scholar. In both respects his college achievement was to be more fully revealed on commencement day.

CHAPTER FOUR

GRADUATION IN CAMBRIDGE

"A nervous style of eloquence"

Although John Quincy Adams was a very proper young man and to be one of the honored graduates at the approaching Harvard Commencement, he had been going about saying, "Oh Lord! oh Lord!" and hoping that it would rain. Like his classmates he had favored a private commencement, and rain would at least spoil the wigs of those dignitaries who had insisted on the traditional public ceremony.[1] The practice of having undergraduates continually demonstrate "laudable emulation" by competing for public favor in "exhibitions," had long caused an undercurrent of bitter resentment among them.[2] Moreover, young Adams, the son of a prominent public figure, had a touchy political topic on which to address the audience. He also dreaded comparison with a particularly gifted classmate who was to deliver the other principal oration of the day.[3]

Yet the commencement seemed to turn out well despite all his apprehensions. For one thing it was not too warm a July day. In fact it was the coldest commencement day on record. People going along the Common in Boston that morning actually clapped their hands on their sides to keep warm.[4] In the late afternoon after the conclusion of the ceremonies another kind of pleasant record was set. In the chambers of John Quincy Adams and his cousin Billy Cranch in Hollis Hall, a mighty repast was spread for guests under the bustling supervision of Mrs. Cranch. She had been planning it for over a year. For two days benches were being installed, while wagon loads of supplies had poured in from Braintree. Two

71

Negro servants and all of the Adams' retainers from two tenant farms were on hand to assist. There were two whole
rounds of beef prepared *à la mode,* four hams and four
tongues, peas and salad, cider punch and porter for over one
hundred guests, with wine and cake for four hundred more.
The feast must have helped to make up for the Spartan-like
"dinner" served at noon by the college. Even Governor Hancock and the college professors dropped in for congratulations, and no doubt a sample. John Quincy recorded in his
journal that another such day would ruin him. This referred
to the congratulations, however, not to the food.[5]

After all such festivity, the unpleasant publicity about the
day's affairs came as something of a shock. The commencement proceedings unfortunately produced some spirited newspaper commentary. The wrath of the humorless Boston *Gazette* on July 23 was aroused by the lampooning account of
the ceremony given two days earlier by the rival *Massachusetts Centinel.* One indignant witness denounced the latter's
"scurrility" in attempting to "pluck the laurel" from the
brows of the youthful performers.[6] The particular cause of
this outburst had been none other than twenty-year-old John
Quincy Adams himself. Such embarrassing publicity was his
introduction to the hazards of public favor, and in this instance it was made in strong words.

The writer in the last Centinel who has published the bombastic,
inflated and ridiculously partial account of the exhibitions of
the young gentlemen who took their degrees last Wednesday at
Cambridge—to say nothing of the other parts of his truly puerile
performance, has dropped a sentiment which in this country
should never be exposed to public view without behing hissed
off the stage as soon as it appears. In noticing one of the youthful
performers, he speaks of him as being *warmly attached* to the
republican system of his father—as if there was anything extraordinary in a young man, or in any body being warmly attached
to the laws and constitution of his country.[7]

The indignant author of this article signed himself "ARIS-
TIDES" and was the kind of a contributor especially prized by
old Benjamin Edes, the bold Whig editor of the *Gazette*. Its
motto was, "A Free Press Maintains the Majesty of the People." The author went on to say at considerable length that
republicanism is naturally the best kind of government since
it defends the poor and weak against the rich and strong, "un-
suspecting ignorance" against the arts of "presuming superiority," all without the "vindictive violence of the sanguinary
despot, and the titled insolence of aristocratic power." "Is it
remarkable then," asked "ARISTIDES," "that a young man,
whose family and fortune have been distinguished and extended by this very system of republicanism should warmly
support its pre-eminence?"

These stirring words were no doubt ostensibly intended to
defend John Quincy against the "scurrility" of the *Centinel*,
the motto of which was, "Uninfluenced by Party we aim to be
JUST." They also revealed how sensitive was the area upon
which his commencement oration had touched. He had
spoken "Upon the importance and necessity of Public Faith,
to the well-being of a community," and had emphasized the
necessity of preserving the public credit in dark and troublesome days.

John Quincy had even applied the expression "critical
period" to the times, thereby furnishing the stuff of which
"history" is made. The topic had not been of his own choos-
ing but was one to which he had been assigned. A month
earlier he had written his father that the subject was indeed
a noble one and badly in need of treatment since public faith
was in a sad condition. He had noted, however, that he had
been "led unaware into political ground." [8] Nevertheless he
had done his best after careful composition and many re-
hearsals, and had won the applause of most of his hearers.
But he also had aroused the derision of some persons, not to
mention the envy of others. This personal rancor had been

amusingly compounded in the *Centinel*'s high-toned account.

Even in the article by "ARISTIDES," however, there were overtones which were intended to do something more than merely "defend" the young graduate. In view of current rumblings in the public press, the remarks of "ARISTIDES" surely implied criticism of no less a person than John Quincy's own father, the American minister to Britain. The article had concluded with a vague but disturbing statement, that "it is truly singular to see certain people whose whole importance has been *created* by the partiality of their countrymen, affect to decry the merits of a democracy, because, forsooth they cannot be noblemen."

The apparent explanation is that old John Adams, in the wake of Shays' Rebellion in the closing weeks of 1786 and obviously still at white heat, had finished the first volume of his *A Defence of the Constitutions of Government of the United States of America*.[9] At first sight this had been hailed with praise by the *Gazette*,[10] which was reprinting portions of it, but whose editorial sympathies must now have been cooling. Embarrassing accusations were beginning to be heard that the elder Adams had become an admirer of the English type of government and was squinting at "aristocracy." An article had appeared in the Boston press on the very day of John Quincy's graduation, reprinting a story from Philadelphia which had concluded, "The gentleman who favours us with this article, asks, whether Mr. Adams' work can so properly be called a *Defence* of our constitutions, as an *encomium* upon the British government?" [11] Within a few more weeks the work was being labeled in some quarters as "political poison." A full scale attack upon its author, however, was to be delayed until 1791 when Thomas Jefferson "innocently" precipitated a major controversy with John Adams. His wife had humorously warned him that his book would lead people to accuse him of wanting to set up a king in America.[12]

Such scattered remarks in the summer of 1787 suggest the

deteriorating political atmosphere to which John Quincy
Adams was exposed as he made his public bow. His audience
must have been thoroughly aware of the delicate situation.
It should not be forgotten that this was the summer when the
Federal Convention was meeting behind closed doors in Philadelphia, when newspapers were still powerfully influenced
by the aftermath of Shays' Rebellion, and when political rumors of all kinds were commonplace. Family, fate, and the
zeal of the press were all at work on young John Quincy
Adams.

Let us return to that cool but clear and pleasant commencement day. The audience was large and impressive.[13] According to custom His Excellency, Governor Hancock, together
with the Lieutenant Governor, the President of the Senate,
and other public dignitaries, had been escorted to Cambridge
in the forenoon by the Sheriff of Suffolk County and by a
company of Horse Guards. Received by the Fellows of the
Corporation and by the professors, they had conferred with
the Overseers in Harvard Hall and had then paraded to the
Meeting House where the young gentlemen graduates spoke
their pieces. So many other distinguished visitors and alumni
were also present that altogether it was enough to make any
performer's knees quake! Of course, a "nervous style of eloquence" was an accepted mode of address in those days and
not peculiar to young Adams as he spoke in eighth place out
of eighteen events. His facial contortions were also regarded
as remarkable by his relatives.[14] In the class of '87 which had
fifty-one bachelor candidates, young Adams was being graduated "second in the scale of rank." Moreover, his selection to
give one of the two "English" orations was an indication of
highest academic honors.[15]

Following these youthful demonstrations, the audience had
repaired to College Hall where a dinner was provided "which,
although *less* elegant than on some former years of public
tranquility, and *far* less expensive, was not less satisfactory

to those sons of science, who meet for *literary* entertainment, and not for luxurious feasting." In the afternoon they all went again to the Meeting House where the candidates for the M.A. performed. All degrees were thereupon duly conferred, the bachelors first. Two honorary doctorates were also recorded, one for Thomas Brand Hollis, Esq., L.L.D., a benefactor of the college and a close friend in England of John Adams; the other for His Excellency, Thomas Jefferson, Esq., L.L.D., the American minister in France. According to one report, "The whole business of the day was conducted with the greatest regularity and harmony. The performance of the young gentlemen gave the highest pleasure to their friends; and to all who have been concerned in their education; and left on the mind of a numerous and splendid assembly, a deep impression of the advantage which may be derived from a truly liberal education." [16]

The account of the proceedings in the *Centinel* on July 21, however, exploded a "harmony" which was in fact more apparent than real. That paper must have had its best reporter on the job; he discussed the commencement in a style that can only be called scintillating.[17] While he congratulated the patrons and graduates on the performance, he urged the university to rid itself completely of "scholastic jargon" in the nature of "fulsome syllogism," a type of exercise much disliked by the students. He also said of President Willard, possibly with more truth than propriety, that his valedictory "deserved merit not only from the matter, but from the brevity"! [18]

Each of the contesting graduates was handled with this same air of superior understanding. A poem spoken by Mr. Harris showed a "degree of formality"; fortunately this "young son of Apollo" displayed a "modest *abord*." The forensic disputation between Messrs. Fiske and Chandler was meritorious but involved a "common fault." Such contestants were advised in the future to stick to *"Argumentum ex absurdo, & ad Hominem."* An address by Mr. William Cranch was "far from being destitute of merit." Mr. Cranch had spoken "Upon the impossibility of civil liberty's long subsisting in a community, without three orders in the Government, vested with such powers as to be mutual checks upon and balances to each other." This was, of course, more or less the substance of John Adams' *Defence of the Constitutions* just beginning to get public notice. Young Mr. Cranch was said to have "read with attention the vindication of the American constitutions, and paraphrased upon some of the principles in an ingenious manner. If he appeared to some persons to have adopted many sentiments of the author, without sufficient examination, they may impute it to circumstances both rational and natural. Mr. [John] Adams is undoubtedly a great man." Then came the inevitable punch line: "He is likewise the orator's uncle"!

The climax of this remarkable piece of reporting was reserved for the end:

The two principal performances were the Orations by Mr. *Adams* and Mr. *Freeman*. The first of these certainly declaimed upon a well chosen subject, in a manly, sensible and nervous style of eloquence. The publick expectations from this gentleman, being the son of an Ambassador, the favourite of the officers of the College, and having enjoyed the highest advantages of European instruction, were greatly inflated. This performance justified the preconceived partiality. He is warmly attached to the republican system of his father, and descanted upon the subject of public justice with great energy. Mr. Adams's indisputable superior, in style, elegance and oratory, is the graceful Mr. *Freeman*. It was thought almost impossible for him to exceed his accomplished rival who spoke before him—but to *Freeman* every thing was easy. They were both considerably agitated when they arose, and seemed to recover a decent confidence after the same interval. . . . In short, these young gentlemen discovered those qualities that must ensure them eminence, and we hope, for the sake of their country, they may be rivals in the cultivation of those talents through life.

Certain of these phrases are worth underscoring. Young Mr. Adams was identified with his father's public station and his "republican system," which was, of course, what outraged "ARISTIDES." As a person John Quincy was called the "favourite" of the officers of the college, which kind of praise would be hard for any student to accept and which was a kind of distinction particularly vexatious for this Harvard class. John Quincy himself called it the "most invidious circumstance that could have been mentioned" and utterly denied that there was any truth in it.[19] His advantages of European instruction were also pointed out, another delicate point since he was anxious to avoid being labeled "foreign." Finally he was declared a remarkably accomplished youth, but young Mr. Freeman was his "indisputable superior, in style, elegance and oratory" to whom "every thing was easy." This certainly took away most of the luster.

What John Quincy himself thought of the comparison was very simple. He said that he liked and admired Freeman but felt neither superior to him nor particularly inferior—although it must be confessed that he had long been dreading public comparison with him. Aunt Shaw rather ungallantly thought that only the young ladies would have preferred Freeman. John Quincy soon began to think himself a mere "cypher in creation," but whether this was on account of all the embarrassing newspaper publicity does not appear.[20] His father wrote him his good opinion of the speech some months later, having just received a copy in London, saying that it was manly and spirited and that if John Quincy lived and died by its sentiments, "I dont care a farthing how many are preferred to you, for style, elegance and mellifluence." [21] From this language, one concludes that John Adams *père* had surely seen a copy of the *Centinel* for the previous July 21.

In any case his son had already informed his mother of its substance.

Two other opinions about the oration are notable. First, the Reverend Mr. Jeremy Belknap, the distinguished historian of New Hampshire, Harvard alumnus and Overseer, and good friend of the Adamses—he had been a spectator at the graduation—promptly wrote John Quincy of his admiration for the speech and requested a copy for publication in the *Columbian Magazine*.[22] (This was a new literary venture in Philadelphia for which Mr. Belknap had recently refused the editorship and in which he was writing an allegorical novel about America from month to month.) It was a strange coincidence that in the aforementioned July 21 issue of the *Centinel,* immediately following the colorful commencement description, there had appeared a long "blurb" about this new magazine in which its growing reputation and popularity was mentioned. An advertisement of it had also appeared in the same issue. After some interesting correspondence, John Quincy's permission to publish finally was secured and the oration on "Public Faith" duly appeared in the September, 1787, issue of the *Columbian.*

Secondly, there appeared in the Boston *Centinel* in September [23] an ironic communication from "THE STUDENTS," burlesquing in horrid terms alleged partiality with regard to academic honors at Harvard. The language of this piece, for all of its spoofing character, expressed some genuine discontent about the prevailing system of scholastic distinctions. The climactic reference to Adams and Freeman in this piece was painfully laudatory and was obviously intended to be funny, no doubt in view of the uproarious newspaper publicity in July.

Reverend Mr. Belknap's request throws considerable light upon the budding interest in "Old John's" son, and likewise on John Quincy's own attitude towards public favor. His concern on this point was honorable, but rather futile. The name of Adams was plainly one with news value, quite apart from the intrinsic worth of the oration. In his first reply to Belknap's query, on July 30, John Quincy agreed to furnish a copy only if his name did not appear and if the English poem read at commencement by a fellow graduate should accompany it. This was in accordance with the proposal of Belknap.

Unfortunately, and rather surprisingly it would seem, John Quincy's fellow graduate refused to appear with him in print. Nevertheless Mr. Belknap wrote again urging young Adams to comply—the copy had already been received—and his argument was distinctly flattering, to put it mildly. He admitted that nothing is more amiable than modesty in a "young Gentleman of acknowledged Genius" but thought that this should yield to proper solicitation.

And why should the name be suppressed? A name which calls up every grateful and affectionate feeling in the breasts of Americans? Without ye name, your Alma Mater will be deprived of half the honor wch [sic] she deserves, but if that be added, the friends of Liberty and Virtue will have ye farther Satisfaction to see ye features of the Parent in the son, and may I not add your Country will have a pledge of a succession of abilities in the same Family still to aid her Cause and espouse her Interest.

When John Quincy replied a second time from Braintree on August 6, giving reluctant consent to publication, he revealed his sensitivity to the idea that public favor might undeservedly be bestowed upon him. "And if my father has been so fortunate as to render services of importance to his countrymen, that is certainly no reason why they should be prejudiced in favor of his son." He stipulated that no mention should be made that there had been any difficulty in obtaining his speech, since this would merely convey an air of false importance. "Apologies of this nature never have any influence upon impartial persons, and these are the only characters I am fearful of offending." Perhaps his most significant

comment, however, was the explanation of his concern lest
the people who had been at commencement, the proper
judges of the various performances, might be displeased to
see him appear in print alone and consider it a breach of decency.[24] In view of what had already appeared in the *Centinel*
and in the *Gazette,* it is readily understandable why he should
have been deeply concerned on this point. But even more unpleasant publicity was about to follow, to the special enjoyment of certain persons who had attended the commencement.

The open letter addressed "To the OVERSEERS of an UNI-
VERSITY" by "THE STUDENTS," appearing in the *Centinel* on
September 15 is surely as amusing a document as can be
found in the history of higher education—or in any other kind
of history, for that matter. It was humorously sensational, but
mysteriously vague as anonymous communications were apt
to be in the eighteenth century. In it the name of proper
John Quincy Adams was again thrust into print, and again
as the butt for "humor."

The lampoon opened with lofty expressions of appreciation to the Overseers whose "laudable intentions appear to
us to be perverted by the partiality and prejudice of a few
individuals, or individual." "THE STUDENTS" loftily excepted
their worthy president from this category. They said that
when they first entered college they had expected that effort
would duly be rewarded; but, alas! they had found just the
opposite: "the hopes of competitors, who have been fired
with noble emulation to obtain the palm, are lost; forever
lost. Is it just, that the very creature of ignorance, inattention,
intemperance and debauchery, should rise upon the ruins of
merit, and assume an unprecedented importance?" Was it
partiality, or bribery, at work? they darkly asked.

"THE STUDENTS" lamented that the "creature of secret influence" had kicked them down from Parnassus "to make room
for his own favourites, or, at least, assigns us an insignificant

station." They begged that "the hydra of C ....t [com-
mencement] may be permitted no longer to poison the foun-
tain of justice, or disturb its waters." They claimed that a
"comparative view of the characters of those who have lately
received a private distinction at the University, with some of
those, who will soon be crowned with its most distinguished
honours, fully demonstrate the drift of our argument—partiality in the extreme." Then came the pious conclusion.

But, thanks be to Heaven, the revolution of an anniversary,
which calls us to depart from our *Alma Mater,* is productive of
the most happy effects. It is then, our illustrious President, aloof
from prejudice, callous or ignoble influence, rewards intrinsick
merit. Could the caprice of an individual have dictated the distribution of honours, at such a period, the publick probably
would not have been delighted with the manly and eloquent
strains of a Freeman and an Adams—No—these reputable youths,
it is likely, would have been pushed behind the scene, and their
abilities, as yet, unknown to their friends and the publick.—
O tempora! O mores!

This silly rag did make some sense in terms of the disturbed character of student life at Harvard in those years, a
situation which was shortly to become riotous.[25] It seems obvious that the "accusations" by "THE STUDENTS" were primarily directed against their tutors or against a particular
tutor, but which particular one is not clear, certainly not
from the testimony of John Quincy Adams' college journal
in which the description of all of them is severe. Student relations with their tutors had become very bad; the latter were a
young lot, certainly not above criticism in their behavior.
They treated the students like "brute beasts" according to
John Quincy Adams, who was not wholly without objectivity
in the matter nor even without a sense of humor on the subject of college discipline. In turn, a favorite sport of drunken
students was to break the tutors' windows. On one occasion
the tutors had been hissed out of the dining room, accom-

panied by a shower of potatoes. Tutors unfortunately were
disciplinarians as well as teachers, and while college rules
were strict the penalties were so ludicrously light as to encourage further disorders. In such circumstances rumors
about the rankest kind of prejudice and favoritism were naturally not unknown, bred in an atmosphere of tense feelings.[26]

John Quincy's contempt for most of his tutors would seem
to have relieved him of any charge of being their "favourite."
It is therefore difficult to see why the *Centinel* in its opinionated account of the commencement on July 21 should have
labeled him "the favourite of the officers of the college" unless—apart from any intended humor or mischief-making—
this referred to college officials other than tutors. Possibly
some such complicated situation as this did exist and had influenced President Willard with regard to commencement
honors. John Quincy had clearly been an exemplary student.
Nevertheless, while acknowledging his favored treatment on
this and several other occasion, he not only denied his ever
having been a "favourite" but said that the college officers
had always known of his critical opinion of them.[27]

Moreover, in the general student feeling against public
performances during the year, as well as against the type of
commencement then in vogue, John Quincy had also taken
the popular view.[28] There apparently had been nothing like
tests or academic ranking of any kind during the students'
undergraduate experience, except for these occasional and
detested "exhibitions." [29] President Willard, a stickler for de-
tails of deportment and an old fashioned scholar, favored
such a system. He refused to give up a public commencement
on the same grounds. Without such demonstrations he believed that there would be no incitement to what he called
"laudable emulation." [30] It will be remembered that "THE
STUDENTS" had spoken sarcastically of their once having been
fired with "noble emulation." The class of '87 had actually

petitioned twice against there being a public graduation ceremony, once to the Corporation and a second time to the Overseers.[31] The expense to the graduate in those hard times seems
to have been one of their reasons. But the general argument
must have been against a type of ceremony in which the schol-
ars would again have to compete for favor, in this case for
commencement applause.

John Quincy had even interviewed President Willard on
the subject of the class' dislike for a public graduation, but of
course to no avail. Not only was "emulation" involved but
President Willard—so he told Adams privately—feared the
resentment of Governor Hancock if he were not given a
chance to show himself off on such a notable occasion.[32] The
egotistical governor continued to be the *bête noire* of the college. He had finally resigned as treasurer but had not settled
his long overdue accounts. Moreover the times were shaky
and Hancock's political power was a source of uneasiness to
many citizens.

The "STUDENTS" protest appeared about the time that the
September *Columbian Magazine* was published in Philadelphia. The August issue had expressed regret that the "ingenious Oration delivered by Mr. Adams arrived too late for
the present number. . . ." It contained thirty items other than
"Public Faith" including such things as "A Description of the
Natural Bridge in Virginia," "The Foresters, an Historical
Tale" by Reverend Jeremy Belknap, and "The New Plan for
a Federal Government proposed by the Convention." This
issue must have reached Boston within several weeks. On
November 7 the *Centinel* reprinted from the magazine the
whole of the Adams' oration, describing the youthful author
in full dress as the "son of his Excellency, the American minister." Perhaps its editor, Major Ben Russell, was trying to
make amends for the previous mischievousness of his paper.

Such was the colorful introduction of John Quincy Adams
to the public. It had come about as it did partly because he

was John Adams' son—and as such reflected upon by a zealous press—but also because his graduation had taken place at a time of considerable undergraduate distemper. He had been thrust into exceptional public notice because Alma Mater had thought well of him, thereby occasioning some jealous ribbing by certain self-styled "STUDENTS," with whom he otherwise seems to have been on generally good terms.[33]

One other question remains to be discussed about John Quincy Adams on his graduation day. What did he actually say?

The keynote of his speech [34]—introducing it he properly, but no doubt truthfully, said that he felt "terrors hitherto unknown"—was the necessity of maintaining the public credit. His high praise of England's example must have further disturbed the Edes crowd, if they bothered to read the address at all. He noted that the situation of Massachusetts for some months past had been truly alarming. There was a lack of circulating medium, the "violent gust of rebellion" was scarcely dispersed, luxury and dissipation were choking out useful virtues, bonds of union with the sister states were shamefully relaxed, and the sails of commerce furled.

"At this critical period, when the whole nation is groaning under the intolerable burden of these accumulated evils," what could have been the cause? Could there have been a loss of honor and patriotism? Some hope, he thought, still arose from the example of the distinguished patriot who headed the government in Massachusetts. (This of course was the grossest flattery. Governor Hancock had in truth discreetly retired the previous year when the domestic situation had really got threatening.)

John Quincy condemned as base and foul the doctrine that nations are not subject to the same laws of honor as individuals. He likened this idea to the principle "which impels the hand of the lawless ruffian, and directs the dagger of the midnight assassin." Survey the history of civilization, he said, and you would find that "public credit has ever been the foundation upon which the fabric of national grandeur has been erected." Read especially the history of Rome whose greatness was due to her "unalterable attachment to the laws of justice, and punctilious observance of all the contracts in which she engaged." In modern times Great Britain exhibited an example of national honor for the admiration and imitation of the American states. "The punctual observance of every contract and the scrupulous fulfillment of every agreement are the only props which have supported the sinking reputation of that ill-fated kingdom."

American women were appealed to for patriotic inspiration by this admiring son of Abigail Adams. He significantly warned his classmates, whenever called upon to defend their country against the "sword of invasion or against the dagger of oppression," to retain severe republican virtues—*i.e.*, to entertain no monarchical notions! Above all they should remember that all the distresses of the Commonwealth were connected with the loss of "national" credit. He said that if everyone would resolve to keep public promises, then happiness would return, commerce would increase, American manufactures vie with those of Europe, and American science enrich the world. The radiant sun of the union would rise again. The muses, disgusted wtih the "depravity of taste and morals" which prevailed abroad, would migrate to America and produce historians and poets to sing her glories. He prayed that honor and integrity might ever distinguish the American states "till the last trump shall announce the dissolution of the world, and the whole frame of nature be consumed in one universal conflagration."

It is evident from these eloquent and burning words that the education of John Quincy Adams had extended far beyond the walls of formal schooling which, indeed, in his case had been rather limited. Two "daggers" and one "midnight assassin" suggest his deep love of the drama, not then to be

had in Boston but acquired by foreign travel and from im-
mersion in Shakespeare at a tender age. They probably reveal
also a fondness for the "Gothic" and "sentimental" novels of
the day with which this young scholar seems to have been
well acquainted.[35]

The political philosophy of his oration, on the other hand,
is deeply rooted in history and morality, not unlike that of
his father's writings. Indeed the whole tenor of "Public Faith"
suggests that the Reverend Mr. Belknap was a keen observer
as well as a flatterer when he detected "ye features of the
Parent in the son," and when he predicted, for the benefit of
his country, "a succession of abilities" in the Adams family.

CHAPTER FIVE

LEGAL STUDIES IN NEWBURYPORT

"Health is all I shall ask"

John Quincy Adams' mother and father and indeed all his relatives had long worried about his health because of his tendency to overstudy and to neglect exercise.[1] As a youth he had been troubled with headaches, and more recently like his mother with spells of "swimming in the head." He had a recurrent illness every spring. His eyes had a tendency to become sore, and he frequently felt unwell apparently from an acid stomach.[2] Extraordinary dreams and insomnia had begun to affect him, although he continued to have a "great propensity" to sleep late in the mornings.[3] Perhaps he was the kind of person who worries too much about himself. A doctor with a "mean" view of human nature once told him that his symptoms were not worth mentioning.[4]

Such a record of general illness could not have been so very unusual even in the eighteenth century, and certainly not for such an intense young student of the law as John Quincy Adams had become in Newburyport, Massachusetts, after graduating from Harvard in 1787. As the eldest son of John Adams he expected a great deal from himself, and was sure that others expected even more. His very graduation address had been sought for publication in addition to provoking controversy in the Boston newspapers.[5] He had been promptly warned by that person dearest to him against thinking too well of himself. "Excellence is comparative," wrote his proud but admonitory mother, who characteristically made a classical reference to conquering Hannibal. She emphasized his need for moderation and above all for exercise, "to brace the nerves and give vigor to the animal functions," thus furnishing a simple maternal diagnosis of the dual nature of his complaint.[6] It did not sound particularly alarming.

Nevertheless at the end of his first year of apprenticeship to the law John Quincy was to suffer a serious crisis in health which necessitated some months of recuperation and at least a year for general recovery.[7] The crisis was to come almost immediately after he had given a public discourse on the disturbing subject of ambition for young men, an oration spoken at the request of the Phi Beta Kappa society of Harvard in September, 1788.[8] A morbid note of philosophical aloofness was to characterize his remarks as he rather insipidly extolled the virtues of the ordinary pursuits of life, or in literary activity free from the "envenomed shafts of rancorous envy." His chaste definition of the worthy lawyer was to be one who disdained "the base and servile arts of chicanery and intrigue" on behalf of "injured innocence and truth." Such words were rather tame in comparison with the vigorous defense of lawyers which he had made as an undergraduate the year before.[9]

All this may not have been resignation from a moral point of view, but for an ambitious young law clerk noted for satire and the son of virile old John Adams, written in the turbulent political year of 1787-88, it must have sounded suspiciously like diffidence. He was to preface his whole puerile performance, moreover, by warning against exaggerated hopes lest an awakening from "fantastic dreams" should in turn be succeeded by a mind settled in "sullen despondency." His experiences of the preceding year afford a partial explanation why such a defeatest attitude was to overtake him.

It had been with very uneasy feelings that John Quincy Adams had contemplated the study of law, begun the previous September in the office of that "great lawyer," Theophilus Parsons of Newburyport.[10] His first three weeks in the North Shore commercial center of Massachusetts had been marked by extraordinary industry, eight hours of study a day in the office and four more in writing forms at his lodgings. He confidently swore—surely a rare thing for him—that the devil would be to pay if he did not learn a great deal of law in the three years ahead. "Health is all I shall ask," he amended, although by this he may have had in mind the sad effects of a recent Saturday night's frolic! He had not actually become intoxicated, but had been left so indisposed that he could neither read nor write nor even attend meeting on Sunday, and he was still suffering considerably on Monday. Apparently it was the first serious hangover he had ever had, and was ample testimony to the enlivening company of young law clerks and doctors' apprentices—and in striking contrast to his sober college days. Yet a few days later he was out dancing until three A.M.! [11]

These were the beginnings of the variegated social life through which John Quincy sought to relieve the tedium of the study of law. When his nerves were in a disagreeable trim several months later he noted that "not even dissipation has been able to help me." [12] However, to do him justice, he never again that year indulged quite so far in wine. He was also trying hard to be prudent in expenditures—he already had a good reputation in that respect—although under the circumstances his money naturally disappeared rapidly.[13]

Life as a law clerk was obviously not to be without its pleasures, yet for John Quincy Adams it was frequently marked by depression.[14] He soon began to have gloomy thoughts about those years of preparation for which he sometimes thought he had little inclination. Although he had finished the second volume of Blackstone's *Commentaries* by November 16, and the fourth only a month later, he continued to lament his slow progress and to ponder his future. "The question, what am I to do in this world recurs to me very frequently; and never without causing great anxiety, and a depression of spirits. My prospects appear darker to me every day, and I am obliged sometimes to drive the subject from my mind to assume some more agreeable train of thought." He began to abhor ambition. "Fortune, I do not covet. Honours, I begin to think are not worth seeking. . . ." [15]

Disquietude frequently invaded his innermost thoughts in those early months in Newburyport. One evening he experienced a depressed feeling different from anything he had ever known before, one which filled him with the deepest dread until he succumbed to a sleep plagued by extravagant dreams. Even in philosophical matters he was unable to relax. A few days later he became involved in a discussion with his fellow clerks on the old subject of self-love, and doggedly stuck to his earlier conviction that there was no such thing as "disinterested benevolence." He could not honestly admit to finding any such motive in himself.[16]

In the latter part of December and during January his general health was better, although he was often critical of himself for what he thought was a lack of diligence. Early in February, however, a few days after the suicide of a young acquaintance, his nerves got into an unhappy tone and his spirits were again depressed owing, he thought, to too intense study and writing. This sometimes lasted until one or two A.M. It was unfortunate that a man had to be either a fool or an invalid, he lamented, as he considered easing up on work.[17] Improvement followed shortly, however, and by early March he was happy to have finished "my Lord Coke" after ten weeks of heavy work, and soon was feeling pleased with a second reading of Blackstone, although his progress was "slow, too slow." [18] This was, relatively, his happiest time of the year. Yet he was soon brooding again in his journal, saying that

the prospects of life which are before me are by far the most frequent employment of my thoughts, and according to the different temperature of my spirits, I am sometimes elated with hope, sometimes contented with indifference, but often tormented with fears, and depressed by the most discouraging appearances.[19]

These uneasy reflections were to be incorporated into his Phi Beta Kappa address in September.

Early in May his regular spring "troubles" commenced, initiating still another phase of depressed spirits. Once again illness was accompanied by pessimism, and sometimes even by "terror" as he contemplated two more years of study before entering a badly crowded profession, attended by no personal fortune. The only good he could draw from his physical condition was that at least it made him get up early! [20] Soon he was not sleeping well again. He began to take long evening walks alone, despite the fact that it had been his custom throughout the spring to take such exercise in company. His imagination became overly active. "I look forward with terror; and by so much the more, as the total exemption from any great evils hitherto leads me to fear that the greatest are laid up in store for me." This morbid introspection extended even to his imaginative sharing in the agony of the death of a child. Since misery is found among virtuous as well as among unprincipled people, what can one expect? this "virtuous" young man asked himself.[21]

Despite the continuance of many social activities including his weekly club, and at least one serenade of the ladies which lasted until three or four in the morning, John Quincy only temporarily pulled out of the doldrums by taking a trip. This was to welcome home his beloved parents from their long sojourn abroad and to help them get settled in the new "mansion" in Braintree. The house had originally been distasteful to him.[22] Could this have been due in part to the fact that it had been bought from that brilliant young playwright, Royall Tyler, who had once hoped to take sister Nabby Adams there? [23] Nevertheless it was apparently a most happy time of reunion. There were boxes of fascinating books from Europe to be unpacked, days of gunning for birds on the marshes, and opportunities for taking in events at Harvard including commencement.

It was with great regret that John Quincy prepared to return to Newburyport after five weeks of "vacation." Despite the loss of so much time he cautiously resolved henceforth not to confine himself so closely to the law but to give more attention to lighter studies. It was a futile resolution. Soon he was industriously at work preparing his Phi Beta Kappa address. After completing this in the first week of August, his eyes became troublesome.[24] Continual interruptions during the month that followed renewed regrets for his loss of time, particularly in view of the "brevity and uncertainty" of life which a funeral brought to mind. His evenings walks now became longer than ever. He had begun to find that visiting was too coldly formal, believing that he was "not upon familiar terms in one house in town," and confessing that in such circumstances he did not wish to be extensively acquainted. Sister Nabby wrote from New York to remonstrate against his anti-social attitude.[25] In view of the active social life which he had earlier led in Newburyport, this was a most significant revelation of his unhappy condition.

At this point, on August 23, just two weeks before he delivered the Phi Beta Kappa oration, his journal abruptly breaks off to be shortly resumed for another month of irregular entries. His only explanation for this remarkable change in habits was that an "indisposition" now prevented him from "writing." [26] This apparently included some other kind of writing than that of keeping a journal, for he had said on August 9 that he was then closely engaged on a matter which had been "accumulating" two months. The reference probably was to a literary matter and something of this nature apparently had had to be abandoned.

It is clear, in any case, that even when John Quincy had been visiting in Braintree in July that personal difficulties had been growing upon him. For example, he had found old Parson Wiberd's sermons more than usually boring, and religious matters at this time were very important to him. When he was in spirits, he admitted to himself that he did not feel completely discouraged about his prospects, but his twenty-first birthday had brought forth the gloomy reflection that he had not strength to stand on his own feet, and that it probably was just as well not to know what the future would bring. More Phi Beta Kappa material! The weather had been unusually hot and fatiguing while he had been at Braintree, and there had been too many insects for the bathing that he normally enjoyed.

It was the Harvard Commencement on July 16, however, which had first given him really serious concern about himself. Perhaps he had been thinking of his own triumph on that occasion the previous year. His spirits had been so exhilarated by the day's events that he could hardly sleep that night, but they were profoundly depressed the next day. "The bow string by being too much extended cannot regain its usual position without an intermediate relaxation," he wrote introspectively in his journal.[27] From this time on he was in grave difficulties, only temporarily checked by the preparation of the oration he had recently been invited to make.

Despite the year's record of misgiving, it is clear that John Quincy had made some real progress in the mastery of books basic to the study of law, in addition to many scholarly works in history and ethics.[28] His unhappiness must therefore have related to the larger area of his total ambition, as this in turn was related to his experience of life. When exploring this area in the Phi Beta Kappa oration, he was to make no mention of government or politics as a proper goal for an ambitious young man. Yet he himself had been deeply absorbed in recent months in the struggle in Massachusetts over the ratification of the Federal Constitution, not to mention the fact that he had been steeped in a political atmosphere almost from the cradle.

One explanation of this curious hiatus lay in the astounding fact that he had been Anti-Federal during that struggle, and had even been surprised to learn in March, 1788, that his own father approved of the Constitution! [29] His attitude may have been due in part to the strong republicanism which had emerged from his European experience. Perhaps it was also due to his admiration for a fellow boarder at Mrs. Leather's on Market Square in Newburyport, Dr. Daniel Kilham, a man of "sense and learning." "I hope the name will not scare you," he once playfully wrote his mother. This fellow Harvard graduate, a bachelor about sixteen years his senior, who had started out in life to be a doctor but had ended up as an apothecary, was a sturdy Anti-Federalist and outspoken delegate from Newburyport to the Massachusetts legislature.[30] Perhaps he was also a good man with whom to discuss problems of health!

John Quincy was to record when he heard the news that ratification had finally carried in the state convention at Boston in February, 1788, that his opinions on the subject had never been passionate or violent and that he was now "converted, though not convinced." [31] However his earlier journal entries clearly indicate that his Anti-Federalism had been deeply held, and that the drawn-out struggle over ratification had contributed to his depressed condition. Several of his friends and eventually even sister Nabby hinted at their disapproval of his views.[32]

In all this, it is important to notice that he had been at odds with his law teacher, Theophilus Parsons, the legal sage of the Essex County conservatives since the days of the Revolution. Parsons was exceedingly pro-Constitution. "Nor do I wonder at all that he should approve of it, as it is calculated to increase the influence, power and wealth of those who have any already. If the Constitution be adopted, it will be a grand point gained in favour of the aristocratic party," John Quincy had stubbornly declared in October. He hated to believe that "free government is inconsistent with human nature," and had approved of Dr. Kilham's independent spirit, which had made him unpopular in the town, in opposing the submission of the Constitution to a state convention.

The struggle over ratification had excited strong opinions. A military man was heard to say that he had been an enthusiast for liberty in '75 but that he now found it all a farce.[33] By late December John Quincy actually thought the country on the eve of a revolution. "Whether it will be effected in silence and without a struggle, or whether it will be carried at the point of a sword is yet a question. . . . I fear [the Constitution] will be adopted." He suspected the parish preacher of Federalist propagandizing.

News of the ultimate triumph of ratification arrived on February 7. There was a noisy celebration in Newburyport to greet the returning delegates, as "the mob huzza'd." It probably was not just a coincidence that a few days later John Quincy noted that his spirits were now by way of improvement.[34] If the theory is correct that politics really meant a great deal to him, only now did he begin to make a partial recovery from what had been an exhausting experience. But his good opinion of his "master" and oracle in the law, Theophilus Parsons, must have been sadly diminished. The tobacco-chewing Parsons, one of the returning delegates, made merry in the office by entertaining visitors with an account of all the tricks which had been employed in the convention to baffle the Anti-Federalists. As John Quincy saw it, Parsons made the "science of politics" one of "little, insignificant intrigue and chicanery." [35] These were to be the identical words employed in the Phi Beta Kappa address to denounce the "servile arts" unworthy of a lawyer!

Ironically, John Quincy himself was to become acquainted at his father's house in July with the Reverend Samuel West, an old college friend of John Adams. West had been the man selected to persuade John Hancock to leave his sickroom in order to offer his famous amendments at the ratifying convention, an action not wholly unconnected with Federalist "intrigue." But young Adams merely found the Reverend to be a most interesting and talkative old gentleman.[36]

His own fingers having been badly scorched and his sagacity rudely shaken, his cynicism about politics naturally reached a new high. The Massachusetts spring election of 1788 was pro-Hancock, but with the "wrong" people supporting the governor. John Quincy dourly recorded the fact without venturing a cause. "The revolution that has taken place in sentiments within one twelve month past must be astonishing to a person unacquainted with the weaknesses, the follies, and the vices of human nature," was all he said,[37] ignoring the obvious explanation that there had been a political bargain.

Nevertheless, John Quincy was now somewhat "Federal" himself, sufficiently so at least as not to please the formidable Mercy Warren of Milton, an old friend of the family whose husband was still under a political cloud from Shays' Rebellion.[38] Perhaps another cynic would have been inclined to have made young Adams himself something of an object lesson in the art of political accommodation! However that might be, the political situation of the entire Adams family could not have been too happy at this time. John Adams *père* had only recently returned from England without having played any part in the work that had made the new Constitution possible, unless, indeed, it had been by having written his book in defence of American state constitutional principles.[39] Of course there were vague rumors beginning to circulate about his being vice presidential material, helped along in the difficult state of Pennsylvania by his old friend

and correspondent, Dr. Benjamin Rush. However, the des-
picable Hancock—like Adams he had originated in Braintree
—was also in the running.

Small wonder that the baffled and unhappy young law
clerk left politics strictly alone in his September address at
Harvard, save to notice that statesmen are remembered for
"noble defeats" as well as for victories, and for an oblique
criticism of the role of military "heroes," which probably reflected his old animus against the Order of the Cincinnati.
Yet his sister was to write him so truly only three weeks later
that "The happiness of our family seems ever to have been so
interwoven with the Politicks of our Country as to be in a
great degree dependent upon them." [40]

Fretting about his slow progress in the law and upset by
political developments, John Quincy in 1788 increasingly
sought solace in literary composition, but also with unsatisfactory results. His difficulty here was doubly compounded
because he was attempting to use an eighteenth century literary device to cope with another problem, his relations with
the ladies. In the field of character study and especially in the
female department, he considered himself an expert since he
had been at it for several years. Seemingly, in his own opinion, he knew a great deal about women. He considered them
easier to understand than men! "It requires a much longer
acquaintance to form a just opinion of the character of a man
than of a woman: the distinguishing traits are deeper and
much more numerous. . . ." [41]

In treating of this and other philosophical questions his
journal had proved disappointing. It had tended to become
more and more of a diary instead of a repository of creative
writing. He sometimes asked himself if he should not put a
stop to all "this nonsense." [42] One difficulty with making his
journal an instrument for the freest expression was the danger that he could not keep the volumes secret. He had learned
this from bitter experience, one instance being when his

brother Charles had been guilty of prying and meddling.[43] In consequence, no doubt, the later journal entries are obviously more carefully guarded with respect to the most sensitive matters than they had been in his Haverhill days, a matter of regret to the reader as well as to John Quincy himself.

To write poetry had always been his dearest ambition. It was a safer medium to employ than the prose of his none-too-secret journal. He said in January, 1788, that he had begun a hundred times to write poetry. "I have tried every measure and every kind of strophe, but of the whole I never finish'd but one of any length, and that was in fact but the work of a day." [44] This presumably referred to his satire on "Delia," i.e., Nancy, written in Haverhill two years before.[45] He was now to try on a more ambitious scale a "design of drawing a number of female characters," perhaps on the model of the "Receipt for a Wife" that he had read in New York on first returning to America.[46] The first of these stanzas appeared in his journal on March 28, the second on April 8, each satirizing a young lady of his acquaintance under the fictitious names of "Lucinda" and "Belinda." The satire on "Delia" was to be converted and bestowed on a certain "Narcissa," another young lady acquaintance in Newburyport. These were the beginnings of a long romantic poem later to be entitled "A Vision." [47]

There was a grave danger of artistic failure in his thus giving expression to his feelings, even in an age noted for its formalized expression—the danger that the experiment could not come off until he had had some sort of deep experience in love himself. Nevertheless, this is what John Quincy Adams in ignorance set out to do between January and March, 1788. His inability to complete his plan may have become apparent to him by mid-summer when he was continually aware of some such problem "accumulating" upon him.

After all, he must have been deadly afraid of a premature love affair such as he had narrowly escaped with "Delia" in the winter of 1785-86. John Quincy was unquestionably a person whose passions were naturally "strong and impetuous" as his mother had long since warned him.[48] This fact, together with his upbringing and the formalities of eighteenth century behavior, must have accounted for his exceptional emphasis on self-restraint. Despite all this he presumably did fancy himself in love at least once during this year. He wrote the initials "M.N." encircled in a heart in his almanac diary for 1788,[49] only to find the young lady, presumably little Mary Newhall, "disdainful," as his scornful characterization of "Narcissa" in "A Vision" was to reveal. The humiliation must have been doubly galling to such an exceedingly egotistical young man. Meantime he must have unhappily kept on trying to write satirical stanzas and no doubt was looking for "Clara," the embodiment of feminine loveliness in his poem.

It was not that he lacked materials for study of the female. On the contrary, the year had been enlivened by a round of social activities, of dancing, card-playing, and sleigh rides, of "kissing games" and singing—the last two he admittedly despised. In all these activities a variety of attractive young ladies had participated. Yet he apparently chose to intellectualize all such relationships, possibly because, as he once confessed, it was difficult for him to be sociable on short acquaintance with unmarried women [50]—and possibly also because of his rejection by "M.N." Consequently a long list of female character studies ensued in his journal for 1788 but with no evidence of any permanent attachment. Miss Knight, Miss Sally Jenkins—he seemed to like her quite well despite her "acquiline" nose—Miss Putnam, and many more. Each was found well-endowed in some respects but each had her shortcomings, often by being "affected," or addicted to reading novels, or subject to woman's principal limitation, which was a deficiency in education. John Quincy actually took pride in being able to "shame" young ladies given to the art of flattery, yet he also knew the keen embarrassment of being "laughed at" by girls.[51]

So the young ladies all became problems to be resolved in his journal. Few were not mercilessly analyzed there. One curious exception occurred. At a tavern dance in January, following a sleighing party, he danced with the eldest Miss Frazier and with two other girls. Both of the latter he carefully described, but of the first he said not a word. The exception probably meant nothing much at the time. As late as August 13, when he passed an evening at Selectman Moses Frazier's, he said of the young misses that they assumed an importance above their years, and as they were handsome he would "rather look at them for five minutes than be with them five hours." So he had not at this time recognized "Clara"—at least not in the person of fourteen-year-old Mary Frazier.[52]

Law, politics, literature, and possibly love all had proved more or less disappointing to John Quincy Adams in 1788. One remaining prop of his self-esteem was also challenged if not over-turned. His "reasonable" religious beliefs became subject to a new kind of questioning. The torrent of religious fundamentalism, a part of the continuing Edwardian revival opposing the doctrine of free will, and known to John Quincy in its derivative form of Hopkinsianism, bore heavily against him. Worst of all, his best friend Thompson was "seduced" by the evangelical gospel during the summer.[53] The weekly meeting of the club, which John Quincy so greatly enjoyed, had to change its evening to permit Thompson to go to lecture.

The instrument of this new torture was the Reverend Samuel Spring—he was graduated from Princeton in 1771—a Congregationalist with the zeal and enthusiasm of a Presbyterian. John Quincy had first gone to hear him in November, 1787. Reverend Spring stressed "disinterested benevolence" because he said that selfishness originated in sin, and he threatened eternal torments for all persons who did not experience saving grace.[54] This sort of teaching John Quincy considered nonsense, not finding the least sign of disinterested benevolence in himself, and no doubt refusing to acknowledge ever having "experienced" salvation.

Nevertheless, throughout the year John Quincy had frequently attended the Reverend Mr. Spring's services because, he confessed, he found them more interesting than some held by other preachers. By late July, however, he had become exceedingly irritated by what he thought was the Reverend's self-interested proselytizing in which "passions" were being paraded as "principles." By August he was bitterly denouncing the sect as promoting a "bigoted, illiberal system of religion" which, professing to follow "purely" the dictates of the Bible, in his opinion contradicted the whole doctrine of the New Testament and went against the idea of a God of mercy as well as against reason.[55] But good friend Thompson, whom he had once described as an "amiable, worthy youth" with a clear head and a sound heart [56]—but whom he now denounced as a person of "violent passion" and "unbounded ambition" —had become thoroughly ensnared. Could Thompson have been an object lesson for the Phi Beta Kappa address? The day following this vehement outburst against his friend, John Quincy's eyes again began to trouble him.

It was in such a state of general irritation, to which his own troubled ambition and affections had led him, that on September 5 he addressed the Phi Beta Kappa society in Cambridge, in self-effacing platitudes. Ironically, one of the scheduled speakers had to be excused at the last minute on grounds of ill health—but it was not courageous John Quincy Adams who thus cried off, no matter how wretchedly he may have felt. (When first agreeing to perform he had made the qualification in his journal, "if I can possibly attend." [57]) For the second time in a year he spoke before an unusually distinguished audience, now of course including his parents. In addition to the college officers and members of the society, Governor Hancock "happened" to be there with the admiral and some other officers of the French squadron which was in Boston harbor. The governor was always fond of such exhibitions for more than literary reasons, and perhaps more than a little curious about young Adams himself. The French officers also had reason to know about John Quincy who had lived so long in their country, and the French consul came up to compliment him after the affair.

Primarily warning in his lofty address against the passions serving as a guide for ambition in young men, and urging lives of quiet service far removed from the "crowd's ignoble strife," unhappy John Quincy Adams had only one vigorous affirmation to advance. The most virtuous ambition, he declared, lay in literature and science. These would not only benefit mankind but would exalt the reputation of America, thus refuting the "insulting" and "presumptuous" attitudes of superiority by Europeans. He boasted of one of the most illustrious of Americans because of his recent achievement in these fields. This was Thomas Jefferson, Esq., author of the recent *Notes On Virginia*.[58] However this identification of his much beloved older friend from Paris days was given only in a footnote to the address. When the curtain finally dropped on the "theatre of human life" John Quincy was sure that cultural distinction would be what a grateful universe would applaud. And, he might have reiterated, for patriotic as well as for literary reasons. This was the only "passionate" note he struck.

Just one week after making this heroic performance, John Quincy visited a doctor in Newburyport to obtain an opiate to quiet his nerves and to enable him to sleep. The humane physician, he had hopefully said in his oration, "administers not only the restoring preparation to the languishing body, but the balm of consolation to the wounded mind." A week later he went to his Uncle Shaw's in Haverhill in a vain effort to recover his health. Aunt Eliza wrote a letter of reassurance to his mother, but confessed that John Quincy's "nervous system" seemed "much effected." He was taking "the bark" that Dr. Swett had recommended as well as some special tea of Aunt Eliza's own brewing and was slowly responding to her maternal care. Since he was the best man to take his medicine that she had ever known she was going to reward him by taking him out riding and visiting. She also revealed that he had not been well since leaving Braintree in July. "What did you do to him?" she quaintly asked. Had they given him too strong coffee or told him some *"woeful Story"*? She significantly underlined the latter.[59]

Ten days later, finding it utterly impossible to study on returning to Newburyport—this was much against his Aunt's advice—John Quincy went home to Braintree for a long period of recuperation. Aunt Eliza, now revealing her full concern to his mother, warned that he must be very careful about diet and exercise and that all study would have to be laid aside for the present. She prayed that his blood would flow on regularly and the roses soon return to his cheeks, but she frankly admitted that he had "alarming complaints." [60]

So "young Hercules" had finally been brought to bay by the hydra-headed monster of despairing ambition. Even his republican idealism had led him astray. His self-communicative journal had also had to be abandoned. Some new directions of interest and new means of expression were clearly demanded for his immediate salvation.

CHAPTER SIX

ROMANCE ON THE NORTH SHORE

> "What bosom burns not
> with poetick fire?"

In the early period of his recuperation from insomnia and nervous afflictions at Braintree in the fall of 1788, John Quincy Adams took a lot of exercise. He tramped the fields and marshes, gunning with brother Tommy until he was tired. Frequently he rode his horse. He also helped in the work of erecting shelves and arranging the great collection of books recently brought from Europe by his father. Other kinds of interests were more slowly resumed. The ministration of religion he found disappointing in the sermons by old Mr. Wiberd but a visiting minister proved to be more engaging. A resumption of intellectual activity was begun with reading in Gibbon's *Decline and Fall,* a work which had long given him great pleasure, although he had never quite approved of that historian's attitude towards Christianity. On November 3 when he tersely recorded "getting well," he had been reading Cicero's *De Senectute,* rather elderly philosophical fare for so young a man but apparently soothing in his present state of mind.[1]

Two weeks later he confided in the brief diary that he still somehow maintained, "My health happily recovered," an overly optimistic calculation of the degree of his recovery. However, his mother had meantime left on a trip to New York where daughter Nabby was "expecting" again. This was probably also a sign of confidence in her son's recovery. Soon it was Thanksgiving and the coming of the first snow of the winter. Early in December John Quincy left Braintree for Newburyport, presumably to consider the renewal of his legal studies, although on the very day of his arrival there his diary mentions "dancing." [2] However, after three weeks, during which he spent a good deal of time visiting in nearby Haverhill, he returned again to Braintree. There he had two more months of outdoor sports and social affairs, as well as light intellectual fare in cultivating "the muse." No doubt Dr. Swett of Newburyport had recommended the former; the last was natural therapy for a convalescing amateur poet.

On the last leaves of his almanac diary for this critical year, 1788, there are several quotations such as he was fond of copying down. One of them queried:

> Perfect he seems & undefiled with sin,
> But is this Saint without, a Saint within.

If this doleful bit of doggerel meant anything at all with regard to John Quincy's state of mind at this time, it suggests not that the young Puritan had been suffering from anything that might reasonably have given rise to an uneasy conscience —certainly he had not yet been guilty of being a Boswell beyond having kept a remarkable journal [3]—but rather that morbid conscientiousness may have contributed to his recent distress. In similar vein, on the fly leaf of his new almanac for 1789 there was written down, "There is small choice in rotten apples." However this gloomy reflection was followed, among other things, with Prince Hal's colorful line, "A fair hot wench in flame-colour'd taffeta." [4] So not all of his reflections were to be gloomy, at least not in the immediate future! Indeed, the "scale" was now to be weighed down on "the other side," [5] and possibly over-weighted.

John Quincy's permanent return to Newburyport in March, 1789, after his mother's return to Braintree and his father's departure to New York to be inaugurated as vice president of the new nation, began a year of unremitting social pleasures during which the study of law seems to have been deliberately relaxed. Whatever had been the exact nature of his illness in the past six months, the remedy universally prescribed was the avoidance of too many "worldly" cares. Society and sociability were obviously indicated.

Back in October, 1788, at the very beginning of John Quincy's illness, his old college chum and fellow law student, James Bridge, had written him a kindly "get well" letter in which he had playfully reminded him that no thoughts "are more concerned with the Flesh than those excited by the Ladies." Bridge had recommended that John Quincy should take some account of them and had thereupon furnished an amusing analysis of several of the Newburyport girls, plus the description of a recent comical serenade by "the lads" which had lasted until three A.M.[6] A similar prescription of light-hearted diversion was made some months later by the practical Billy Cranch, who responded to cousin John Quincy's request for a remedy to relax the mind, by advising, first, to reason gloom away, but if that failed to seize upon some trifle to divert one's thought. Cranch then related a conversation he had just had with excited little Betsy Foster concerning a copy of John Quincy's satirical and romantic poem about the local girls, entitled "A Vision." [7] An interest in girls was obviously not a bad prescription for melancholy.

Although his weekly club of fellow law clerks and doctors' apprentices—that "little chosen flock" [8]—continued to be an important diversion for John Quincy after his return to Newburyport, his essential concern was with "the Ladies." There was a continual round of sociable evenings at Judge Bradbury's, Colonel Wigglesworth's, or Mr. Moses Frazier's, with the young ladies always in attendance for dining, cards, or dancing, and for parties in the "grove" when the weather grew warmer. John Quincy's daily walks were of course continued, usually with other young men but sometimes in mixed company. The signs of his illness dropped off; occasional fatigue or drowsiness usually followed late hours at dancing or serenades; and he said in April, 1789, that scarcely anything of his complaints remained except for occasional "spasms." [9]

Life for the Newburyport law clerk seemed to have settled down to the old routine. Inwardly, however, his muse had taken new wing. His introspective journal had, of course, been abandoned months before. It was during this period of convalescence that he first sent to the public press some examples of his literary wit and poetry. These were also contributions to a little renaissance of literary sentimentality then taking place in Boston and the North Shore towns.

The sour soil of belles lettres in Boston had been dubiously enriched in late 1788 by the establishment of the *Herald of Freedom,* a bi-weekly newspaper unusually receptive to literary effulgia. In January, 1789, the ambitious *Massachusetts Magazine* was founded by that worldly wise and patriotic printer, Isaiah Thomas, who saw no inconsistency in the simultaneous publication of salacious broadsides and of sober, useful literature.[10] The appearance of this magazine coincided in January with the publication, also by Thomas, of the so-called "first American novel," *The Power of Sympathy: or, the Triumph of Nature* by William Hill Brown. This was a florid literary extravaganza dedicated to "the young ladies of America" which included titillating references to a recent scandal in Boston, a horrid tale of seduction and suicide.[11]

The entire Boston press almost simultaneously broke into a rash of romantic poems and sarcastic essays, the latter invariably on the theme of the deceptive wiles of women, some of it downright vulgar. A veritable battle of the sexes ensued! [12] Also included were literary puzzles in the form of poems which furnished clues through classical references to the names of local nymphs, done in the most insipid manner. These so-called "rebuses" may have been the eighteenth century's equivalent of modern crossword puzzles, but they were also presented at the time in the guise of advertising "Columbian" prowess in the "arts and sciences."

For that recuperating young satirist, twenty-one-year-old John Quincy Adams, at once nationalistic and literary and romantic, all such nonsense must have been a wonderfully diverting interest while he was slowly resuming his legal studies. He became a mighty composer in his own right of puzzling rebuses, of which at least three were published in the *Massachusetts Magazine* in 1789.[13] On another occasion, as "Celadon" in the Boston *Herald*,[14] he achieved a short-lived fame as a magisterial and puckish critic of female literary "genius," thereby evoking a scad of rebuttals and remonstrances. While his name as a contributor of these and other offerings never appeared publicly, he unquestionably gained quite a private literary reputation among his friends. In any case he must have gotten a lot of innocent amusement out of it.

Possibly this sort of thing was not so innocent on the part of all contributors. The game of character identification and analysis must have sometimes seemed perilously close to character assassination. Indeed it began to be a public complaint that scurrility—scribbling of all kinds was reaching a record high. A new work on libel was currently being advertised in the newspapers! The *Essex Journal* of Newburyport even ran a series of "Mirror" portraits in the spring of 1789 under such insinuating titles as "Prudence," "Curiosius," and the like. It would appear that John Quincy Adams in late April contributed one of these ponderous satires himself.[15]

Even more sensational was an "Enigmatical list" of young ladies which was also published in the *Journal* that day.[16] It offered character clues to various of the local Newburyport belles in quite the best Boston manner. In some way or other young Adams was deeply involved in the tempest of protest which blew up in the local teapot, although the whole thing smacks of a jolly rag perpetrated by devilish young law clerks.

Apparently it was he who submitted a grave, admonitory communication to the *Journal* under the signature of "Lelius" on May 6, self-righteously identifying the author of the "list" with one of his fellow clerks. He declared that the author was more conspicuous for idleness than for literary ability, and said that his time might be better employed in studying the cause of justice than in slandering his female acquaintances.[17] Perhaps John Quincy was writing about himself, tongue in cheek! Of course, there were literary neophytes other than himself around town. On several occasions Alice Tucker, daughter of the minister in Newbury, had to listen to a "conceited coxcomb" read his poems to her.[18]

All of Newburyport was up in arms over the sensational "Enigmatical" descriptions. Much of the *Journal* for May 6 was devoted to vociferous criticism of such ungentlemanly tactics. It was loudly—almost too loudly—asserted by "Eugenio" that the "villain," "abandoned wretch," and "ruffian" who had produced the "malicious effusions" was one who would have been better off reading "Galen, or Coke on Littleton." Members of "a certain club" were advised to be "better employed in their usual noise and intemperance, than in striking their heated Craniums together, and by the concussion producing fire to blast the reputation of our fair," piously called "the loveliest work of God." [19]

Unless John Quincy and his fellow club members were simply having a "game" as well as great sport with the "coterie" of local nymphs, he was but one of many local citizens who disapproved of innuendos on young ladies being made public under cover of poet's license. In that case, however, it is doubly ironical that his own satirical writings about the local girls should soon have gotten into private circulation. Perhaps his satires were already being bruited about, like Shakespeare's "sugred sonnets" among his private friends. Only a few weeks before he had had to make some kind of an "explanation" to poor Rebecca Cazneau, that unfortunate

friend of Alice Tucker, about whom he had already written
a wicked satire as a part of his "Vision":

> Belinda next advanç'd with rapid stride
> A compound strange of Vanity and Pride
> Around her face no wanton Cupids play,
> Her tawny skin, defies the God of Day.
> Loud was her laugh, undaunted was her look,
> And folly seem'd to dictate what she spoke.
> In vain the Poet's and musician's art
> Combine to move the Passions of the heart,
> Belinda's voice like grating hinges groans,
> And in harsh thunder roars a lover's moans.[20]

His talent for making such critical verses on young ladies
of his acquaintance went back at least to his Haverhill days,
as his sarcastic "Epistle to Delia" (*i.e.*, Nancy) of December,
1785, proves.[21] As for the delightful task of putting the initials of female names into verse, he had composed two acrostics—one presumably kind and one unkind and "both un-
true"—on the name of Catherine Jones back in January, 1787,
when that disturbing young Newburyporter had been visiting in Cambridge.[22] The "kind" acrostic had gone like this.

> C—ould all the powers of rhetoric combin'd
> A—ssist to show the beauties of her mind,
> T—he poets efforts would be all in vain,
> H—er mind is fair without one single stain.
> A—ll the soft Passions which improve the heart,
> R—eign in her breast, and every thought impart.
> I—n such a breast no foible can reside,
> N—o little art, for prudence is her guide.
> E—ach moral beauty, which adorns the soul,
> J—oinéd to each grace completes her soft controul.
> O—f siren charms, the poets often tell,
> N—o goddess e'er employ'd them half so well;
> E—nvy itself, must drop a tear to find,
> S—o fair a face, with such a beauteous mind.[23]

John Quincy subsequently made an acrostic on the name of Mary Frazier, and doubtless on many other girls during his Newburyport residence. Some of these apparently got into print along with his other writings.

An almost endless amount of similar nonsense and literary high jinks was appearing in the Boston newspapers that year. One might conjecture that some of this originated in Newburyport. Perhaps that was the place from which "Julia," a young lady in the country, reproached "Delia" in the Boston *Herald* in December, 1788, for preferring the amusements of the town and delaying her stay. Several months later when "Julia" arose to the defense of her sex, which had been taking such a merciless going over in the Boston press by "Gyges," "Horatio," and "Civil Spy," she contributed some observations on human nature in "our small village" by coolly dissecting the characters of "Narcissa" and "Maria," [24] pseudonyms also employed by John Quincy Adams about Newburyport girls. A few days before, "Belinda" had published a scornful reply to "Mr. Civil Spy" in which she scathingly referred to a member of a family of "rising greatness" which was looking for a coach and coronet as befitted a "Peer of the American republick." One thinks of Abigail Adams ordering a chaise with coat of arms inscribed for the Adams family before returning from England the previous year! [25] One remembers also that John Quincy had started off his "Vision" with a particularly vicious satire on poor "Belinda." [26]

Meantime, in January and February, 1789, the first two numbers of Mr. Thomas' *Massachusetts Magazine* had appeared, with "charades," an "enigmatical list of young gentlemen of Boston," and puzzling "rebuses" furnished by "Julia and Emma" and others. The epidemic of fulsome "rebuses" which now ran riot in the local newspapers invited public identification of numerous nymphs. The whole thing had delightful overtones for young people as one "rustic" poet made clear.

What's meant by a REBUS
   Come tell me, I pray,
Says Dolly to Enos,
   While raking of hay.
Let me BUSS you again,
   And again, says the youth,
And that will explain,
   What's a RE-BUS in truth.[27]

Such whimsical matter was grist for the literary mill of John Quincy Adams. The "rebus" especially appealed to his talents.[28] The one he wrote on "Maria" (*i.e.*, Mary) Frazier which appeared in the *Massachusetts Magazine* in May, 1789, may be taken as a sample, not that it had any particular significance either as poetry or so far as the girl went at the time.

Take the word by which silver fac'd Cynthia's nam'd
An animal always for Industry fam'd
An object which most men with ardor pursue,
With a colour which gives to fair Iris a hue.
Add a substance to these, which for hardness is known
And say that her heart is worth more than a throne.
Then take the light Goddess, capricious and blind,
A pleasing and useful employ for the mind.
The friendship, which Nations in Treaties profess
And what for a friend we should ever possess.
A country encircled, by Ocean around,
And the part which receives the impression of sound.
Join the City which once o'er the universe sway'd,
Then tell me the name of a beautiful maid.[29]

His solution, also in verse, appeared in the same magazine several months later. It was composed of the first letters of the "clue" words and of course spelled "MARIA FRAZIER."

The rage for "rebuses" gave John Quincy another idea. As "Scipio Africanus" in the Boston *Herald* for February 27, 1789,[30] he published a mock rebuke to those persons who like himself—this of course was part of the humor—were concealing the names of their loves in the form of "rebuses." He gravely asseverated that he, for his part, wanted to proclaim openly his love for "Dinah," thereby proving that "the force of sentiment depends not upon the tincture of the skin." This latter was a slam on poetic comparisons between "white skin" and "innocence within," then much in vogue with amateur versifiers like himself. His would-be humorous performance was in fact a parody or foreshadowing of the "Clara" portion of his long poem, "A Vision," and read, in part:

> My DINAH's charms no vulgar poet claim,
> No servile bard, that clips the wings of fame,
> To vile acrostics, tunes, unmeaning lays,
> Or in a rebus centers all his praise.
> The partial gods, presiding at her birth,
> Gave DINAH beauty, and yet gave her worth;
> Kind nature ting'd with blackest hue her skin,
> An emblem of her innocence within.
> A jetty fleece adorns her lovely head,
> Her sparkling eyes are border'd round with red,
> Her nose is flatten'd by the hand of love,
> By Cupid's self, descending from above.

The last two lines of this burlesque are precisely those which he was to use in closing "A Vision":

> Thy choice alone, can make my anxious breast,
> Supremely wretched, or supremely blest.

One can only conclude from this sad performance that had young John Quincy Adams lived two centuries later, he would have been publicly pilloried for triple prejudice on grounds of race, color, and creed. He apparently had them all.[31]

While "Scipio Africanus" did not go entirely unnoticed, it caused nothing like the uproar that followed the publication of his "Celadon" contribution to that paper on March 10. The appearance of "Celadon"—the name implies a casualty of romantic warfare [32]—was carefully noted in John Quincy's diary the next day with the quizzical observation, "Laid to me," something he acknowledged as true many months later. The following evening at Mr. Russell's in Boston—he was still recuperating at nearby Braintree—he heard an "Attack on C. & Poetry" which revealed the considerable public reaction, at least among his friends.

What he had done in a long mocking essay was to make a pretended defense against the complaints of "Gyges," most vulgar of all the scribblers, of those *"learned Ladies"* who had recently contributed to Mr. Thomas' *Magazine*. Tongue in cheek, he declared that they had reflected no small honor upon their country, and he had then proceeded, with lofty superiority, to criticize their various offerings, graciously admitting that it was quite natural for young ladies to have young gentlemen as the "most prevalent" objects on their minds. On the whole, he declared, their offerings excited such hopes for "Columbian science" that the imagination could scarcely conceive of the wonderful future ahead! He himself was so "fired with the thought" as to break into poetic rhapsody:

> Proceed, ye fair, pursue the glorious end—
> Oh! may success your efforts still attend!
> Behold the laurel and the myrtle join'd,
> In sweetest union happily combin'd.
> While beauty's fingers sweep the sounding lyre,
> What bosom burns not with Poetick fire?
> What morbid miser would not give his gold
> To hear his beauties in a *Rebus* told?
> Who would not sigh to have his virtues made
> The pleasing subject of a soft charade?
> What youth aspires not to behold his name
> Borne on enigmas, to eternal fame?
> Proceed, ye fair, pursue the glorious end,
> And bright success your efforts shall attend.
> Tis yours alone to please with varied charms,

> Whose *wit* entices, and whose beauty warms.
> In you alone with wonder we may find
> The *loves,* the *graces,* and the muses join'd.
> CELADON [33]

Here again the conclusion, with its emphasis on "you alone," is reminiscent of the conclusion to "A Vision." Apparently it was a part of John Quincy's stock in trade.

Within three days the replies were coming in. "Don Quixote" facetiously asked just when *"this fire broke out,"* and advised with mock gravity, "Allay, thou potent sorcerer! allay sublime Celadon! thy wonder working wand—let thy pen sleep quietly in thy inkhorn, so shall thy memory never upbraid thee with the follies of thy youth." Another critic replied in poetry, lamenting the poor champions of feminine genius who had stepped forth in Thomas' "Museum."

> But Celadon, *cruel,* employed satire's pen,
> To clip the bright laurels the "champions" had won.

"Horatio" ironically lamented, "O, had I the pen of Celadon!" and slyly queried whether it would not be shattering to discover that "Julia and Emma" had been educated in England and possibly assisted by one who had "seen the academies of France," probably a poke at young Adams because of his foreign education. "Sancho" said on March 31 that "Celadon" must have a "Tyger's heart"—like Shakespeare's?—to be so cruel. All of this had a large element of good natured spoofing in it. But the communication of "Laconic" on April 3 sounded like the view of an outraged feminist, for it angrily called "Celadon" and others "peurile scribblers" whose bark like a puppy's is heard but not felt.[34] The controversy lingered on. By the end of the year the *nom de plume* "Celadon" was being employed by someone other than John Quincy Adams, someone of considerably less delicacy, and whose coarse satire he thoroughly disliked.[35]

What did John Quincy's composition of these and other

"Fugitive Pieces," as he called them, reveal about the young man's romantic relationships in Newburyport? His principal poetic production of that period was of course "A Vision," which he had begun in early 1788, the concluding portion of which he had parodied or anticipated in the "Scipio Africanus" satire in February, 1789. A copy of "A Vision" was surely in circulation among the young ladies by June, 1790.[36] The presumption is that by his elimination of one girl after another in his strictures on the eight characters which make up the bulk of the poem, he revealed himself as being continuously in search of an ideal female personality. This he is eventually supposed to have found in the lovely sixteen-year-old Mary Frazier, enabling him to complete his "Vision" by writing a rhapsody to "Clara." [37] However, since the Frazier infatuation apparently came to a head only in the spring of 1790, this theory would suggest that "A Vision" was not completed until that late date.

But supposing, as the "Scipio Africanus" performance suggests, that the "Clara" portion of "A Vision" was written much earlier? In that case, either John Quincy actually finished his poem before he became deeply interested in any particular girl, and was merely indulging in a literary *tour de force,* or he first identified "Clara" with some other "blue-eyed blonde" than Mary Frazier. However poetically unsatisfying the first suggestion might seem, it is possibly the true explanation and may even throw light on the artificial character of the poem's conclusion. He unquestionably did utilize some earlier writing for another part of the production, for the "Narcissa" portion contains much of his old "Epistle to Delia." Perhaps "Clara" also was a type rather than a spontaneous creation. In other words, from time to time certain girls may have looked very much alike to the poet.

As for the second supposition, the record of his "rebus"-making together with other things [38] does suggest that John Quincy had been rather deeply interested in several other

girls before his attention became seriously fixed upon Mary
Frazier. Some of his contemporaries certainly thought that
"Clara" was originally someone else. When Betsy Foster discussed her copy of "A Vision" with Billy Cranch in June,
1790, declaring that she was charmed with it but quite fright-
ened of the satirical author, she "read" several of the characters and said that the one on "Miss Jones was very *beautiful.*" She also hoped that Miss Frazier had "profited by the
advice," although she understood that John Quincy "now"
saw her "in quite a different point of view." Cranch, who
probably knew a good deal about his cousin, expressed himself as "not displeased to find that she discover'd so good a
Judgment." [39]

When John Quincy's most intimate friend, James Bridge,
heard from him in September, 1790, of his feelings for Mary
Frazier he was simply bowled over, even though he knew that
Adams had lately been giving her particular attention. Bridge
immediately fell into elaborate apologies for having expressed
the opinion that the "Goddess" was cold and badly spoiled,
adding that it probably was natural for one so beautiful to
have become vain "in that region of flattery—Newbury-
Port." [40]

The case for John Quincy's earlier interest in Catherine
Jones is thus fairly convincing. He had not been originally on
too favorable terms with her, as he tells us in his journal, and
had written a "double" acrostic about her while he was still
at Harvard, as already noted. Later his opinion admittedly
changed and the "rebus" he wrote—but apparently never published—in October, 1789, revealed

That name, which gives a nymph beyond compare
Whose mind is lovely, as her face is fair. [41]

Moreover Catherine Jones had become deeply interested
in him, enough to make his friend Bridge affect envy in February, 1789. Bridge and Miss Jones had had occasion to speak

of John Quincy and "Katy spouted away upon her favourite topic with so much tenderness & warmth of friendship that I was in doubt whether to be vexed or pleased." [42] On October 3 of that year James Putnam, another close associate, reporting airily on "the beauties of Temple Street," said that he had given John Quincy's best wishes to "Maria" (*i.e.*, Mary, but which Mary is not clear) and "to the rest your compliments at large." He added, however, that "Katherine" had arrived, the "same best girl & has improved by absence—she speaks of you as the best of the sex—she observes with a degree of warmth which almost exceeds the tenderness of *friendship.*" [43] It has already been noted that as late as June, 1790, it was taken for granted by some persons that Catherine Jones had been the original of "Clara" in the circulating manuscript of "A Vision."

Of John Quincy's earlier interest in a girl named Mary Newhall there also can be little doubt. He had put her initials in a heart drawn on the flyleaf of his diary for 1788; and it has always been agreed that she was "Narcissa" in "A Vision," *i.e.,* the girl who had been disdainful of his affection and for whom he vengefully predicted an unhappy future. Mary Newhall was also one of the three girls who had a "rebus" by John Quincy published in the *Massachusetts Magazine* in 1789, and one of the four whose "rebuses" were copied into his book of "Fugitive Pieces." Two of the other girls so honored in his private book were, of course, Mary Frazier and Catherine Jones. The fourth was Harriet Bradbury, the too affectionate "Corinna" of "A Vision," and a much closer friend of several of the other lads than she ever was of his. However, when John Quincy's "rebus" about Harriet appeared in print in September it was accompanied by a "pastoral ode" undoubtedly also of his composition. This was addressed to "Emma: Or, the Rose," and had a charmingly plaintive conclusion.

All beauteous maid, angelick fair,
Oh! save a soul from deep despair,
And draw the *thorn* from love:
'Tis thine to pour the sovereign balm,
Bind up the wound, dissolve the charm,
And ev'ry pang remove.

All these literary strivings, including his known compositions about Mary Frazier herself, reveal a picture of John
Quincy Adams as a very susceptible young law clerk, one
rapidly proceeding down the primrose path of sentimentality
to an "attachment" of some kind. He had indeed always
denied that his character was phlegmatic in romantic matters
as his appearance must have suggested. He had long been suspected by at least one friend of being as capable of strong
attachments as any person he knew.[44] A little tragedy therefore lay in store for romantic John Quincy, in the unhappy
culmination of the Frazier affair in the fall of 1790 when he
was miserably trying to settle down to practice law in Boston.
There was also to be a decline of his poetic interests thereafter. In April, 1791, a chastened John Quincy was to write
one of his brothers:

The Magazines will I believe never present you with any more
Rebuses, Acrostics Elegies or other poetical effusions of my production. I must bid a long and lasting farewell to the juvenile
Misses. It is to the severer toils of the Historic Matron that I must
henceforth direct all the attention that I can allow to that lovely
company. Happy if they do not exclude me altogether from their
train: and command me to offer all my devotions to the eyeless
dame, who holds the balance and the sword.[45]

Just how had the final culmination and demolition of his
"Vision" come about? To complete the tale it is first necessary
to take up the narrative of that last year in Newburyport.

John Quincy's summer in 1789 had been briefly broken
in its round of parties and "chowders"—and it is to be hoped,
some study—only by a visit to the Harvard Commencement

in July. He picked up a diploma for his brother Charles who
had hurried off to New York. In September John Quincy also
made a visit to Gotham to visit his parents for a month. There
he saw stage plays and met many officials of the federal government in both their official and unofficial capacities.[46]

His return to Newburyport in October was highlighted by
President Washington's triumphal visit, a gala affair. John
Quincy himself had a major hand in preparing the local wel-
coming address, a task that must have strained his imagination since he had once observed that the subject of eulogizing
Washington was well-nigh exhausted! Despite his seemingly
high spirits he was still occasionally threatened by "the ancient quarrel between the powers of drowsiness and me," and
sometimes had "nervous twitches" which reminded him of
the constant need for exercise. He also got the "Washington
cough" which was going around, but fortunately not the influenza which was so prevalent in Massachusetts in November.[47]

Social activities now, if anything, increased. The first assembly ball of the season in Newburyport was on November
24, and others followed every two weeks thereafter. These
John Quincy usually enjoyed. His visits to the household
of the Fraziers became particularly numerous, although he
found his visit there on November 9 "somewhat dull and
silly." By December 21 he apparently was suffering from
heartache since he wrote the word "dull" and then drew a
heart after it in his diary. Four days later he recorded the
intriguing Christmas entry, "Love Letter." [48] But who the
favored one was does not appear. Presumably he was still very
much the unattached young man.[49]

The spring and early summer of 1790 were roughly a con-
tinuation of the previous year with the usual round of entertainment and a few legal matters. He also participated in a
"forensic disputation" on the subject of the unalienability of
citizenship at the Harvard Commencement in July, thereby

earning an M.A., or "second" degree, as was the easy custom of the times. A few days before this he had been admitted as an attorney in the court of Common Pleas for the County of Essex. A week later he engaged an "office" in Court Street, Boston, actually the front parlor of one of his father's houses. He went to Boston reluctantly, fearing the "temptations to dissipation" in that place, but Newburyport was overcrowded with able lawyers and Braintree offered little in the way of prospects.[50]

In Boston John Quincy boarded with the family of Dr. Thomas Welch, an old friend and confidential agent of the family. The very day after engaging his office, however, he retraced the forty miles to Newburyport where he spent the evening at Mr. Frazier's. On August 9 he opened his office but soon found himself in low spirits, although he was meeting many old friends and taking sociable walks of an evening "in the Mall." On September 29 he again returned to Newburyport, spending evenings at Bradburys' and Fraziers'. Obviously he was finding it hard to leave!

Back in Boston he addressed his first jury in October and, according to his own account, was "too much agitated" and cut a very poor figure. (He never had had any confidence in his talent for extemporizing.) His report of this sad event seems almost to have given apoplexy to old John Adams in New York. The latter immediately jumped to the conclusion that John Quincy had had a "downfall," and, although he later wrote him several letters of encouragement, rather unkindly told him that his "diffidence" and "tremor" had been remarked upon when he had opened at the bar. It was kindly brother Charles who wrote John Quincy a fine letter of reassurance and common sense and tried to play down his apprehensions.[51]

Scarcely two weeks after this fumbling start at the law, on October 29, John Quincy's diary contained the interesting entry, "M.F. came to town." The truth is that Mary Frazier of Newburyport had been "visiting" at nearby Medford. John Quincy himself had been there on several occasions during the past week, as had also another old friend, the ubiquitous Miss Jones! Four days later he recorded, "Conversation with M.F." These are the first occasions in his writings of any extraordinary reference to Mary Frazier, the "Clara" with whom he had finally fallen in love. The next day he found the club at Mr. Elliott's "very dull" and got "no sleep." He attended the first assembly ball of the season and said that it was "agreeable enough." But on November 8 he was still "perplexed," and three days later was "in anxious expectation." [52]

On the thirteenth day of November he noted in his diary, *"Letter from my mother. N.B."* That forbidding letter meant the end of the Newburyport romance of John Quincy Adams and the end of Mary Frazier as the realization of his "Vision." As he abruptly terminated the affair he lost a fair-haired girl said to have had only one rival for beauty in all New England. She was to be remembered for both beauty and charm by some people for many years after her death, only twelve years later. She was to be remembered by John Quincy Adams also, even in his old age, according to a letter said to have been written by him in 1840. He had once written about her, or someone similar, in his "Vision":

> Come, and before the lovely Clara's shrine,
> The mingled tribute of your praises join;
> My Clara's charms no vulgar poets claim,
> No servile bard that clips the wings of fame,
> To vile acrostics tunes' unmeaning lays,
> Or in a rebus centers all his praise.
> The partial gods presiding at her birth
> Gave Clara beauty and yet gave her worth;
> Kind Nature formed of purest white her skin,
> An emblem of her innocence within;
> And called on cheerful Health her aid to lend,

> The roses' colors in her cheeks to blend,
> While Venus added, to complete the fair,
> The eyes blue languish and the golden hair;
> But far superior charms exalt her mind,
> Adorned by nature, and by art refined,
> Hers are the lasting beauties of the heart,
> The charms which Virtue only can impart.

And the conclusion:

> On thee thy ardent lover's fate depends,
> From thee the evil or the boon descends;
> Thy choice alone can make my anxious breast
> Supremely wretched, or supremely blest.[53]

A major factor in this little tragedy was that the Age of Manners was opposed to long engagements; a "declaration" was supposed to be followed by early marriage.[54] This John Quincy was not prepared to carry out. Dependency upon his parents had been a long-standing grievance, never more so than at this period of starting on a dubious law career while his thoughts were turning to matrimony. His father had always preached economic independence to his son, although both parents had warned against early success, and had even expressed dire forebodings about the difficulties which malice and envy would put in his way.[55]

John Quincy felt, however, that independence had been unfairly delayed in his case by his long years of residence abroad. As far back as the critical summer of 1788, sister Nabby had tried to reassure him on this point, vainly attempting to combat the depression then growing upon him by saying that dependency was a very natural thing, and that it had not been his fault that he had been in Europe when he might have been advancing his education more rapidly at home.[56] He himself had reminded his father in Angust, 1790, of the peculiar circumstances which had retarded his career. Now, in October, temporarily viewing

politics with disgust—one of the interests which his father
was feverishly urging upon him—he again identified his unhappy lot with those "sacrifices" to the public welfare which
had "deprived me of my fundamental support, and have left
me exposed to the most humiliating neglect from all the
world around me." [57] So he nursed a bitter grievance.

Unfortunately the entire Adams family at this time was
in a high state of anxiety about finances, although one would
suppose that their government securities, at least, must have
appreciated greatly in recent months. In addition to John
Adams' eternal lamenting about the miserable salary of a
Vice President and the poor returns from his several "estates," [58] the problem of daughter Nabby became particularly pressing. Her husband, the impressive Colonel Smith
whom her parents had once regarded as so "solid," had become a perpetual source of worry because he had no regular
employment.

Moreover, Nabby had recently added a third infant son
to the roster of family dependents. "Heaven grant that she
may add no more to the stock until her prospects brighten,"
wrote Madam Abigail to John Quincy on August 20, giving
him a stern admonition never to form a connection until he
saw his way clear to supporting a family, at the same time
indignantly denying his playful insinuation that she had
been trying to interest him in a wealthy girl.[59] Not long
afterwards sister Shaw romantically rhapsodized over delightful rumors in Haverhill that Abigail's young "Hercules" had
been conquered in love by a sixteen-year-old. She reminded
Abigail how wonderful it was for a young girl to find a
"faithful friend," but added fuel to the flames by wittily
congratulating her on her new grandson. "There will be
statesmen in plenty, if Mrs. Smith goes on from year to year
in this way." [60] How Abigail must have longed to box the
ears of her loving but silly sister.

Finances were no laughing matter. John Quincy had always been exceedingly careful about his own accounts, even earning the praise of the family treasurer. He was therefore deeply concerned about Nabby's prospects even though depressed himself. Moreover in September his father had bluntly emphasized the financial crisis by saying that while he meant to assist John Quincy as long as might be necessary, "I only ask you to recollect that my Circumstances are not affluent; that you have Brothers and a Sister who are equally entitled. . . ." [61] The implication was overwhelming. All that his father could suggest for his idle time, while waiting for cases to appear, was to study politics at town meeting, to try to figure out how to make the "estates" pay better and *mirable dictu* how to study Latin authors more effectively.

His mother's torrent of good advice for his proper conduct had continued throughout the summer, although she once half-apologized for "moralizing": there is a tide in the affairs of men; you must learn to cope with jealousy; never let a woman be indebted to you for poverty; marriage is chargeable; and so on. He had countered what he had amusingly suggested was her worldly attitude on marriage by proudly asserting that he would never marry for wealth. He had then played into her hands, however, by simultaneously declaring that he would never "connect a woman to desperate fortune." [62] That was all the assurance she really needed. In September when she said that she had heard from Tom that John Quincy was in love—had she really known nothing of it before?—she again warned him to keep free from entanglements, playfully adding that it might help to improve his careless toilet but no more.[63]

His resentment about his depressing and lonely situation had reached a pitch by October 17. But his mother's masterful reply, written from a sick bed on November 7—the fatal letter that was received on the thirteenth—was adamant on the subject of love. Common report had reached her that he was attached to a young lady. Since he had no means to warrant his entering into a formal engagement and since he had told her that he had no idea of connecting himself at present, he was in danger of making himself miserable for life as well as being most cruel to the young lady herself by continuing his attentions. "Perhaps I ought not to have delay'd being explicit so long." Her strength, she declared, would not permit her to say more; but she had said a plenty.

So the axe of parental disapproval fell, and the affair was abruptly ended. John Quincy replied a week later, express-ing anxiety for his mother's health and saying that he had been a child to complain of his situation. As for the young lady, "I wish to give you full satisfaction by assuring you that there shall never more be any cause on my part for the continuance of it. The Lady will henceforth be at the dis-tance of 40 miles from me and I shall have no further oppor-tunities to indulge a weakness, which you may perhaps cen-sure," but which, he pathetically added, "if you knew the object, I am sure you would excuse." It was his only cry of anguish, and the most human thing he ever said on the sub-ject.

Several weeks later John Quincy wrote again to ease his mother's mind, stating that he was perfectly free and would remain so. "I believe I may add I was never in less danger of any entanglement, which can give you pain, than at the present." [64] His decision had been made with a strange finality. He had not only buried his love but had jumped on the grave with both feet.

Yet he had written his friend Bridge as recently as Septem-ber that "all my hopes of future happiness in this life, center in the possession of that girl," or so Bridge had quoted him in his reply.[65] When he once bitterly reminded his mother of what he had suffered at the "monition of parental solici-tude and tenderness," she soothingly acknowledged the "sac-rifice" he had made.[66] A similar diagnosis was held by his Aunt Eliza who some years later told of how she could have shed "tear for tear" when she saw him struggling with his passions in making his sacrifice to *"Situation & filial Duty."* [67] It was an acknowledgment of self-denial in which he heartily concurred.

Nevertheless, regardless of his parents' attitude and maneuvering, it is clear that it was also in keeping with John Quincy's own character for him to have made a prudent decision. When he had first confessed to sister Nabby of his attachment back in April—how ridiculous to believe that his parents did not know about it during the summer—he had admitted that reason and prudence would oppose their influence; and he had promptly reassured her in his very next letter of his discretion in the matter. Indeed it was Nabby herself who had then sweetly warned against the danger of a "too wise maxim of Prudence" in effacing early romantic impressions. Perhaps she had in mind her own miserable experience of having been thwarted in love.[68]

Had not John Quincy himself proudly told his mother in August—he was plainly driven to it—that he would never commit a woman to desperate fortune? He had also rather oddly written his father in the critical month of September on the danger of early matrimonial connections, saying sagely that "a foundation must be laid before the superstructure can be erected. I hope I am in no danger from this quarter." [69] Such worldly restraint in so delicate a matter, even in the eighteenth century, and so reminiscent of John Quincy's reasoning on a faintly similar occasion four years previous, casts the shadow of a doubt as to how completely in love he had been, or at least how truly candid he was with himself.

At any rate he was to stay away from Newburyport for a long, long time and seems never to have even considered renewing the Frazier connection, although Mary herself remained single for many years until—according to legend— after John Quincy himself had married. Indeed when he

was considering marriage in England in 1796 and his mother
—of all people!—defensively and "patriotically" suggested
that "Maria" might still have some "claims," he answered in
the negative with something like polite anger. When they
had parted, it had been with "a mutual dissolution of affection" and with the tragic promise that neither would ever
marry anyone unworthy of the other. For her own sake, he
now loftily said, he hoped that she would keep the bargain
as well as he had.[70]

It is probable also that he had been disappointed in Mary's
own attitude, perhaps on the suject of "waiting." She was
no doubt influenced by the solicitation of *her* family and
friends—of course including the helpful Catherine Jones.
This explanation, for what it is worth, was the one advanced
long afterwards by Adams himself.[71] It certainly would seem
that Mary was looking for something like a showdown, and
very probably had come to Medford in October for that purpose. James Bridge had jocularly said of her intended visit
there, before he knew of John Quincy's real feelings, that it
seemed as though John could not escape "the coils" even by
moving to Boston.[72]

Five months after this little tragedy of November, 1790,
when John Quincy briefly attempted to resume his old practice of analyzing female character, he strangely criticized the
quality of prudence! He acknowledged that it was a rare
and valuable virtue in young ladies, and that his own taste
was "naturally depraved," but he denied that prudence and
discretion would ever possess any peculiar charm for him.
"Should my Heart ever yield itself to the voice of Love, I
hope my Judgment will approve, though it must never pre-
tend to direct the Passion." [73] Such reckless language, for it
was diametrically opposed to all his earlier distrust of "passion," suggests that he had been through a bitter experience
of something like rejection. It also suggests a confused attempt at evading responsibility for having acquiesced in a

prudent decision himself. A few days before he had been out walking with his old friend Phillips who was well-informed of the romantic goings on in Newburyport and who now expressed wonder at his "apostacy." [74] So he was suffering no doubt from a broken heart, but very likely also from wounded esteem. In any case he was sadly perplexed—he symbolically lost his cloak at a New Year's Eve party—and in need of new interests. It is significant that he was soon "writing for the printer's boy." [75] It was an Adams' habit in times of stress as his own brief literary career had shown.

There is no evidence that he had a recurrence of serious illness at this time. His experience may even have been beneficial, if bitter, medicine for his excessive sensibility. However, his Aunt Eliza later said she knew that his health had suffered; and in January, 1791, his mother was writing her sister Mary at Braintree to thank her for her kind care of John Quincy. "He wanted it I believe." She said that he worried over lack of legal employment and that he would have to have more patience.[76] John Quincy soon left on a trip to Philadelphia where the Adamses had recently moved to the new seat of the federal government. His mother, who had been ill herself on and off for the year past, noticed that he had lost much of his vitality and again attributed it to his fretting over lack of practice and to his dislike of economic dependency! [77]

To give John Quincy Adams his due, however, on the trip home by packet from New York in March he noticed among the passengers "the prettiest Quaker girl" he had ever seen.[78] Perhaps his later complaints about having "blunted sensations" as a result of his disappointment in love were to be somewhat exaggerated. However that may have been, his days of dalliance were clearly over. His days of public contention were now to begin.

CHAPTER SEVEN

THE RIGHTS OF MAN IN BOSTON

"A blasphemous doubt of
Tom Paine's infallibility"

A grandson of John Quincy Adams once wrote that politics was the "systematic organization of hatreds," and that in Massachusetts it had always been as harsh as the climate.[1] This accurately reflected the views of his forebears, who in particular took any criticism of a member of the Adams family as almost an appeal to human depravity. Their attitude stemmed primarily from their extraordinarily low opinion of human nature. John Quincy went so far in 1791 as to speak of "that state of individual imbecility in which man is supposed to have existed, previous to the formation of the social compact."[2] Despite the optimism of the Age of Reason, their opinion was confirmed even more by certain developments following the American and French revolutions.

To an Adams, fearing tyranny in case of a breakdown of the compact, everything obviously depended on the proper organization of government, strengthened by whatever assistance morality and education could bring to checkmate the evil consequences of passionate human nature. To many other persons such an attitude suggested that the Adamses apparently considered themselves exceptions to the rule; or it raised the suspicion that they were ambitious people trying to pose as new American aristocrats, probably as a result of their long residence in England.

The role of political parties as an auxiliary device for handling political differences between men had once been appreciated by young John Quincy Adams. In June, 1787, viewing the turbulence in local affairs, he had written that it is impossible for a free nation to subsist without parties which, unfortunately, were not yet formed. The following year, however, after his discomfiture on the issue of the Federal Constitution, he sarcastically remarked of the shifting situation in Massachusetts, "We have not yet got sufficiently settled to have stated parties; but we shall soon, I have no doubt obtain the blessing." [3]

It was ironical that only three years later John Quincy himself helped to precipitate political cleavage on a national scale by becoming the precocious spokesman for a new American conservatism. The issue which he seized upon in June, 1791, in his "Publicola Letters" had been created by the "rashness" of Thomas Jefferson, the Secretary of State, through an "innocent" endorsement of the American edition of Tom Paine's *The Rights of Man*. This work, an answer to Edmund Burke's strictures on the French Revolution, had been reprinted in Philadelphia in the first week of May. The Adamses correctly interpreted the wording of the endorsement as implying criticism of the political pontificating of the Honorable John Adams, Vice President of the United States of America. John Quincy vigorously rose to his father's defense despite his earlier admiration for Jefferson.

As a highly effective newspaper controversialist in 1791, John Quincy at the age of twenty-three stood in striking contrast to the sickly if courageous youth of three years before. Yet he still had occasional trouble with his eyes and suffered from morbidity of spirits. After returning to the study of law in Newburyport, Massachusetts, in March, 1789, he had resumed a remarkably active social life which had culminated in a romantic attachment. This he had ultimately put aside at the expense of personal happiness, thus re-affirming the highly disciplined life that he had so long accepted.[4] Years before when as a boy John Quincy had gone abroad a second time, against his wishes, his implacable mother had written him, "The habits of a vigorous mind are formed in contending with difficulties." [5] If by "vigorous" she meant combative, as she plainly did in the heroic sense, her eldest son's life at least was to be a testament to the correctness of her theory, especially from the time of the "Publicola" affair.

When John Quincy returned to his law practice in Boston in March, 1791, after visiting his parents and the new seat of government in Philadelphia, time hung heavily on his hands. There was a conspicuous lack of clients. Despite frequent dining out, attending of assemblies, and reading at his office, ofttimes at night, there was ample leisure for sad reflection about his recent, untimely venture into love. He copied out bits of the romantic poetry of Shenstone into the blank leaves of his diary.[6] Beginning on April 1 he fitfully tried to renew the elaborate journal he had abandoned when he became seriously ill in 1788, but succeeded in making only a few entries.[7] There was an eclipse of the sun he viewed from Beacon Hill but which hurt his eyes because he had no glass. He took to re-reading history, and set about making resolutions including—after reading Cicero—"Never to be perf.[ect]." [8] It was all very bitter and dull.

The last entry in his abortive effort to revive his journal that spring had to do with a subject that was to be the turning point in his public life. It was also a subject which was to siphon off some of his excess energy. One evening in April at the home of Mr. Foster, the room was so crowded that he had no opportunity of conversing with the ladies, so he fell into conversation with several men. He found that Mr. Sargeant had been reading Edmund Burke's pamphlet on the Revolution in France. "He made some judicious remarks upon the subject and appeared to agree in the opinion which I had entertained of the Work." [9] John Quincy's hand probably already itched for a pen to add his comments about a country he knew so well and about its revolution concerning which he had long had misgivings.

Indeed he had been thinking for some time about "venturing upon some speculations in our Newspapers," as he had confided to his brother Tom. He had intended to write on some topics relating to the American "national" government which was still only precariously settled. To this end he had already started to collect books and newspapers.[10] Apparently the pen which had previously served as a solace was to do so again during this intolerable spring. After all, he was an Adams. As his sister had once written him, their "destiny" seemed "inescapably" tied up with public affairs.[11] When John Quincy subsequently "apologized" to his friend James Bridge for having taken to politics, he asked forgiveness for "Publicola" on the grounds of his "situation and connexions." [12] It might also be noted that at his mother's suggestion his father had recently put him on a regular allowance.[13]

John Quincy's desperate plunge into political controversy began on May 24, a day significant also because the "V.P." was in town. His diary contained the important word, "Wrote." The "V.P." was of course his father, the Vice President, who had recently returned from Philadelphia with Mrs. Adams who was unwell. No doubt the "V.P." was hot with wrath because of Jefferson's recent "endorsement" of *The Rights of Man.* Jefferson's note to the American printer had contained some pointed remarks "to take off a little of the dryness" about the political "heresies" that had recently sprung up in America. He said he hoped that a reprinting of Paine's pamphlet would help to contradict these, although he later protested that he had had no idea that the printer would use his note. John Adams had openly expressed his detestation of Paine's work and he was generally understood to be the author of the ponderous "Discourses on Davila," a recent series of newspaper articles more or less continuing the conservative tone of his *Defence of the Constitutions*. Since Jefferson confessedly had "Davila" in mind as principal among the "heresies" of the times, an ominous atmosphere had arisen in official Philadelphia which was greatly disturbing to President Washington, to whom Paine had unfortunately dedicated his pamphlet.[14]

As for old John Adams himself, he seems by 1791 to have generously assumed that he was becoming a lightning rod for the whole Washington administration, the success of which he identified with the survival of the federal experiment itself. Hence he had become doubly suspicious of any personal criticism. He even congratulated himself in July as serving as whipping boy for Hamilton during the rage of opposition to the "glory and success of his bank." In both public and private affairs John Adams had had reason to become aware of the economic benefits which the new government had effected under the leadership of the gifted secretary of the treasury.[15]

Between May 24 and July 5 John Quincy Adams worked busily on as "Publicola"—a Roman cognomen signifying "a friend of the people," but in this instance perhaps more properly referring to the consul who had helped suppress the Catilinarian conspiracy. His diary has almost daily entries of "wrote" and "writing on." During this time he generally stayed at Braintree where his mother was ill, trying to keep up his physical stamina by frequent bathing and walking. But when he had finished with the last number he found himself thoroughly exhausted for the rest of the summer. His articles first appeared, beginning on June 8, in the enterprising *Columbian Centinel* of Boston, under the editorship of the friendly Ben Russell. They then spread throughout the newspapers of the land. "Publicola" was hailed as the "American Burke." It was immediately assumed by Jefferson and others that John Adams himself was the author. Some crude vilification of the vice president resulted, thus adding fuel to the flames, all of which the Jeffersonians promptly blamed on "Publicola" for not having let the controversy smolder.

The beginnings of an unfavorable reaction to the French Revolution soon followed in the American press, although not for this reason alone. With the few exceptions of such persons as John Adams and his eldest son, that tumultuous event had been almost universally approved in America in its early stages. An unfavorable reaction to Edmund Burke's "apostasy" was now also to some extent revised. All this, however, was at the expense of a division of American political opinion that was eventually to break into open political warfare in 1793, when the "rights of man" became a factor in American foreign affairs. It was "Publicola" who began the first counter-offensive against the new version of the political doctrines of the Age of Reason, soon to be identified with the power of the French revolutionary imperium.[16]

To many Americans, especially those persons who had never been willing to face the political and economic realities that had accompanied their own Revolution—many were likewise suspicious of the centralizing activities of the new federal government—the ponderous writings of John Adams had long been regarded with irritation. The courageous stand of "Publicola" was precipitated as a by-product of this situation, although John Quincy himself had asserted as early as October, 1790, that "In France it appears to me the National Assembly in tearing the lace from the garb of government, will tear the coat itself into a thousand rags." He had not thought that the sweeping activities of a "triumphant democracy" was a good omen for "an equitable government of laws." [17]

As far back as 1787, within six months of the publication of the *Defence of the Constitutions of Government of the United States of America,* the political ideas of old John Adams had been considered as "poison" in some parts of the American press because of their alleged aristocratic bias. Such an inference had even accompanied some newspaper comments on his eldest son's graduation at Harvard that year.[18] The strong note of caution in the political thinking of John Adams had been sharpened by Shays' Rebellion, but it was implicit in what he had been preaching since '76 with respect to the need for proper governments. Of course his view of human nature may not have been quite so jaundiced at that early date. Some "checks" in the political process he had always considered necessary, particularly in the way of strong executives and two-chambered legislatures. Among his political enemies in 1791 he numbered not only the "Stone House" faction of Hancockian demagogues in Massachusetts, together with the remnants of the Shaysites, but also those Pennsylvanians who since 1776 had advocated a single chambered legislature and other specious forms of political democracy. The latter had originally included old Dr. Franklin with his easy tolerance of human nature and fondness for the French school of doctrinaires. Indeed Adams suspected that Franklin's ideas had been an indirect source of inspiration for the omnipotent pretensions of the French Assembly in 1790.[19]

Old John Adams had come to feel so strongly about putting brakes on human nature in politics that in addition to writing the *Defence* and the "unpolished"—but highly cherished—"Discourses on Davila" he had ventured in 1789 and 1790 to press his ideas upon such republican stalwarts as Roger Sherman and Sam Adams. He had learnedly argued with them that the new American government was really a "monarchical republic" like that of England, except for the hereditary principle, and that the executive would eventually have to be made an integral part of the legislature—thus presumably favoring "balance" at the expense of "checks." All history proved, according to John Adams, that only the aristocracy of mankind has ever prevented the onslaught of despotism. Though governments should of course be republican, the term itself was "fraudulent," and was always in danger of being distorted to the point where people would prefer monarchy. The events in France had excited these extreme ideas together with Adams' prediction that the developing struggle in Europe would be nothing more than "a change of impostors and impositions." [20] Years later he was to boast that he had been the only leading American, not excluding Washington, to predict so early the true course of events in Revolutionary France.[21]

Consequently a certain unpopularity of John Adams in America was quite understandable, to put it mildly. The strongest weapon in his arsenal of historical arguments was none other than the British constitution itself.[22] Yet Tom Paine had had the gall to say in his *Rights of Man* that the English did not even have a constitution because it was not written down on paper in the way the French were doing it—and of course in the way Americans themselves had done. Thomas Jefferson had endorsed all such nonsense and slurred John Adams at the same time for "political heresies"!

The vulnerability of the Adamses to charges of aristocratic tendencies and English notions had been amusingly revealed by a satire appearing in a Boston paper in 1789. It stemmed from the discussion in New York as to how to address President Washington and other officials of the new union. The battle of "titles" had been a brief but comical episode in the organization of the government. Pompous John Adams had been particularly suspected of entertaining high-flung notions. In the *Columbian Centinel* for August 22, 1789, there had been a contribution by "A REPUBLICAN" purporting to furnish parts of a poem written by a gentleman "formerly of Boston" on the subject, "Resist the Vice*****."

> Gads! how they'd stare! should fickle Fortune drop
> Those mushroom lordlings where she pick'd them up,
> In tinker's, cobler's, or b - - k b - - - - r's shop.

Be grateful then YE CHOSEN! mod'rate, wise,
Nor stretch your claims to such preposterous size,
Lest your too partial country—wise grown—
Shou'd on your native dunghills set you down.
Ape not the fashions of the foreign great,
Nor make your betters at your *levees* wait.
Resign your awkward pomp, parade and pride,
And lay that useless *etiquette* aside;

The faithful guardians of the country were implored to

Resist the VICE—and that couragious pride
To that o'erweening VICE—so near ally'd.

The poem concluded with praise of Washington, and the lament,

Successors we can find—but tell us where
Of ALL thy virtues we shall find THE HEIR?

Abigail Adams was relieved to learn that this slander on her husband, the "Vice" President, was not the product of the pen of an embittered female. (Doubtless she had in mind Mercy Warren of Plymouth who had unsuccessfully solicited a federal job for her husband.) Abigail considered the author a brute to have attacked her for allegedly favoring routs and plays, which she said she had never attended in America —but had of course attended abroad.[23] As for the political charges, her husband was not without defenders. The *Centinel* itself immediately carried a reply. Editor Ben Russell was a staunch Federalist, but also a man of broad vision who was always looking for exciting newspaper material. In an article by "TOGATUS" in his next issue the "dunghill" reference was deplored as impudent and malicious. The writer condemned the leveling of "arrows of obloquy" at a man "on whom the eyes of the whole continent" had been "deservedly fixed."[24]

The flare up over titles had reappeared in the spring of

1791 at the time of the general attack in American news-papers on Burke's "phillipick." An editorial from London was reprinted in the *Centinel* on April 2, saying that the "plain" people understood some matters better than Burke and that perhaps "THE BRIGHTEST MEN ARE OFTEN THE GREAT-EST FOOLS." The French people, it was said in a later issue, had good reason to abhor almost anything distinguished by titles. "RUSTICUS" in the Boston *Independent Chronicle* on April 28 attacked a defense of Burke in Philadelphia and hinted that possibly some of the "*old leaven,*" or a few "apos-tates from their original creed," would like to see a limited monarchy established in America. The reference to John Adams is unmistakable. The radical *Federal Gazette* of Phila-delphia on May 19 called for a veneration of the "*Rights of Man.*" The "endorsed" American edition of Paine's pam-phlet had meantime come out and the *Gazette* itself had been reproducing it. The *Gazette* left it to the "would-be *aristo-cratic few* to propagate the abominable *political heresy,* that civil government was instituted for the purpose of *enslaving men,* and for the creation of kings, bishops, lords, and dukes. . . ." It hailed the secretary of state for retaining his "manly republican sentiments" and sneered at a detractor who had recently sneered at *him*. In Boston a satirical edi-torial from Philadelphia was reprinted on May 26 on the subject of "TITLES," ending up with the patriotic exhortation, "*Goddess of Liberty!* kick down these *gewgaws.*"

Two of the most direct attacks on the vice president were aired in Boston and Philadelphia on June 18. Since both articles had been printed elsewhere some time before, they cannot be attributed to the effect of the "Publicola" articles, as Jefferson was later to insist had generally been the case. On the other hand there is no proof that they were part of the "abuse" that resulted from Jefferson's "endorsement" of Paine, of which John Adams so bitterly complained. The first attack had been published in the Poughkeepsie *Journal,* originally submitted there on May 21 by a subscriber who attributed it to a foreign correspondent. It said that while John Adams should be given credit for his learning, it was plain to see that he was attached to "aristocratical and monarchical principles." His "Davila" was said to re-assert the need for balanced government, but also to uphold the idea that distinctions of property, aristocracy, and monarchy "have their foundation in the original constitution of our nature." [25]

What angered John Adams more than anything else was a satire in a Connecticut paper which was republished in the Boston *Centinel* on June 18 under the heading "Antifederal Abuse." He said that this was the first time he had heard of the "Lye." It was based on a story of the vice president's alleged stingy action in "rewarding" with a dollar some workers on a bridge while returning home with Mrs. Adams in a coach from Philadelphia in May. There was also a pointed reference to the vice president's well-known complaints about the small size of his salary. By implication this satire compared the "poor *American* sons of the hoe and broad-ax" to French peasants doing *corvée,* saying that in some people's opinion these "Yahoos" were expected to receive pleasure by "feasting their rustic eyes on him who had shone at European courts, even at the British—that model of perfection. . . ."

What! that children of the third generation may be able to say (when wooden spoons and shoes will be in fashion) by way of exultation, My father's father's father laid the last board on such a bridge, and had the honour to lead the horses (and with his hat on too) of the grandfather of the present, puissant, consummate, and most honourable Duke of Braintree—and he smiled *at him* so *pretty.*

The *Centinel* gravely added that such abuse of so distinguished a patriot needed no comment. *"Its cloven-foot is sufficiently visible.*" But it was wonderful newspaper copy! [26]

Confronted by such spirited journalism, the task of John Quincy Adams as "Publicola" clearly called for something more than an academic defense of his father's rambling scholarship. Entering upon the newspaper forum, the liveliest stage of controversy of the time, where manners had been sadly eroded by a generation of irreverent revolutionists headed by the redoubtable Thomas Paine himself, John Quincy had need of plenty of partisan wit to make "Publicola" a formidable antagonist. His success in so doing was a tribute to something more than to an acquaintance with the best scholarship of the eighteenth century.

Despite occasional awkwardness, "Publicola" revealed the deft phrase and cutting expression of one who for years had disciplined himself to write terse criticism of men and events. It also revealed a young man who had recently learned the bitter, conservative truth that in life it is necessary to cut your coat to fit your cloth. In opposing the thrusts of Paine, the supreme romanticist of the age, John Quincy necessarily fought with the weapons of conservatism. In the Puritan context to which he had been bred this meant preaching moral principles reinforced by dry humor. Without the latter he would have failed. Moral principles alone would never have enabled him to challenge successfully the scintillating author of *The Rights of Man.*

This does not mean that John Quincy Adams was in the same class with Tom Paine as a pamphleteer, but only that his newspaper writing had certain pungent qualities that made a real appeal to the public. When Jefferson first identified "Publicola" as the work of the elder Adams, the careful James Madison disagreed on the basis of information that had reached him, but also because "there is more method also in the arguments, and much less of clumsiness and heaviness in the style." [27]

To say that young Adams "answered" Paine is also not

quite correct. The first question he asked was about Thomas
Jefferson himself. By what right had that "very respectable
gentleman," the secretary of state, set out to adjudicate what
were "political heresies"? When had Americans set up an
"infallible criterion of *orthodoxy*" or practised "slavery of
the mind" under the "sanction of a venerable name"? Did
the secretary of state consider Paine's pamphlet the "canon-
ical book of political scripture" containing the "true doctrine of popular infallibility"? Was Mr. Paine to be adopted
as "the holy father of our political faith" and his pamphlet
to be considered a "Papal bull of infallible virtue"? Surely
that "friend to free inquiry upon every subject," *i.e.,* the
secretary of state, would not be opposed to further inquiry
"consistent with the reverence due his character." [28]

In short, although John Quincy did not make the accusation directly or even mention Jefferson by name, he did suggest in the most ironic terms that the free-thinking secretary
of state was inclined to be a "heresy hunter." Indeed, the
whole of "Publicola" suggests that misrepresentation of liberty was being made by friends of the secretary of state.
Small wonder that in one of the first and best known of
the replies to "Publicola," that of "AGRICOLA" in Boston on
June 23, bitter resentment was expressed on behalf of the
secretary. "Your attack in your first paper upon Mr. Jefferson, was very warm indeed; and as the author of your production is concealed, it was very unmanly." [29]

Despite his own success in making pungent observations,
John Quincy scorned Paine for his literary cleverness. *The
Rights of Man* he termed "historical, political, miscellaneous,
satirical, and panegyrical"—the last an old favorite word of
John Quincy's. He said that Paine tried to turn "sallies of
wit" into "maxims of truth" and to be more interested in
"flippant witticism" than in sober reasoning.[30] Flippancy
in an author had always irritated John Quincy Adams and
now he was trying to cross swords with a master of the art.

In one place he complained that it was impossible to do justice to the wit of Paine as the latter had brilliantly done with Burke in employing the famous epigram, "loaves and and fishes." Paine seemed to prefer epigrams to arguments, he said, thereby exposing the absurdity of his pretence at "reasoning." [31]

Irritability with facile and flippant criticism on such a serious subject was a leading characteristic of "Publicola." But the major problem he raised pertained to moral standards in government and to the immoral behavior of men who spurned the law. John Quincy attacked the fatuous pretensions of the French Assembly and Paine's own irresponsible demand for a similar revolution in England. "The principle that a whole nation has the right to do whatever it pleases, cannot in any sense whatever be admitted as true." It was his fear that liberty might become "the sport of arbitrary power, and the hideous form of despotism . . . assume the party-colored garments of democracy." In the name of the "unalienable rights" of the majority, the rights both of minorities and of individuals could be extinguished, he said.[32]

In support of this attitude, John Quincy cited the British constitution and the traditional nature of the common law. These seemed to him to be the backbone of the American political system despite the abuses and corruptions which had necessitated the American revolt.[33] Respect for an orderly delegation of powers also led "Publicola" to defend the English system against the French, along lines previously laid down in John Adams' writings. It also opened "Publicola" to the charge by "AGRICOLA" and others of being Anglophile. Apparently assuming that the elder Adams was the author of "Publicola" (as had already been openly asserted in the Philadelphia *Federal Gazette*) "AGRICOLA" demanded to know, "Pray, Sir, who made you, as an American, the guardian of the British government?" And it led to the direct charge that "your whole labor is pointed to this one object—*the introduction of a mixed Monarchy* into the United States." [34]

As an earnest young student of law, John Quincy Adams preferred Blackstone, whom he had spent three years in reading and re-reading, to Tom Paine as an authority on the British constitution. In a rather amusing way this revealed what he thought was basically wrong with Paine's theories. The latter had a lifelong obsession, shown as far back as *Common Sense,* that the leading fact in British history was that William the Conqueror had been a scoundrel! "Publicola" dryly noted that "Mr. Paine always refers the origin of the English Government" to William of Normandy.[35] Similar ignorance, John Quincy thought, was displayed in Paine's curious prejudice against "game laws" in England, on the ground that they operated unequally among the people and were no doubt reminiscent of the abuses committed by the French nobles. To an old gunner of birds on the marshes of eastern Massachusetts such as John Quincy Adams, this was an exaggerated argument. All American states had such laws and he thought them to good advantage. The argument on this point in "Publicola" might have been directly inspired by an entry made in John Quincy's journal many years before: "I went with my gun down upon the marshes; but had no sport. Game laws are said to be directly opposed to the liberties of the subject: I am well persuaded that they may be carried too far, and that they really are in most parts of Europe. But it is equally certain that where there are none, there never is any game. . . ." [36]

Witticism and ignorance supporting immoral pretentions of the majority to do whatever it pleased was the political spectre in Paine's writings that John Quincy Adams held up to abhorrence. Finally he asked—most significantly in view of his life-long concern with foreign affairs—what trust could be put in treaties with any nation subject to Paine's ideas? [37]

He congratulated the thrice happy people of America who, as he pointed out, had with difficulty survived their own "critical period," but not by abandoning fundamental principles; who had a legislative system representing an equality really existing among them and not one based upon "the metaphysical speculations of fanciful politicians, vainly contending against the unalterable course of events, and the established order of nature." [38]

Some years later old John Adams was to speak of the fiery ordeal through which he had passed when once "suspected of a blasphemous doubt of Tom Paine's infallibility, in consequence of Publicola's eloquence and Jefferson's rashness." [39] It was an understatement on all counts. His son John Quincy had been more than eloquent as "Publicola"; he had been publicly mean for the first time in his life, and at the expense, moreover, of a man he had venerated since the days of his boyhood acquaintance in France. As for coming through the ordeal, John Quincy's eyes were affected to the point where on August 29 he was "almost blind." That same day he also recorded, "my father unwell." [40]

One wonders what effect the reception of an unbelievable letter from Jefferson a few days later may have had upon the recovery of father and son? On August 30 Jefferson wrote John Adams at great length, going even beyond his original rashness in blaming "Publicola" for all the unfortunate publicity that had arisen to make a breach between them.[41] This letter was never answered, possibly because John Adams continued to feel unwell, but more likely because he did not think it worthwhile. Time surely confirmed him in his attitude of scornful silence and made him doubly glad for the impassioned eloquence of his son.

Yet a certain lesson may have been learned. John Adams sarcastically wrote a political confidant in September, 1791, about securing a residence in Philadelphia. He hoped that the house would be "Democratical" enough but not too expensive for a "simple Duke"! Less than a year later daughter Nabby was lamenting that "Poppa" had temporarily given up wearing a wig.[42]

CHAPTER EIGHT

THE LAW AND THE DRAMA

"Like Dogberry in the play"

Despite their implacable New England character, the Adamses developed an interest in the theater which was blossoming at the time of their return to America. Accompanying President and Mrs. Washington they occasionally attended plays in Philadelphia. Abigail with her special admiration for the French stage was properly critical.[1] A needy actor even wrote the Honorable John Adams in April, 1792, beseeching money, patronage, and favor. This unfortunate man had found himself financially embarrassed partly due to the death of a child while on his way to joining the old American Company in New York. He had a scheme for showing the patriots of America on the stage in "transparent paintings" as large as life, accompanied by eulogies and music.[2] One would like to think that the vice president was to be one of the patriots so honored—and that he furnished the "little money" so eloquently requested.

The sympathetic interest of young John Quincy Adams in the "gentle agitation" stirred in Boston that year by the plays of a new American Company in the guise of "moral lectures," is readily understandable. John Quincy had been steeped in Shakespeare from childhood. His mother had kept the plays of the Bard in a closet of her bedchamber. By the age of ten he was already familiar with many of them, although such characters as Falstaff, Nym, and Ancient Pistol were then quite beyond his comprehension.[3] The Bard was forever on his mother's lips, or at least in her let-

ters, foremost among those poets so generously quoted by
"Portia" in the expression of her ardent affections, or in
giving moral and patriotic instructions to her children. The
very first night that the Adams boys and their father reached
Port Ferrot in Spain in December, 1779, they had gone
ashore to attend a play, and they had continued to do so
every night during their stay.[4]

Theatrical entertainment had been endlessly repeated for
Master John in Paris, St. Petersburg, and London during
the next six years. The Russian ballet became familiar to
him as did the offerings of Drury Lane and Covent Garden.
He knew the French and Italian actors in Molière, Racine,
and Voltaire, to say nothing of Mrs. Siddons, the "Divine
Ferron," and other celebrities in English productions of the
whole Shakespearean repertory. Light comedies and farces
also abounded. Such an international favorite as "Love à la
Mode" was a staple offering. John Quincy attended the
Italian Comedy in Paris with the Hon. Thomas Jefferson,
and no doubt the Théâtre Française, perhaps in company
with his distinguished mother after she came over in 1784.[5]
Madam Adams had been equally delighted and shocked in
Paris by her first sight of dancing girls, clad in the thinnest
gauze and "showing their garters" in the most diverting
manner. She had been moved to grave moral reflection when
she considered "the tendency of these things." [6]

In many leading American cities and even to some extent
in Boston a revival of interest in the drama had taken place
after the American Revolution. Such old stage favorites as
"Miss in Her Teens" had been supplemented in New York
in 1787 with the amazingly popular and patriotic "The Contrast" by Royall Tyler. This talented young playwright had
once practiced law in Braintree, Massachusetts, and had only
narrowly missed becoming a son-in-law of the Adamses. Perhaps he even had been moved to write his satire as a result
of that experience.[7]

It may be that the older John Adams was never quite such an admirer of the stage—or of Royall Tyler either, for that matter—as some other members of his family; but his eldest son became a life-long devotee and student of the drama, although not of actresses after the age of fourteen! [8] In the dispute which arose over the exhibitions given in a building in "Board-Alley" in Boston in 1792, John Quincy came to the defense of the players when they were being hounded out of town. However, it must be confessed that his argument was based not upon the players' intrinsic worth to the community but on more prosaic and legal grounds, that the law prohibiting their offerings as well as the action taken against them was unconstitutional. In this as in so many other things his personal feelings were subordinated to "principles." Strong bias did lead him, however, into taking a position in which he was embarrassingly wrong. He rashly accepted the silly rumor that old Governor Hancock had abetted an act of violence against the players.

It was ironical that public controversy should have thus ensnared John Quincy in 1792, since he professed to have been trying hard to avoid it. Earlier in the year his chief public concern had been the mundane matter of improving local government. Of course it was a year of exciting federal elections during which his father's fortunes were reviewed *ad nauseam* by the entire family; and John Quincy himself still basked in the reflected glory of his recent political writings. His admiring friend Bridge jokingly reproached "Dear Publicola" for his "apostacy'" in having taken to politics, a career that Bridge had always predicted he would follow.[9] Yet John Quincy sturdily professed an abhorrence of public attention lest it should injure his rise in the law. He wrote his father that he was apprehensive of becoming politically known before he could establish a professional reputation.[10] He had now reached the age of twenty-five.

Why then, late in the year, did he plunge into print again

over such a minor issue? No doubt the theater meant a great
deal to him, perhaps more than he realized. Although he was
not in regular attendance in the fall of 1792, two years later
when a new and much better theater had been organized in
Boston with himself as one of the sponsors, he was to attend
three and four times a week.[11] Its seemingly non-political
character also appealed to him. When he apologized to his
father in December for trifling away his time in discussing
theatrical questions and in translating articles on French
politics for a local paper, he gave the excuse that his pen
having lain dormant for nearly a year and a half might best
be revived upon subjects not of the first importance. Certain
topics were closed to him. Reasons of delicacy, he said, prevented him from publicly airing his filial indignation over
election slanders against his father.[12] Belles lettres, of course,
had long since proved an unsatisfactory outlet for his ener-
gies—not to mention that his vein of romance had run thin.[13]
Finally he had immediately bristled in opposition to what
he must have considered an almost personal challenge on
the subject of the theater laid down in the public press by
the Attorney General of Massachusetts, the Hon. James Sullivan. Not only had John Quincy himself been an accomplice
to "breaking the law" by occasionally attending the theater,
but Sullivan was considered to be a deadly enemy of his
father and himself.

The antipathy of the Adamses at this time for that sturdy
Revolutionary patriot, James Sullivan, probably stemmed
from the fact that he had backed the despised Hancock for
the vice presidency in 1788, apparently even to the extent of
taking a trip south for that purpose. To John Adams his
old Revolutionary associate Sullivan was now like a pesti-
lence to be avoided, a "savage" false and faithless whom old
John swore he might "cross" sometime if he did not mend
his ways! John Quincy had been warned almost hysterically
when he set up his law office in Boston that summer to

beware of Sullivan lest he do him a mischief, and accordingly had been exceedingly prudent in all relations with him.[14] Admittedly the most popular civil lawyer in Boston, and a model of deportment and industry despite his fits of epilepsy, Sullivan was serving in the second year of what was to be a long and distinguished career as attorney general of the state. Not only had he taken the first official action against the players with that "intrepidity of face peculiar to himself," but had had the temerity to defend the right of majority rule in matters of state. This he had done in the Boston *Independent Chronicle* on December 13, 1792, over the signature "A Friend to Peace." [15] Defending the voice of the majority was like waving a red flag in front of young "Publicola," who promptly responded in the *Columbian Centinel* under the pen name of "Menander," the Athenian dramatist and poet.[16]

Many citizens of Boston had long wanted a theater. A very considerable number, however, led by redoubtable Sam Adams and "Old Honestus" Ben Austin, opposing aristocratic habits and "moral degeneracy," stood firm on the old colonial statute which had prohibited theaters. This law had been renewed in Massachusetts in 1785, a year during which a "Vauxhall" type of entertainment together with some amateur theatricals had appeared in Boston. Agitation on the subject nevertheless continued. Sponsorship of a theater project was made by "Candidus" in the *Centinel* in 1789 on the grounds that it would be good for business and also give young people something to do besides carousel [17] The following year the managers of the old American Company, who already had theaters in three northern cities including Providence, presented a petition to the Massachusetts legislature for leave to open a playhouse. This petition, however, had been denied.[18]

The matter came to a head at a Boston town meeting in Faneuil Hall on October 26, 1791. A large majority voted

to petition for a repeal of the state prohibition. A minority
of over three hundred moved a counter petition.[19] Political
confusion reigned on an issue that cut across ancient loyal-
ties. Dr. Charles Jarvis, a popular leader, quarreled with old
Sam Adams who for once in his life could not get attention
at a town meeting:

> To blast a wicked stage his voice he raised,
> And yet that thundering voice could not be heard.[20]

Thus was he satirized by one of the Hartford Wits.

Nevertheless, "the mighty Samuel" and moral principles
prevailed in the state legislature the next January, despite
the Boston petition and a remarkable speech by the eccentric
John Gardiner. The proceedings were promptly published
by Isaiah Thomas in his sympathetic *Massachusetts Magazine.* Gardiner, a man of long foreign residence like John
Quincy himself, and a one-time friend of "Squinting Jack"
Wilkes in London, had been enabled to return to America
in 1783 through the efforts of James Sullivan, no less, among
others.[21] Although Abigail Adams had once called Gardiner
a "madman," he held to the same views as her son in matters
pertaining to literature and the theater.[22]

Meanwhile the local journals had taken up the issue in
earnest. The mighty Boston *Gazette,* always jealous about
the rights of the people, published a grave warning that
three dollars for a seat in the pit of a theater might be but
a trifle to speculators in scripts, but not to honest men! It
said further that "STRANGERS" were threatening to damage
"CITIZENS"—the "new" American Company had been import-
ing a number of English actors—and that though "NOISE and
HISSING may possibly gratify the *dissolute,* and *abandoned,*"
it would ever be condemned by "the *considerate,* and *virtuous.*" This last was a reference to the town meeting which
had treated Sam Adams so rudely. According to the *Gazette*

it had lasted for hours during which "many very ingenious & animated arguments ensued." [23]

Despite the law and the attitude of the legislature, construction of an "Exhibition Room" in "Board-Alley" was begun in 1792, financed by a number of local citizens including Dr. Jarvis and several merchants. The building was a remodeled livery stable situated on a muddy short-cut between State and Summer streets and, strange to say, only a short distance from where James Sullivan had recently bought land on which to build himself a house.[24] The theatre, which had a pit, rows of boxes on three sides, and a gallery, accommodating altogether about 500 persons, was finally opened in August. Even before it was finished the English actor Charles Stewart Powell had arrived from the "Theatre Royal, Covent Garden," to join the new company, and had begun to give "concert plays" in Boston's Concert Hall. The first exhibitions in the new "Room," however, were of the Sadler's Wells variety—tumbling, tightrope walking, a "dancing ballet," and the "Gallery of Portraits." John Quincy Adams termed it all "miserable stuff." [25] After about two months of this sort of entertainment, real plays began to appear. John Quincy intended to see "The Beaux Stratagem" on October 3 and did get to see "The Miser" and a pantomime a week later. "The best bad, the worst inexplicable," he caustically remarked.[26] On October 20 there was another town meeting on the subject of the theater. On the thirtieth John Quincy saw "Hamlet," "a play called a moral lecture," in which Powell surprised him by the excellence of his performance; but "Love à la Mode"—they always gave double features in "Board-Alley"—he thought miserably done.

Matters were now moving rapidly towards a crisis. On December 5 the players were "routed by the governor" who had already complained to the legislature about the situa-

tion and had demanded that the reluctant Sullivan take
action. Since no grand jury would indict and since complaint
by an informer was lacking, this was done by arresting an
actor during a performance, catching him in *flagrante delicto*
so to speak. This not unnaturally caused a riot by the audience. Although no one would appear in court next day
against the players, they thought it prudent to shut up shop
for the present in "Board-Alley." [27] Young Adams bet an
acquaintance a beaver hat on December 13 that the anti-
theatrical statute would not be repealed in two years.[28] The
fact is that for all practical purposes it was done the next
spring. Incidentally, December 13 was the same day that
Sullivan wrote in the *Chronicle* to explain the administration's attitude towards the players. The day following, John
Quincy himself started writing and as "Menander" first appeared in the *Centinel* on December 19.

John Quincy made three principal points in his rebuttal
to Sullivan. (1) "In a free government the minority never
can be under an obligation to sacrifice *their rights* to the
will of the majority. . . ." (2) ". . . the conduct of those citizens of Boston, who from a cold and deliberate opinion
that the law prohibiting theatrical entertainments is unconstitutional, have attended the exhibitions in Board-Alley,
is not unjustifiable." (3) ". . . if they had not Hibernian
blood enough in their veins to turn State witness against
themselves, they had enough of American spirit about them
not to avoid by any subterfuge a legal investigation."

The first point about protection against majority rule was
a carryover from John Quincy's argument the previous year
against Paine's *The Rights of Man,* and his whole detestation of French Revolutionary doctrines. The second point
voiced his understanding of the individual's right of private
judgment. The third was plainly an expression of contempt
for the reasoning of that "Hibernian," James Sullivan, a
son of Irish redemptioners, who had suggested that the pro-

testors should make a test case of themselves in order to bring the matter to court. Young Adams had obviously been re-examining his stock of convictions about American rights. Indeed, he had recently been steeping himself in works on American history,[29] but at the same time obviously retaining certain "un-American" prejudices. He noted in his diary that at his club where "Menander" was the topic of conversation—the authorship was wrongly attributed to Dr. Jarvis—the expression, "Hibernian blood," was disapproved.[30] The implication is obvious.

The second of the "Menander" articles in the *Centinel*, on December 22, directly attacked the legality of the proceedings against the players. It transferred the major blame from Sullivan to Hancock who was accused of having acted unconstitutionally in first calling the subject to the attention of the legislature. While the *ex officio* character of the warrant used by the attorney general was roundly denounced, this too was attributed to the haste which "the passion of an important personage gave to the whole affair."

That passion, Sir, if common report may be credited proceeded so far, as to sanction other measures, where the substance and the forms of law were equally disregarded. It is well-known that on the Friday evening after the interruption of the entertainment, a number of people, were unlawfully collected, with the professed intention of pulling down the building where the performances had been exhibited. That they declared they had the express permission of the Chief Magistrate to put their design in execution is beyond a doubt; and this permission, it is said was given at his own house, where they went in a body to request it.

Thus had Governor Hancock been guilty of countenancing popular fury, according to young "Menander"!

John Quincy Adams never made a worse mistake in his whole life than in this instance of letting his passion run away with the sober facts. Madam Adams proudly wrote about the second "Menander" number, saying wittily that

the governor had certainly burnt his fingers and that as soon
as the general court convened he would surely have the gout
as was his habit in time of trouble. Old John Adams in New
York, however, was properly sceptical. While appreciating
hearing about the "History of Tragedy, Comedy, and Farce,"
the old gentleman had too much common sense to think that
Governor Hancock had given encouragement to the rioters
to meddle with the playhouse or the board fences; if the
mob said so, the mob had lied.[31] And such, indeed, proved to
have been the case. The rioters had in fact been checked,
rather than encouraged, by the governor.

So "Menander" now had to write an apologetic third
piece.[32] The *Gazette* had meantime come to Hancock's defense with a blistering attack upon those "idle scribblers
under fictitious signatures" who were trying to tear down
good government in favor of one "more congenial to their
views of a *mixed monarchy*." (Who but an Adams could have
been indicated?) The "atrocious falsehood" of "Menander"
was said to have been made worse by his methods of insinuation, "like a *coward, and an assassin.* . . ."[33] Another article
in the same issue sarcastically asked where the rights of the
minority were now, in view of the action of a recent town
meeting which had denounced counter-petitions as irregular.
The article sneeringly requested that those who chose to
exercise the *"Rights of Man"* might at least have the liberty
the constitution gave them, of petitioning the legislature
against a repeal of the act prohibiting theatrical entertainments. This was something like turning "Menander's" argument against himself.

What could John Quincy Adams say? The despotic action
of the town meeting he simply ignored;[34] but he had to eat
humble pie in admitting that he was happy to find that the
report against the governor was without any foundation.
However he pointed out that he had "cautiously avoided"
stating this as a positive fact. As to the epithets of "coward"

and "assassin," these he called the usual terms employed by the humble friends of "great men." He said that he had had no intention of fixing false charges upon the chief magistrate, but that this did not do away with the larger question as to the propriety of the whole proceeding in which the governor had been engaged.

With such a defiant "apology" did young "Menander" conclude his sorry career, marked first by crudely insulting Sullivan and then by repeating unfounded rumors against the governor. But his doting mother, while acknowledging that his father had been right in doubting the libel against Hancock, still thought that two of the three "Menander" atricles were in a "masterly style"—that of December 19 and the other of unknown date because the tell-tale date is blotted out! [35]

This unfortunate affair reveals John Quincy Adams in late 1792 to have been in a most unhappy and confused state of mind. A matter not of the first magnitude, as he himself had termed it,[36] had first enticed him into print and had then become the occasion for permitting spleen to undermine his judgment. It is significant that on the day before the first "Menander" article appeared, he had confessed that a weight of anxiety lay heavily on his mind. He had been reading Livy, lamenting that time was fleeting but protesting, "Yet for what am I to blame?" The old bitter thought had been growing upon him that his situation in so many ways was not of his own making. No doubt he was seeking excuses for having sent his first "Menander" communication to the press, though he was man enough to reproach himself for whining.[37]

It is not to be wondered at that a person in such a state of mental turmoil should have committed errors of judgment. Confusion in his sense of values must have excited such irresponsible passion. To explain how this confusion had come about, let us review his twelve months past. The year had actually started off rather well, but had grown increasingly distasteful to him.

The aftermath of the "Publicola" incident in 1791 had left John Quincy physically exhausted, his eyes remaining sore until September; but one suspects that the incident had given him enormous satisfaction. Within a month, moreover, he was writing in a rarely optimistic vein to his younger brother, Thomas Boylston Adams. He had been surprisingly pleased by his performance in October at the Court of Common Pleas. "I found my satisfaction in myself growing much stronger, and acquitted myself more to my satisfaction than I had ever done before." [38] This was high praise indeed from an old practitioner of "nervous eloquence," one so eternally critical of himself. He even hoped to improve his capacity for forensic contention. For fifteen months this had been one of the greatest sources of his anxiety and apprehension. Thomas Boylston knew of his fear on this score and how fatal it could be in the legal profession. The future professor of oratory at Harvard and future author of two volumes on that subject [39] was apparently beginning to feel that he was making some progress along the rocky road of public speaking.

Another reason for this brief outburst of confidence was an extemporaneous speech he had recently delivered before a committee of the general court. The subject was the incorporation of the North Parish of Braintree into the separate town of Quincy. This important but troublesome affair had come to a head after fifty years of agitation, and now was to engage his attention for several months. Although he said that "like Dogberry in the play" he had bestowed all his "tediousness" on their honors, the incident obviously had not gone off badly.[40]

Despite renewal of his usual bouts of doubting and dullness, another local matter also attracted his attention at this time. In a town meeting held in Boston in December, 1791, he had been chosen a member of a committee to report on measures for reform of the town police. This was a part of the larger question of reforming the whole town government, perhaps even of the town's becoming incorporated. To John Quincy's astonishment his nomination for a place on the committee had been made by Dr. Jarvis—"Dr. Demigog" to his critics—one of the local politicians detested by the Adamses. On being questioned the doctor surprisingly said that the country was under great obligations to John Adams and that it was proper to pay some notice to his sons. Also, John Quincy seemed to him to be a sensible young man.[41]

This was the beginning of a split in town affairs that helps to explain some of the confusion over the question of the theater in the months following. Together with a dispute over an appointment to the state Supreme Court, the split temporarily drove a wedge between Hancock, Sam Adams, Ben Austin and some of their nominal supporters. "Old Honestus" Austin now took the lead against reforming the constabulary in opposition to both Jarvis and Sullivan. In a tempestuous town meeting in January—it confirmed John Quincy in his "contempt of simple democracy as a Government"—Austin became so insulting in his manner that a street fight resulted the next day. Ben Russell, stalwart publisher of the *Centinel,* pulled Austin's nose and spit in his face thereby bringing on an action for assault and battery.[42] It is interesting to note that when the suit was settled a year later, John Quincy was to report the nominal jury settlement as a victory for his friend Russell. In a long newspaper contribution he was to excoriate Austin as a local Jacobin.[43]

This question about the police kept John Quincy occupied with committee meetings in early 1792, but actually he got very little satisfaction out of it. Not only did the final committee report displease him, since it cut out the part he considered most important,[44] but Austin and his followers at the stormy meeting had overthrown what remained. When he later thought over the events of this unhappy year, John Quincy gloomily concluded that he would do well to keep clear of politics altogether. All of his views seemed to be as unpopular as his conduct had been on the subjects of the police and the theater. His father then tried to comfort him by saying he rejoiced that his son had taken such positions, not that he wished him to be unpopular but that his views were right. In any case, a setback in his political career would give him time for his profession.[45] Apparently his father always took for granted his son's ultimate political career. How John Quincy must have wished that the same could be said for his legal practice!

Even in this respect, in early 1792 he seems temporarily to have enjoyed more business than heretofore. He even argued several cases in court, winning one in January but losing an important one in April. He also settled several matters out of court including the affairs of an estate. A little business even necessitated his taking an overnight trip to Worcester. But soon he was again "busy with nothing." His sole public activity now was to serve as one of the clerks of the market, a kind of office primarily concerned with dining and drinking. Melancholy grew upon him. By mid April, the day after he lost the Titcomb case, he was "very unwell" and lamenting with all his old time fervor about his insufficiency at the law. That day he resolved again to resume writing a journal, a practice given up during his illness in the fall of 1788. It was a resolution, he glumly said, which he had adopted the year before and "perhaps for the fiftieth time." [46]

"Why continue with a journal?" he querulously asked himself on that unhappy day. Trivial events, scarcely rising above insipidity, together with painful occurrences and mortifying reflections, were surely not worth recording. The last year had not been without its instruction, but the "difficulties, and perplexities under which I laboured twelve months

since" still continued, and were increased by the considera-
tion that "I have now gone through another annual revolution in my progress to the grave, without advancing a step
in my career, as it relates to this world." Yet he saw no use
in complaining and resolved to try to do better.

His journal was dropped again after a few days, only to
be briefly resumed a month later with a brave effort at self-
exhortation. He denounced his lack of application and the
childish opinion that "extraordinary genius" is incompatible
with plodding. (This criticism was directed at some of his
fellows but the "genius" referred to must have included his
own!) Since he could scarcely hold any expectations of pur-
suing a public career either from his present situation or
from that of his country, and since his thoughts of undertaking a "useful literary performance" would interfere with
his profession, he concluded that he must continue to make
the law his first interest.[47] Yet only a few days earlier he had
called "these sandy desarts of legal study" an "unnatural
cultivation." [48] It is clear that both politics and literature
continued to be secretly cherished ambitions.

It is only fair to bear in mind that such self-deprecation
by John Quincy Adams was only one man's opinion, that of
his severest critic. These were secret thoughts and plainly
exaggerated. They were made also during a bitter period
following a serious set-back at the bar. Nevertheless, it seems
significant that it was general reading rather than legal
studies which attracted him in the months that followed.
After his parents' return to Quincy in May, he spent his
weekends there and principally employed his "idle" time
in reading literature. He read Milton and Pope that summer,
supplementing these authors with numerous works on American history, such as the Reverend Jeremy Belknap's *History
of New Hampshire,* Hutchinson's *History of Massachusetts-
Bay,* and Winthrop's *Journal.* Later in the year he read a
good deal of Jonathan Swift, including the *Tale of a Tub.*

He seems to have preferred satire as that unhappy year progressed.[49]

As for his repeated "failures" to renew his journal, we
should note in John Quincy's favor that he never had failed
even during the period of his worst illness to record at least
a line or two each day in his almanac diary. This was an
achievement remarkable in itself. Moreover his life in this
year of confusion, as well as at other times, must be eval-
uated not only in the light of his pessimistic reflections about
his lack of professional success, but in the sum total of all
his activities. On the social side, these activities had continued to be as heavy as ever, although with increasing emphasis on male companionship.

Foremost among his social engagements had been faithful
attendance at his club, a meeting of eight or ten young men
with an occasional older person. The club met on Saturday
evenings at one of the member's home. Vinous conviviality
and lively conversation held sway. An eighteenth century
English institution, the club must have been an idea that
John Quincy had picked up abroad. Surely none could have
been more regularly attended than his. After he left Boston
in 1794 it speedily degenerated into a Saturday night tavern
affair.[50]

Foremost among his rakish associates at the "Crackbrain
Club," or visiting for an occasional chat at his office, were
sons of local men of affairs. There was the facetious Tom
Crafts, son of a prominent judge and politician; Nathan
Frazier, Jr., a cousin of the beautiful and "lost" Mary; John
Gardner, Jr., and the Sargent brothers, all sons of local mer-
chants. From these and other boon companions—they nick-
named each other "Starveling," "The Fat Knight," "Sir
John," "The Squire," "Longwharf" and so forth—John
Quincy seems to have learned unnatural, raffish talk.[51] These
were his boisterous friends for evening walks, for supping at
Julien's, or for bowling and drinking at Birds—the latter in

John Quincy's overly-heated imagination probably the local equivalent of the fabled Boar's Head Tavern! Not only was he their leading spirit but he seems to have gained their warm affection, as had also been true with certain members of his old club in Newburyport. John Gardner was an especially admiring friend, somewhat in the same way James Bridge had been earlier.[52] One fellow named Hall was especially noteworthy because a meeting at his home usually meant heavy drinking. John Quincy invariably regretted these particular bouts and swore to avoid them henceforth.

Although the club meetings were of increasing importance to John Quincy, they were still infrequent affairs compared with his many teas and "evenings at home" in Boston. These were old pleasures dating from the moment he had arrived back in America. Of peculiar interest at this time, however, was his rather negative reaction to the young ladies he met on such occasions, or at assembly balls during the winter. Many prominent families of Boston, including Cushing, Gray, Amory, Breck, and Higginson, had one or more eligible daughters with whom he became well acquainted. If he had a favorite among them in the spring of 1792 it was probably Sally Gray with whom he occasionally held a private conversation. This might even be called his "Sally Gray year"; but it was a mild affair at best. He recorded on May 24 that he had talked with Sally upon a subject "once very interesting"; but he laconically added, "at present indifferent." [53] And that seems to be about as far as it went.

Romance was still a baneful topic. As he remarked, following a party in February, "nothing could a charm impart." Female society was only tolerable, and it did not tend to improve. Perhaps he was not too popular with the ladies himself, with the possible exception of Miss Gray. At one assembly in the fall he actually could not get a single partner to dance, and at another he got but one.[54] Nevertheless, these were exceptional occasions at the close of a most depressing

year. Like Job he had even suffered an affliction of boils on
his face.

The aftermath of the Frazier affair unquestionably still
rankled. Indeed, John Quincy was to describe its effects
strongly several years later. Perhaps he even met Mary on
several occasions in Boston since one of the homes he occasionally visited there was that of a certain "Miss Frazier," presumably some relation of the Newburyport family.[55] However, there seems to have been no attempt by John Quincy to
renew the Mary Frazier affair at this or at any other time,
although he had become an almost daily associate of her
cousin Nathan, with whom he sometimes reproached himself
for being "imprudent" in conversation.[56]

If the young man suffered the pangs of love in 1792, it
apparently was love of a varied kind if the remnants of his
poetical strivings may serve as evidence. In his private book
of poems there are two "Elegies to Miranda" which relate
to this period.[57] The first is of little consequence. It was
addressed to "Miranda" on her birthday wherein she is ac-
claimed the acme of all perfection, but one whose heart
"never can be mine." The second elegy is much more suggestive for an understanding of its author in this troublesome
year. It is a humorously ironic lament about his proneness to
fall in love! It is a satire about his ability to be attracted by
females of all descriptions, regardless of person, manners, or
even color.

> Imperious Beauty's ever varying forms,
>> By turns assume their empire o'er my heart,
> Each new attraction, my fond bosom warms,
>> Now nature's bloom, and now the grace of Art.

Be she fair fifteen or some fearless widow who "her ripe
charms displays," the fair coquette, or even the prude who
treats one with disdain, he declared he could love them all.
Whether learned or vulgar they made their appeal, he said,

for " 'Tis simple Nature, and can be no sin." One stanza was reminiscent of the "theme" of "Scipio Africanus":

> All colours please me, black or brown or white
>   For 'black though comely' was the wise man's flame;
> A fair complexion yields me vast delight,
>   And yet, how just the nut-brown maiden's fame.

And then the anguished conclusion:

> Blame not the Bard because the objects change,
>   But Oh! Miranda, lend thy generous aid
> To fix one heart, that fain would cease to range;
>   Tempt him with beauties that will never fade.

If the poem is taken to mean anything at all in a personal sense, all that can reasonably be concluded is that John Quincy Adams in 1792 was revolving wildly between various objects of his affection. That he should have truly wished that there was someone like "Miranda" is readily understandable. That there was not may have been a part of his unhappiness. But the "Bard," as was his wont, was unwilling to blame himself for his own condition.

For whatever reasons, as the year progressed his melancholic moods increased. The heat of summer as usual depressed him, although he did manage to do a lot of bowling as a supplement to his daily regimen of walking. There was also frequent convivial supping at Birds Tavern. He sullenly asked himself, "Time misspent, but why should it be otherwise?" He even failed to go to his beloved Harvard in September for the annual Phi Beta Kappa "exhibition" at which, we recall, he had been the stellar attraction just prior to his illness in 1788. That had been a year in many ways unhappily similar to this. Soon he was miserably confessing to himself that he had done wrong not to have gone.[58]

The almost daily walks that he took in the evening or at night, sometimes after his club and as late as one or two A.M., also brought experiences that seem to have heightened his

growing tension. These walks were a form of the exercise so
necessary to maintain his health and were invariably taken
on the Boston "Mall," usually with a friend but sometimes
alone. The great mall ran the length of the Boston Common
from the old Burying Ground to the Public Granary, then
into the little mall, or "Paddock's Walk," or into a path behind the granary which crossed obliquely to Beacon Street
and ran westward up that side of the Common, terminating
in the region facetiously called "Mt. Whoredom." [59]

For some strange reason beginning in August, 1792, these
nightly walks on the mall developed reactions of repugnance
and even of danger in young John Quincy Adams. Perhaps
in referring to extraordinary experiences he may have been
overly fond, as was Dr. Watson, of words such as "adventure."
When he lamented "dissipation," for example, it invariably
meant no more than his having drunk too much wine. Yet
some of his experiences in the mall were admittedly odd. On
August 27 following his walk he noted, "N B & avoid!" A
week later, "Walking in the Mall all the Eve[g]. Fortunately
unsuccessful." Four days after this he went walking with
Daniel Sargent but "parted accidentally, and I got fortunately
home." A month later he recorded another sort of titillating
experience, "Disconcerted madame in walk in the Mall."
This was after he and some of his rakish friends had dined
and perhaps wined together too well.[60]

No doubt such cryptic utterances—they were to be even
more frequently recorded the next year—are capable of various interpretations. At the least they do suggest occasional
excessive concern in connection with these nightly strolls.
There can be little doubt that poor John Quincy was in an
unusually tense state of mind in the fall of 1792. In October
he suffered several bad nights of sleeplessness reminiscent of
those of October, 1788.[61] Perhaps like some Puritan Boswell
—another young gentleman famous for recording his thoughts
and experiences—John Quincy was being subjected to all the

dangers from footpads and other designing persons who commonly beset gentlemen on their nightly perambulations in the eighteenth century. Perhaps the mall in Boston was not so greatly different from that in St. James's Park in London. In any case, John Quincy Adams plainly feared it, despite the vicarious thrills it may have given him.

So the theater controversy in the fall of the year must have been a very welcome if "trifling" diversion to this generally unemployed and badly upset young man. But it is evident that he was not in a judicial mood for the proper appraisal of this or any other emotionally charged issue. It should further be remembered that he was incessantly being exposed in the latter part of this year to the torrent of his father's suspicions about political "treachery." These included the machinations of Clinton of New York to replace him as vice president—Alexander Hamilton had warned as early as June of this—and the malicious talent which Thomas Jefferson was displaying for the spirit of "faction." [62] The political enemies of the father were natural objects of attack by a loyal son. Among those local enemies were the unspeakable Hancock and his first lieutenant, Attorney General James Sullivan. It was certainly revealing how John Quincy had concluded there was significance in Governor Hancock's decision to vent his "peevishness" on the players on the very day that the results of the federal elections in Masachusetts became known!

At the beginning of 1792, John Quincy had humorously summed up his unprofitable business situation and his inability to get along in local affairs by quoting his beloved Shakespeare, saying with Ancient Pistol, " '*si fortuna me tormenta, il sperare me contenta.*' " [63] By the end of this trying year, although he was more deeply involved in "Shakespearean" things than ever, his sense of humor had pretty well evaporated. As he sourly wrote his father shortly after the beginning of the action against the theater, "All the actors are now gone." [64]

However he was just as wrong in thinking that the players would not soon be back as he had been in "accusing" the governor of abetting a riot against them. He had wagered wrongly on both counts and had lost a beaver hat, at least! What he had accomplished by his passionate efforts was scarcely to be described, to borrow one of Dogberry's words, as "suffigance." But he had clearly demonstrated another step forward in his development as a controversial participant in the hurly-burly of public affairs.

CHAPTER NINE

NEUTRALITY AND L'ENVOI

> "I am on the bridge between
> wisdom and folly"

The unsuspected and surprising news reached John Quincy Adams on June 3, 1794, that President Washington had determined to send him abroad as minister resident at The Hague. He had never sought public office and knew that his father had never sought it for him. A few days later, however, he did ask him whether he had had any prior knowledge of the appointment. His father's satisfaction at the appointment was in fact much greater than his own. John Quincy said that he rather wished it had not been made at all! [1]

Within several days he began to suffer bouts of serious ill health, even necessitating his being bled. These bouts continued throughout the early part of the summer. Sailing was put off until September because of unavoidable delays. [2] In July he had to make an official visit to Philadelphia. There his father warned him to attend to his dress a little since "No man alive is more attentive to these things than the President." [3] This was not the first time in recent years, however, that John Quincy had been warned about his careless appearance. He suffered continuously on the trip south; as always, the heat of the summer affected him. The prospect of leaving the country was also depressing. He hated to think of parting from friends, although as a matter of fact the companionable Tom Crafts had left for Europe only a few weeks before and at least four other members of the "Crackbrain Club" in Boston were to follow there shortly. In addition to reasons of sentiment, John Quincy felt it a duty to live in one's own country, and anticipated returning as soon as possible. Above all he feared that his leaving would be a serious check to his career in law that finally had begun to develop after three long years of waiting.[4]

So, in 1794 John Quincy Adams at the age of twenty-seven was to leave his native land somewhat as he had done as a lad fifteen years earlier—as an act of duty and against his personal wishes! Now as always his private life seemed to be sacrificed to his country's needs. He would go at the President's behest and would serve at pleasure, but he himself had not sought the appointment.

Nevertheless the situation had been of his own making. In the year preceding his appointment, despite all his desperate devotion to the law, John Quincy had made himself one of the foremost controversialists in the American newspaper press on the subject of foreign affairs and French relations. He had written first as "Marcellus" in April, 1793, and then as "Columbus" and as "Barneveld" in December '93 and January '94. Many of his articles, originally appearing in the Boston papers, were reprinted in New York and elsewhere. Although he wrote under pseudonyms, his authorship became well known. His mother, the irrepressible Abigail, even coyly but unsuccessfully tried to get Senator George Cabot of Massachusetts, already titular head of a nascent "Essex Junto," to have "Columbus's" writings published in Philadelphia. Cabot had expressed a hope the previous summer that John Quincy would take up his pen against "Citizen Genet"; but he was not now impressed with the need for republication.[5] Genet had already bowed out.

Public distinction if not a foreign appointment must have been something that John Quincy craved, possibly even more than he himself knew. In his long lamentation of May, 1792, he had mentioned the lack of prospects in his country's service as well as in his profession.[6] Nor had all of his public con-

tributions consisted of "anonymous" writings or of committee work for the town. In January, 1793, he had made some
remarks at a town meeting in Faneuil Hall that had attracted
favorable attention, even though he was on the unpopular
side of the issue.[7] Certainly his love of public controversy
reached a new high that year, despite all his apprehensions
about its effect on his legal career. Shortly after the first "Marcellus" number appeared in the *Centinel* in April, 1793, he
fretfully recorded in his diary, "I am on the bridge between
wisdom and folly." [8] This may have been an expression of
anxiety on some other score—he had several matters to worry
him as we shall see—but it probably showed apprehension
caused by his having again yielded to his love of print. He
probably felt a good deal like his father who, between outbursts of delight over his son's public writings, would assev-
erate that there was no future for a lawyer in a printer's
office.[9]

It seems to have been true for 1793, as for the year immediately preceding, that public controversy not only was cherished by young Adams for its own sake—contentiousness was
plainly growing upon him—but it had become a real necessity
as he champed on the bit of fancied idleness. Not until 1794
did his law practice improve to the point where he could dis-
pense with an allowance from his family. Curiously, this improvement came in part owing to the kindness of his old
"enemy," James Sullivan, whom recently he had been abus-
ing so badly in the press.[10] Even at that juncture, however, he
was yet lamenting that his practice amounted to so little.

Meantime the tempo of his private life seemed to have become more strident and unsatisfactory than ever. It is interesting to note that he had again begun to put on weight. He
sometimes worried about his legal work, but his greater concern was with his life of clubbing, roistering, keeping late
hours, and occasionally drinking too much wine with ill effects the next day—with all kinds of "dissipation," in short,

that wasted time and led to inefficiency. It always seemed to be his luck to get some business the day after one of those nights! Despite his general record of devotion to serious matters he was continually engaged in self-recrimination and in making resolutions to do better. On New Year's Eve in 1793, for example, he deliberately stayed away from his friends only to have them come to his lodgings to drink champagne, so that, as he disgustedly recorded, he "ended the year with folly." [11]

The mightiest effort he made to reform himself was shortly before the arrival of the unexpected news of his appointment to The Hague. In his diary for May 13, 1794, he had noted, "temperance compulsive." He commended a "new regimen" to himself a week later, but with the gloomiest forebodings. He forced himself to come home early to "self-inflicted employment" and to "new application," finding himself within a few days reduced to the point where he was dangling between "hope and fear." Perhaps such desperate self-discipline included an effort—his annual spring effort—to revive his journal or possibly to turn his hand to some new kind of writing. But whatever it was he came perilously close to grief. Although he had been fairly prudent at the club on May 31, after taking supper at Hall's he again fell by the wayside and arrived home late at night with his heart "unfit for examination." [12]

Fortunately, only three days afterwards the news came of his appointment to The Hague. Surely this was a saving act of providence if there ever was one, despite all his half-hearted protests to the contrary. However it was to turn back into Puritan channels the main stream of his life-long hopes for literary distinction. For the first time since his illness in 1788, he now by a mighty effort of will did successfully revive his journal,[13] to be continued for the rest of his life as "memoirs." Its old motto was more significant than ever: "La molèsse est douce, et sa suite est cruelle." It was like an echo from a childhood reproach against idleness: "I make but a poor figure at composition, my head is much too fickle, my thoughts running after birds eggs play and trifles, till I get vexed with myself." [14]

While John Quincy had been struggling through those early years of "painful suspense and tedious expectation" at the law,[15] an unusual amount of latitude in conduct had no doubt been a very natural thing, encouraged as it was by the bitter memory of things lost or at least never renewed. On hearing in 1795 of his younger brother Charles' marriage to someone he himself admired and goaded by a singularly inept remark by his father, John Quincy wrote his mother a most revealing letter. He fiercely lamented the struggle he had once had to go through as a result of his "prudential sacrifice" in giving up the lovely Mary Frazier in 1790. He had done all this at a cost to himself, he said, that he alone knew, including the price of "blunted sensations." He acknowledged that he had lived through the ordeal and had "never intended not to." But he declared that his success had been "perhaps principally due to facilities in its execution which might have failed, and which were more serviceable to my intentions than flattering to my pride." [16]

Here is one explanation of the occasional "dissipation" he had so uneasily enjoyed in Boston. Had he not bitterly resolved in 1791 never to be perfect? [17] Mild as such "facilities" must have appeared to many persons in the eighteenth century, to this young Puritan—for Puritan he was despite all his European experience—such activities unquestionably represented a grave danger. Not only were they allied to idleness, but the evils of loose companions had already been amply demonstrated by his charming but luckless brother Charles. Tavern-drinking in particular had been a life-long abomination to his father, who certainly was no teetotaler since he enjoyed a tankard of hard cider each morning before breakfast. There was also his mother's unfortunate brother to stand as a family warning.[18] For a time such "facilities" may well

have seemed necessary for survival to young John Quincy
Adams; but if so, he had never been proud of them. As he
later wrote to a friend from abroad, he had never been cut
out to be a "rake." When he had been thrown into that character he had performed the part with "as little grace as enjoyment." From the "damnable" attractions of some of his
friends and his own perennial failures at reformation, he
then found himself happily in Holland "once more my own
man again," in firm control of those habits which he had "in
some measure lost" in Boston.[19]

This private quarrel between prudence and folly continued to agitate him all the time he was writing in 1793 on
the need for prudence in the conduct of foreign affairs. The
two problems were somehow connected in his thinking! A
parallel is at least suggested in "Columbus No. II," in the
remark that "parties are to the public body, what the passions
are to the individual." [20] His character had begun to harden
—perhaps it even became too hard—as he sought to assert himself more effectively in both private and public matters.

One of the most revealing personal items he ever wrote in
his diary was his confession on March 12, 1793, that at a dance
that night he "made intentionally an offensive reply." [21] This
had unpleasant implications. In public affairs it recalls the
offensive tone in his recent "Menander" articles, and it foreshadowed the invective in his newspaper writings a year later.
His satire had plainly begun to turn to spleen. Cutting and
caustic remarks, so characteristic of his mature style of composition, were to become blatant in the "Barneveld" articles
against James Sullivan, beginning in the Boston papers in
December, 1793.[22] These ultimately were to bring precautionary warnings even from his proud parents, but surely they
demonstrated a new skill at partisan abuse. However, no such
personal characteristics can be detected in either the "Marcellus" articles or in his statesman-like Fourth of July oration
that year, the latter delivered in a lofty tone of non-partisan-

ship—unless indeed "statesmanship" can somehow be identified with that hardening of the private affections of which he
was later to complain so bitterly.[23]

Alternations between indulgence and regret were now so
continual with John Quincy Adams as to become as monoto-
nous as they were disturbing. He had started off the new year
with his customary round of dining and assemblies, and with
only an occasional self-reproach. But on March 31 he was
injudicious at his club and subsequently became ill. Yet he
succeeded in avoiding another drinking bout and even with-
drew from a party the next day when he found himself in
bad company.[24] Henceforth he seems to have found less pleasure in mixed affairs than before. But sometimes he still attended affairs with young ladies, particularly those that included Sally Gray, or at least until he rudely spoiled their
friendly relations by refusing to take Sally home from a party
one night in June.[25]

Other social activities were unabated. He was continually
dining out with male companions. In addition to occasional
visits to the theater, which was briefly revived in Boston that
spring, there were also the dutiful meetings at church and
visits to Quincy over the weekends. More interest and excitement attended his nightly strolls and his convivial club. For
example in the evening of April 23 he was involved in a "fool-
ish adventure" in which however "discretion prevailed." Just
what this refers to is unfortunately not clear. Two weeks later
he tried to console himself for an "error" by committing a
"folly," leaving himself with the most painful reflections. Yet
he considered himself a "sport of chance" and would not admit that it had been altogether his fault. A walk at two A.M.
in the mall several nights later was rather "fortunate than
otherwise." On May 27 he was "guilty of extravagance" at
Birds Tavern; and the next day "silly again," apparently in
conversation during a walk in the mall. On another walk on
June 4 he recorded that he was prudent; but on the twentieth

in the mall he was "not so wise as sometimes. Home this evening almost despairing." [26]

Some of these remarks suggest that John Quincy had become almost pathetically self-conscious about a tendency to speak too freely. "Too tonguey" would have been the Yankee expression. An occasional lack of prudence in speech had indeed troubled him for some time past, along with a tendency to feel "silly." Perhaps he had developed an embarrasing penchant for using "macaroni" expressions as a part of that new rakish behavior so unbecoming to him. When he met several young men and women out walking one evening in June he "made a lamentable mistake again"; and on July 5 he parted in the mall from his old friend Gardner "very foolishly." But embarrassment arising from loose speech could have been only a part of his anxiety. A few days later he again experienced some kind of an "adventure" in the mall, but again suffered no harm.[27] And so, to a lesser extent, did his difficulties continue throughout the fall. One can only guess at their meaning. On a lamentable night in November he said that he indulged "beyond all hazards" and was left two days later still "trembling" for the wages of his sins.[28] Such activities were soon to be interrupted, however, by his preoccupation in writing "Columbus," and then "Barneveld."

Yet one of his most curious personal experiences came at this very time. In early December, at eight o'clock in the evenings of three days running, he had appointments of some kind in front of the porch of the Brattle Street Church. Presumably this was the one which then stood in the vicinity of present day Scollay Square. Each night he was "fortunate" that there was a lack of "correspondent punctuality"; he was "luckily unsuccessful" and escaped "unhurt." [29] For whom could he have been waiting those cold nights in the winter's snow? He was to have a similar experience at another mysterious appointment in the evening of March 4, 1794, but which he said was "very well" with him. Three days earlier, it may be noted, on one of his evening walks in the mall he had again met with several adventures, one of which he said was "really affecting." [30] Since this obviously had to do with some unfortunate creature, it suggests that being solicited by a streetwalker may have been one of the things that he meant by "adventure." In such a topsy-turvy fashion did his escapades and lucky escapes continue.

So, too, did his lamentations and resolutions continue. When he dined at Hall's one February evening in 1794, he said that he could not possibly "have done worse." In late March he recorded the unhappy conviction that life in this state was "no blessing," and sternly asked himself why he did not maintain his spirit "while under sentence." Two days later he despairingly cried, "When will the vulture leave my bosom?" On April 1, following some keen disappointment—perhaps over hopes which had excited these outbursts—he declared all his expectations fruitless. Soon he became involved in a "double folly" at Hall's, only to try and brace himself for another go at reformation. He was still miserably asking himself on April 22, "Anticipations for futurity—what?" [31]

His principal diversion in these troubled months of early 1794 had been an almost day to day attendence at the newly built theater which had opened in "Board-Alley" in February, and of which he was one of the financial patrons. It became an oasis in a desert of desolation, helping to quench his inordinate thirst for diversion, although not always in fullest measure. One of the last performances he saw was on May 26, "The Virgin Unmasked," the old Fielding farce about marriage which he tersely dismissed as the "worst play I ever saw or read." [32]

It is doubly clear, then, that in the spring of 1794 just prior to his last Herculean attempt at reform and prior to the salutary appointment abroad, the young man had been suffering an almost intolerable disturbance of spirits. This may have been due in part to worry about his law cases and almost certainly to his indiscretions. Possibly involved, too, was bitter disappointment over the failure of President Washington to appoint him Federal Attorney General for New England. There had been some foundation for such hope,[33] and if news of this had somehow leaked out then ambition for public distinction had also been a "vulture" that was tearing at his liver. He scarcely could have been his father's son had it been otherwise, as his Aunt Mary Cranch had long ago observed upon his return from Europe.[34]

Yet he had always denied that ambition had prompted the writing of any of his newspaper articles. On one occasion he said rather grimly that he hoped at the very least what he was doing was for the benefit of his country; and it was one of his favorite maxims that it is an individual's right and duty to express himself on momentous affairs. Indeed, it was by quoting this self-justifying assertion, together with an expression taken from John Quincy's 1793 Fourth of July oration, that James Sullivan was to open the first of his "Americanus" numbers in rebuttal to "Columbus" that fall.[35]

The emphasis in the "Marcellus" newspaper articles—the first of which John Quincy published over the name of the famous Roman general in Boston on April 24, 1793, must have been written before news of Washington's proclamation of "neutrality"—was likewise on individual duty.[36] As already suggested, John Quincy's concept of international relations was closely related to that of personal morality. This he emphasized in referring to the need for people to refrain from the "avariciousness" of privateering—to help preserve American neutrality following the arrival of Citizen Genet—and in stating that the rights of nations "are nothing more than an extension of the rights of individuals. . . ." This idea, akin to his old argument in "Publicola," he related to the Christian teaching of the Golden Rule. In international as in private affairs he wanted morality to be the basis for conduct.

As for American treaty obligations towards the French, while John Quincy reluctantly admitted that it was the law of nations that such obligations do survive revolutions, he thought that French activity in the West Indies, placed by "nature" so far from France, had been so abominable as not to warrant American intervention in their behalf. To help the French subject the islands to still greater oppression would be to subvert all moral and political decency. Also in being guided by self-preservation to avoid involvement in war, America was merely obeying the higher law of nature which is paramount to all human legislation. It was the same law of self-preservation that he was applying to himself, no matter how unsuccessfully, in these troubled months.

This argument that the natural state of nations is a state of peace for reasons of self-survival, John Quincy had derived from the teachings of Vattel, the famous French author of *The Law of Nature and of Nations*. He had once personally known Dumas, the editor of Vattel, as his pupil in Paris and had even lived in the Dumas household for a time. While still a law clerk in Newburyport he had carefully noted that Vattel preached an international gospel of "Do as you would be done by" and "Honesty is the best policy," which supported his view that the law of nature, together with common sense and honesty, is the true basis for international conduct.[37]

By a mere coincidence, John Quincy's mother had written him from England only a month after he had made these observations in 1787, saying that in the general flames of war which then threatened Europe she hoped and prayed that America would have "wisdom sufficient to keep out of the fire," being already a sufficiently "burnt child." [38] While Madam Adams' observations dealt rather cavalierly with the diplomatic facts of the American Revolution, her bias and good sense had surely been absorbed by her son together with the teachings of Vattel and other authorities.

The immediate reply to "Marcellus" by "A DEMOCRAT" in the *Independent Chronicle* in May, 1793, likewise invoked morality if not natural law.[39] The clever efforts by "Marcellus" and others at *"smoothing* over matters" were said to be pro-English and not productive of true neutrality at all so far as our friends the French were concerned. As announced by Citizen Genet, the French had recently thrown open their ports to American shipping, something the English had denied them after the Revolution, to say nothing of their never having surrendered the fur trading posts. As for the observance of the "sacred" French treaty of 1778, "A DEMOCRAT" wanted to know how American security holders would have felt if such a concept of honor had been applied to paying off the old public debt? A similar question was raised in the *Gazette* by "Marcellus, jun.", while "PLAIN DEALING" asked "Marcellus" insultingly how America could "sneak" out of her French engagements? He denounced those "reptile" upstarts in Boston whose social origins two generations back were lost in a "stench," but who having acquired a little money were now contemptuous of the "Rights of Man." A few weeks earlier the *Chronicle* had carried the lofty definition of an Antifederalist as an independent citizen who was totally detached from lucrative expectations in government, whether from appointments, bank dividends, or funded stock.[40] The implication of much of the criticism of "Marcellus," in short, was that a double standard of morality was being invoked for foreign affairs.

However, there was less of morality than of patriotic statesmanship in the oration that John Quincy made at the request of the selectmen of Boston on the Fourth of July that year.[41] The critical sentiments of his "Publicola" letters and of his first "Marcellus" communication must have encouraged his choice as speaker. But his acknowledgment that the American Revolution had first taught the French to cherish the cause of liberty and to discover for themselves that the "consent of the people" is the only legitimate source of authority, could scarcely have pleased all admirers of his earlier writings. He admitted the horrors of the guillotine, "smoking with the blood of a fallen monarch," and of the wars which the French Revolution had unleashed; but he accepted as inevitable the ultimate triumph in Europe of liberty based on social equality. The absurdities of feudalism were toppling and all such governments must eventually fall, he said. Surely such politics even on the Fourth of July in 1793 were somewhat equivocal. According to his brother Charles, who had become vociferously anti-Jacobin, John Quincy had prudently steered between the Scylla and Charybdis of public opinion. Charles was polite enough to allow that no doubt it had been his "duty to offend no one"! [42]

The ostensible theme of his oration had been the causes of the American Revolution. These he attributed to the acts of an adventurous British ministry. With the perfidious encouragement of its American sycophants, he said, the ministry had abandoned the monopolistic commercial policy of its predecessors, which was tolerated in America as the price of protection, in favor of a system of internal taxation and tyranny to support political corruption. John Quincy said that Americans—he called them descendants of people who had fled to the "new world" to escape oppression in Europe—had even "anticipated" tyranny in their ardent defense of liberty. But he supported the larger thesis that seeds of liberty in the old world itself would be nourished by the example of America, the "first-born offspring of Freedom."

Small wonder that Benjamin Edes of the "Old Whig" Boston *Gazette* immediately sought the privilege of printing John Quincy's oration. [43] On the other hand, the *Independent Chronicle* either scornful or stunned by the whole affair, did not even mention that celebration of the Fourth that year. However, the *Columbian Centinel,* staunchly loyal to Federalist policy—and loyal also to good newspaper copy—gave a rousing description of the day's affairs: the firing of guns in the morning, the ceremonies in Universal Hall, and finally the "ORATION" delivered at noon by John Quincy Adams in the Old South Meeting House. The oration was said to have been "for purity of style and rectitude of principle" equal if not superior to all previous addresses on the Fourth. At the liberal entertainment that followed at the Green Dragon Tavern, one of the fifteen toasts was drunk to the hope that every nation might have a Washington with a "sword of Marcellus." This was followed by three cheers and three guns.[44] The coolness of "Marcellus" towards France in foreign affairs had obviously not been completely obliterated by the non-partisan address. But some of the Federalist politicians present must have begun to wonder just what sort of a person this not-so-young Adams was!

To give John Quincy credit, or at least to credit his human nature, the oration on which he had worked so hard and rehearsed so earnestly, and which at first had seemed to him full of brilliant sentiments, had become dull and commonplace by the time of delivery.[45] However the applause had undeniably pleased him. But some of his sweeping generalizations were to prove anything but dull in the controversial months ahead. His boast that the American Revolution had borne a character "different from any other civil contest that had ever arisen among men," was to be ironically quoted against him in James Sullivan's first "Americanus" number in December.[46]

The summer and fall of 1793 saw the mounting fury of the controversy over the actions of Citizen Genet. As early as August the Washington cabinet had resolved to ask for his recall, following the escape, despite Genet's assurances, of the French privateer *The Little Democrat* from Philadelphia. The cabinet was also outraged by the public insults in which the "Citizen" had indulged while challenging the authority of President Washington on the subject of neutrality. The President's official warning on September 7 that he would revoke the commission of *exequatur* of any French consul who tried to assume powers of admiralty on French "prizes" in American ports, as Genet was urging all consuls to do, furnished the final issue. In October the French vice-consul in Boston, Duplaine, seized by force from a United States marshal a vessel brought in as a prize, and promptly had his *exequatur* revoked. Since public opinion in Boston favored the consul an indictment could not be secured, to the glee of Genet who in the meantime had again publicly protested the President's authority by denying his right to issue a revocation.[47] Genet's irresponsible conduct was of course the way things were being done in revolutionary France.

Like his father but unlike most other Americans, John Quincy Adams had from the first looked with a jaundiced eye upon the mounting enthusiasm for Jacobinism in America. In January he had courageously avoided attending a "Civic Feast" in Boston which was chaired by none other than old Sam Adams.[48] As "Lelius" in the Boston *American Apollo* on March 29 he had rejoiced in the nominal jury verdict in the case of assault and battery brought against Ben Russell, editor of the *Centinel*, by that local expounder of liberty, equality, and the rights of man, "Old Honestus" Ben Austin, the enemy of lawyers.[49] Although enthusiasm for the French began to wane in some American quarters with news of the beheading of Louis XVI and the outbreak of the "Terror," the applause for Genet had been accompanied during the summer of 1793 by the formation of numerous "Constitutional" and "Democratic" societies. Anti-British feeling also had mounted since June with news of the orders in council for the seizing of all American foodships bound for France. Meetings of protest by merchants had been held in Boston and elsewhere.[50]

As a lawyer, John Quincy Adams became interested in several cases in 1793 involving admiralty proceedings, including the attachment of a ship in July for the protection of the sailors' wages. In such matters he had become "very busy" in examining books upon the law of nations. Despite what would seem to have been his special interest in protecting the rights of workers, he was "posted" on August 10 on the masthead of the French frigate *La Concorde* in Boston harbor and threatened with death along with other "aristocrats" and supporters of neutrality. He expostulated in his diary, "Defamed; proscribed;—what next?" [51]

What next, indeed, but stories of rioting in New York and other places, together with the expression of fears by some people that Citizen Genet would soon be making the laws of the United States! The whole Adams family was in a high state of indignation at news of still more privateering, now on behalf of both England and France, and at other acts of insubordination towards national authority. This was being put to a real test for the first time.[52] John Quincy might have taken up his pen even earlier to denounce such activities had it not been for a long-drawn out spell of influenza which he suffered in September. Also the scourge of yellow fever in Philadelphia had meantime put a damper on national affairs. He apparently did make several false starts at writing, but it was not until after the Duplaine incident in Boston that he submitted his masterful "Columbus" letters to the *Centinel*. While writing the first number to appear on November 22, he deprecatingly asked himself if his effort would really benefit his country! [53]

John Quincy wrote as "Columbus" to expose the follies of Genet, that "beardless foreigner" and "Petulent stripling"— it is said that John Quincy had once known him as a schoolboy in France—who had openly defied all rules for ministerial conduct and even had tried to play off the authority of "the people" against that of Washington.[54] The danger of such foreign intervention in American affairs, resulting from do-

mestic divisions, was precisely the "noxious weed"—shades of
his old commencement address—which he declared the Constitution had sought to root out by giving control of foreign
affairs to the Union. See how the liberties of Sweden, Geneva,
Holland, and Poland had recently been lost, he said. Internal
factions, like passions, might sometimes be necessary; but like
passions they could be a source of misery as well as enjoyment, requiring "continual restraint and regulation." Here
again private and public standards coincided, for John
Quincy Adams plainly considered passions to be a danger to
both.[55]

To this young student of the law of nations perhaps Genet's
greatest crime had been his scornful rejection of such "worm-
eaten" authorities as Grotius, Pufendorf, and Vattel whose
teachings Genet thanked God he had forgotten. Closely connected with such heretical ideas was the sweeping denial that
"sovereignty" could ever be surrendered by "the people" to
the executive of any government or nation—hence Genet's
claim that President Washington did not have the authority
to rescind Duplaine's *exequatur*. In answering all such nonsense, "Columbus" vigorously defended the actions of the
venerable President—declaring, however, that he was totally
unconnected either with him or the American government—
by a learned exposition of the constitutional powers of the
presidential office.[56]

The achievement of "Columbus" was intrinsically very
impressive, quite apart from its popularity with the Federalists in Boston and New York. It once again underscored
the morality theme of "Marcellus" but with plenty of additional patriotic fire unchecked by the non-partisanship of the
oration on the Fourth. The sallies were cleverly expressive
and the whole style was lighter than anything that John
Quincy had done before, including "Publicola." It was natural that Attorney General James Sullivan, himself a mighty
contributor to the press on popular issues and a previous tar-

get of John Quincy's pen, should have been aroused to prepare a series of replies under the signature of "Americanus,"
beginning in the Boston *Independent Chronicle* on December 19.[57] By that date four of the five "Columbus" numbers
had already appeared but "Americanus" started off slowly,
taking up his opponent's articles one at a time.

On the day that "Americanus No. III" appeared, December 26, John Quincy in turn began a series of unnumbered
rebuttals under the new signature of "Barneveld." Curiously,
these also appeared in the *Chronicle,* perhaps at the solicitation of its editor. (Several years later John Quincy said that
the editor would never forgive him for having put a little
truth in his paper.[58]) The sixth and last number of "Americanus" appeared on January 6, 1794; the fourth and last number of "Barneveld" did not appear until January 16.[59] The
order of publication is important to notice. While John
Quincy had the first and last words in the controversy, Sullivan's series overlapped both those of his opponent. It also
overlapped two quite different styles of expression. Where
"Columbus" had been thoughtfully if vigorously critical,
"Barneveld" was downright insultingly so. Indeed, the latter
finally ended not unlike the unfortunate "Menander" in the
previous year, in something of a state of embarrassment to
the reader if not to the author.[60]

The Hon. James Sullivan had begun his argument by
ironically quoting John Quincy twice, as already noted: first
as to the true character of the American Revolution and secondly on the citizen's duty of self-expression.[61] It is therefore
clear that young Adams' authorship of "Columbus" must
have been known almost from the start. Sullivan's argument
was similar to that of Citizen Genet, but more cogently expressed. He agreed that all "authorities" on the law of nations were *passé* because they had all written before the
American Revolution, that glorious event which John Quincy
Adams himself had declared to have a unique character and

to have in turn inspired the French. Before 1776 all governments had been tyrannical—but now "the people" were supreme! Not even the popular Washington could do things
against their sovereign will, according to "Americanus." Such
criticism was strangely like certain newspaper strictures which
had been raised against "Publicola" back in 1791: that the
President was a "man of the people" and that the Adamses
had seemingly forgotten the real reasons for the American
Revolution.[62]

It is not hard to believe that one reason "Barneveld" immediately showed so much spleen in his rejoinders to "Americanus" was because he suspected from the beginning that the
detested Sullivan was the author. Surely John Quincy suspected it, even if he did not know it for a fact. In the odd,
apologetic paragraph in the last number of "Barneveld" on
January 16, he flatly stated that he did not know with whom
he had been contending; but he had written his father on
January 5 that Sullivan was "said" to be "Americanus."[63]
One can therefore only suppose that he was employing tech-
nical language in his last number. By that time even his
parents thought he had gone too far in his castigation of the
opponent they knew was Sullivan. "Americanus" had age to
respect if nothing else, warned Madam Adams.[64]

To explain clearly what "Barneveld" was really getting at
is an almost impossible task, for he plainly overshot the mark.
In his first article he arrogantly accused his opponent of discussing "authorities" on international law either out of ignorance or "wilful falsehood." The "American Eagle," he
boasted, disdained to shine in such plumes. (Madam Adams
rather inelegantly thought that the contest henceforth should
be labeled one between "the Eagle and the Snake."[65]) The
discussion all presumably related to the question of the sovereignty of the people, and whether sovereignty can be transferred. However "Barneveld" spent much of his time simply
denouncing what he said were the self-revelatory tactics of

his opponent: his complaining about things of which he knew himself to be guilty, and his saying that his motives were good because he knew that they were false.[66] In short, "Barneveld" from beginning to end accused "Americanus" of being a practitioner of reverse psychology.

All this was accompanied, moreover, with accusations of "confusion," of "incoherence," and of "contemptible" ideas which John Quincy said he found in his opponent. In the third isue of "Barneveld" he even declared that he had as little opinion of "Americanus's" veracity as the latter appeared "to have himself," and referred to the "copious source of his inconsistencies, his absurdities and falsehoods." This was pretty sharp language even for an eighteenth century pamphleteer.

What angered "Barneveld" most of all and led to some of his strongest expressions was the allegation that a false quotation had been made in his first number. A false quotation, indeed! Thin-skinned "Barneveld" said that "Americanus" obviously did not know a paraphrase when he saw one; [67] but he was bitter and angry at the accusation. This may have accounted for his savage description on January 2 of his "false-reasoning" opponent: "No half-fledged spurless chickling on a dunghill, could strut and crow, and flap his wings, with more insulting exultation." So eloquent had John Quincy Adams become!

To all such abuse "Americanus" rather mildly and humorously protested that while he had not affected either elegance of style or "hard, unintelligible words" in his writings, neither had he descended to vulgar expressions by calling his opponent ignorant, false, or even a scoundrel.[68] As has been pointed out, "Barneveld" did insert in his last number an apology of sorts, after his mother had gently reminded him that even Dean Swift was said to have read his pieces to "an old woman" for criticism.[69] He concluded with considerable pomposity that he would not bother to answer insinuations

against him, being willing to submit himself to the "JUDG-
MENT OF MY PEERS" and requesting only the privilege of not
resorting to *"personal abuse."* And making this remarkably
inept statement he added the bland assertion, already noted,
that he did not know with whom he was contending. If he
had been justly charged in any particular, he said that he
owed an apology to the public but none to "Americanus."
This must have been what his mother had in mind two days
later when she noted with satisfaction that her son had "cor-
rected himself."

Old John Adams had meantime written from Philadelphia
that he hoped "Barneveld" would not render himself cheap,
although he rejoiced that that "blockhead" Sullivan had received the "flagellation" he deserved. A few days earlier, after
delivering himself of the opinion that Sullivan was "the least
of a Gentleman of any one in Boston," he had also expressed
the hope that John Quincy would not forget that he was
one.[70]

What did the public think of all these pleasantries? One
communication in the *Chronicle* on January 2 furnished glee-
ful material for the Adamses in their letters to each other for
some time to come. This unknown critic had hailed what he
called the manly arguments of "Americanus," as contrasted
with the petulance and affected wit of his opponent. He also
labeled John Quincy's writing a sort of "literary plagiarism"
from *Junius*—this had been quoted in "Columbus No. I"—
and said that the "juvenile writer" who showed the "aspirations of family pride" ought not to be protected by that "high
station conferred on his Sire by a free and generous people"!
For such caustic comment, John Quincy said that he was indebted to the "saturnine genius of the *Chronicle*"; and his
mother identified those lines with the pen of "Americanus,"
who "whines and cants like the Hypocrite he is. . . ." [71]

Even some of John Quincy's friends, however, received his
pieces without exactly clamorous praise. He suspected that

they, too, were jealously disposed to "check the *aspirations* of the writer"! The public in general, he dourly thought, was like a lady with too many admirers.[72]

A more judicious contributor to one of the Boston papers was inclined to suspend judgment on both writers until it might be seen what hopes of public reward they might have. John Quincy was said to have been accused of the "crime" of being the "Son of a man *High in Office*," while Sullivan had acquired a reputation of being a "humble seeker" of office. Surely this was criticism not too severe on John Quincy. But on January 9 a more scathing critic demanded to know what that "rude Boy" who signed himself "Barneveld" meant by his abuse of men of genius and learning? He was asked if he remembered the Fourth of July oration which he had delivered with such "affected skill," and whether he had ever read his sire's famous letter to George Wythe of Virginia in 1776 on the subject of liberty? Declaring that both sire and son had changed, he warned "Barneveld" that "billingsgate" should never be confused with satire.[73]

The unkindest cut of all came a week after the last of the controversy. A correspondent in the *Chronicle* addressed a poem to "Columbus alias Barneveld" on a certain subject to remind him of his father. The subject, from which an eloquent extract on liberty was quoted, was old John Adams' pre-Revolutionary *Dissertation on the Canon and Feudal Law*. The correspondent added, ironically, that all printers of "Columbus" or "Barneveld" were requested to reprint the extract.[74]

Yet if "Barneveld" had done little more than reveal a very impassioned young man, "Columbus" undeniably had been an enormous success. The time would come, exulted Abigail Adams, when its author would be sought as "a Jewel of great price." Although her husband was afraid in January to ask President Washington directly whether he had read "Columbus" or not, they had been having several "interesting and affectionate" conversations together about which he unfortunately could give no hint. Old John was still fairly roaring with delight a month later over Abigail's witty letters on the subject, saying that if their selfish young "rogue" in Boston had any "family pride" in him, "his Pa" renounced and abjured all responsibility for it! But he advised John Quincy to stick close to the law for the present since unfortunately there were doubts of his great services to his country's being recognized.[75]

Although the spring of 1794 was a season of private misery for "victorious" John Quincy Adams—he even distinguished himself one night at a town meeting [76]—it was in general a happy time for his parents, separated though they were by the continuance of Abigail's indisposition to leave Quincy. The tide of Jacobinism had temporarily ebbed, and the troublesome Jefferson whose soul was "poisoned with ambition" had finally resigned from the cabinet and left Philadelphia. "Good riddance of bad mare," old John Adams uncharitably commented. Although that "born rebel" Sam Adams had succeeded the late, unlamented Hancock as governor of Massachusetts, this was at least in some measure his due. The Federalists in New England were scarcely showing wisdom by associating with the "Old Tories" in the spring elections, but otherwise things seemed to go rather well for the Adams family.[77] Of course there were some personal problems. "Silly" Charles had wanted to get married. Tommy who had just been admitted to the Philadelphia bar had aroused his mother's indignation in his first jury address by allegedly making remarks derogatory of female character! [78]

Nor had the President forgotten John Quincy Adams. Although a judicial appointment had not materialized, apparently to that young man's great sorrow, on May 26 Secretary of State Randolph informed the vice president of Washington's intention to appoint his son to The Hague. John Adams immediately sat down to write his "dearest Friend" the news, to enable her to recollect herself and to prepare for the event. To Abigail also came a letter from Martha Washington, mingling condolence and congratulations but praising the abilities and future prospects of the meritorious youth about whom she had heard from no less an authority than Washington himself.

There was also a letter of great joy for John Quincy from Aunt Eliza in Haverhill. She knew that he had obtained "the Palm" by following the path of virtue, but she expressed her heartfelt sympathy for the agonizing sacrifice of love to duty she knew he had once had to make. The whole matter was elegantly summed up by old John Adams himself when he wrote his son that the appointment was "Proof that Sound Principles in Morals and Government, are cherished by the executive of the United States, and that Study, Science and Literature are recommendations which will not be overlooked." [79] It sounded almost like the awarding of an honorary degree.

Amid such general rejoicing there seems never to have been a doubt in anyone's mind about John Quincy's accepting the appointment. His father almost in the same breath with which he informed him of the event began to give him advice for his "cautious" behavior abroad, particularly in view of the intricacies of Dutch politics.[80] Everybody seemed happy; everybody, that is, with the apparent exception of John Quincy Adams himself.[81] On top of illness and depression of spirits he had to take passage in a leaky old tub because no other vessel was available from Boston. Fortunately he had Thomas Boylston Adams along. As the brothers sailed on September 13, two close friends of John Quincy accompanied them as far as the lighthouse: Nathan Frazier, Jr., a cousin of the once-beloved Mary, and Daniel Sargent, Jr., Mary's future husband. There was something ironic as well as symbolic about the parting.

Within a few months, on his own word, John Quincy

Adams was to experience enormous relief from the unsatisfactory kind of life he had been living in Boston.[82] He was also about to enjoy a greater portion of that economic independence he had always cherished, despite the check to his practice of law. In addition to having a salary he now possessed a handsome sum of money which had been presented to him on sailing by his father.[83] He was also on the way at last to finding himself a wife. After nine increasingly difficult personal years at home, he was fortunate to be taking voyage again.

He was nevertheless leaving his country as a publicly recognized figure, in contrast to the juvenile hopeful who had returned from Europe so long ago. If the years in between had not all been happy, in them he had done some remarkable things that had attracted wide attention. In the face of personal difficulties, he had developed those assertive qualities so necessary for his self-expression and so useful for public affairs. This son of distinguished parents had made his own mark in the critical years he was now leaving behind him.

BIBLIOGRAPHICAL AIDS

I. Abbreviations frequently used in footnotes

APM   Adams Papers Microfilm, followed by reel numbers (*e.g.*, APM 13 refers to the microfilm of the first volume of the journal that John Quincy Adams began in January, 1785, shortly before his return to America). This is a microfilm of the Adams Family Papers deposited in the Massachusetts Historical Society. The microfilm, consisting of hundreds of reels, has been issued in four parts, and is described in accompanying brochures in the possession of repository libraries.

JA   John Adams

AA   Abigail Adams

JQA   John Quincy Adams

AA2   "Nabby" or "Abby" Adams, an older sister of John Quincy Adams, named Abigail after her mother.

AAS   "Nabby" after her marriage in 1786 to Colonel William Smith.

CA   Charles Adams, a younger brother of John Quincy Adams.

TBA   Thomas Boylston Adams, the youngest brother of John Quincy Adams.

MC   Mary Cranch, an older sister of Abigail Adams, married to Richard Cranch of Braintree.

ES   Elizabeth Shaw, a younger sister of Abigail Adams, married first to the Reverend John Shaw of Haverhill.

Memoirs   *Memoirs of John Quincy Adams Comprising Portions of his Diary from 1795 to 1848*. Edited by Charles Francis Adams. Twelve volumes. Philadelphia, 1874-1877.

Writings   *The Writings of John Quincy Adams*. Edited by Worthington Chauncey Ford. Seven volumes. New York, 1913-1917.

LNET   *Life in a New England Town: 1787, 1788. Dairy of John Quincy Adams, While a Student in the Office of Theophilus Parsons at Newburyport.* Edited by Charles Francis Adams, Jr., with the assistance of Miss J. C. Watts. Boston, 1903.

"H.C."   "Harvard College. 1786-1787" in *Historical Essays* by Henry Adams. New York, 1891. This contains numerous extracts from the journal kept by JQA while a student at Harvard. It is substantially the same article which first appeared in the *North American Review,* Vol. 114, January, 1872, pp. 110-147.

II. Other source material

The Works of John Adams. Edited by his Grandson, Charles Francis Adams. Eight volumes. Boston, 1856.

Letters of John Adams, Addressed to His Wife. Edited by his Grandson, Charles Francis Adams. Two volumes. Boston, 1841.

Letters of Mrs. Adams, the Wife of John Adams. With an Introductory Memoir by her Grandson, Charles Francis Adams. Fourth edition, revised and enlarged, with an Appendix containing the Letters Addressed by John Q. Adams to his Son on the Study of the Bible. Boston, 1848.

Familiar Letters of John Adams and His Wife Abigail Adams, During the Revolution. With a Memoir of Mrs. Adams. By Charles Francis Adams. Boston, 1875. This is principally a compilation of the two foregoing works, for the years 1774-1783.

New Letters of Abigail Adams, 1788-1801. Edited with an Introduction by Stewart Mitchell. Boston, 1947.

Poems of Religion and Society. By John Quincy Adams. With Notices of his Life and Character by John Davis and T. H. Benton. Auburn, 1850. This edition contains an incomplete copy of "A Vision." The original edition of 1848 had it not at all.

"The Journal of Elizabeth Cranch, October 5, 1785—March 4, 1786" In the *Collections* of the Essex Historical Institute, Vol. 80, No. 1, January, 1944.

III. Special works

John Adams's Book, Being Notes on a Record of the Births, Marriages, & Deaths of Three Generations of the Adams Family, 1734-1807. Compiled by Henry Adams. Printed for the Boston Athenaeum, 1934.

A Catalogue of the Books of John Quincy Adams Deposited in the Boston Athenaeum. With Notes on Books, Adams Seals, and Book-Plates. With an Introduction by Worthington Chauncey Ford. Printed for the Athenaeum. Boston, 1938.

IV. Selected Adams biographies

Bemis, Samuel Flagg *John Quincy Adams and the Foundations of American Foreign Policy.* New York, 1949.

Bobbé, Dorothie *Mr. and Mrs. John Quincy Adams. An Adventure in Patriotism.* New York, 1930.

Bowen, Catherine Drinker *John Adams and the American Revolution.* Boston, 1949.

Chinard, Gilbert *Honest John Adams.* Boston, 1933.

Clark, Bennett Champ *John Quincy Adams, "Old Man Eloquent."* Boston, 1932.

Morse, John T., Jr. *John Quincy Adams.* Boston and New York, 1898.

Quincy, Josiah *Memoir of the Life of John Quincy Adams.* Boston, 1859.

Roof, Katherine Metcalf *Colonel William Smith and Lady. The Romance of Washington's Aide and Young Abigail Adams.* Boston, 1929.

Seward, William H. *The Life and Public Services of John Quincy Adams, Sixth President of the United States.* With the Eulogy delivered before the Legislature of New York. Auburn, 1849.

Whitney, Janet *Abigail Adams.* Boston, 1947.

V. Selected secondary works

Adams, Charles Francis, Jr. *Three Episodes of Massachusetts History.* Two volumes. Boston and New York, 1892. Volume two contains a social history of Braintree, with many valuable references to the Adams family.

Amory, Thomas C. *The Life of James Sullivan with Selections from His Writings.* Two volumes. Boston, 1859.

Buckingham, Joseph T. *Specimens of Newspaper Literature: With Personal Memoirs, Anecdotes, and Reminiscences.* Two volumes. Boston, 1850.

Crawford, Mary Caroline *The Romance of the American Theater.* Boston, 1913.

Cresson, W. P. *Francis Dana, A Puritan Diplomat at the Court of Catherine the Great.* Toronto, 1930.

Currier, John J. *The History of Newburyport, Massachusetts.* Two volumes. Newburyport, 1906-1909.

Hazen, Charles Downer *Contemporary American Opinion of the French Revolution.* Baltimore, 1897.

Lipsky, George A. *John Quincy Adams, His Theory and Ideas.* New York, 1950.

Matthews, Albert *Harvard Commencement Days, 1642-1916.* (Reprinted from the *Publications* of the Colonial Society of Massachusetts, Vol. XVIII.) Cambridge, 1916.

Mayo, Lawrence Shaw "Jeremy Belknap and J. Q. Adams, 1787," in the *Proceedings* of the Massachusetts Historical Society, Vol. LIX, 1925-1926.

Morison, Samuel Eliot *The Life and Letters of Harrison Gray Otis.* Two volumes. Boston, 1913.

Three Centuries of Harvard, 1636-1936. Cambridge, 1936.

Seilhamer, George O. *History of the American Theater.* Three volumes. Philadelphia, 1889.

NOTES

Chapter One

1. The account of his persuasion is given in Samuel Flagg Bemis, *John Quincy Adams and the Foundations of American Foreign Policy,* p. 11. The boy had wanted to enter Andover as preparatory for Harvard. To do his mother justice, she had passionately wanted to accompany her husband and elder children abroad, according to Janet Whitney, *Abigail Adams,* p. 150. The pages of Professor Bemis' valuable work, which includes a brief account of JQA's early years, as well as those of Mrs. Whitney, are enriched with material from the Adams Papers in the Massachusetts Historical Society.

2. The quotations in this and in the preceding sentence are from AA to JQA, June, 1778, and January 12, 1780, in *Letters of Mrs. Adams,* pp. 95, 96, 111. The first letter was on the occasion of his first voyage to Europe. The moral authority of imperious Abigail Adams was evident throughout her life. Even in old age, she could reduce her teenage grandsons to tears by reproving them for some trifling misconduct. See C. F. Adams, Jr., *Charles Francis Adams* (Boston and New York, 1900), p. 10.

3. JA to Benjamin Waterhouse, April 24, 1785, In John Adams, *Works,* IX, 530. His mother also acknowledged that he was deficient in "many branches of knowledge." *Letters of Mrs. Adams,* p. 219.

4. His mother's constant exhortations for him to cultivate virtue and to restrain passion, venerate religion, etc., were invariably identified with the idea that these things affect the greatness of nations as well as the individual himself. See *Letters of Mrs. Adams,* pp. 95, 96, 114, 115, 154. His father had been especially concerned about his son's morals and "innocence" in 1782 when JQA was in St. Petersburg, a sen-

timent echoed by his mother some months later. *Ibid.,* pp. 426, 427, and 147.

5. *Memoirs,* I, 19; JA to President Willard of Harvard, in *Publications* of the Colonial Society of Massachusetts, Vol. XIII, pp. 114, 115.
6. Journal, February 26, March 5, 7, 1785, APM 13.
7. Journal, April 26, 1785, APM 13; also quoted in *Memoirs,* I, 21.
8. Henry Adams, *A Catalogue of the Books of John Quincy Adams,* p. 7.
9. *Memoirs,* I, 21.
10. The opinion of Francis Dana of Cambridge, Massachusetts, who had been his "mentor" and employer in St. Petersburg in 1782, is quoted in W. P. Cresson, *Dana,* p. 310. His father's fears of JQA's airs of superiority when he should go to college are in his letter to Professor Waterhouse, in John Adams, *Works,* IX, 531. JQA's self-reproach for not having paid enough attention to Dana's advice is in his journal for March 10, 1787, APM 14.
11. His shortness may be inferred from a humorous reference in *Letters of Mrs. Adams,* p. 233. His stoutness was evident some months later, even after he had lost weight, as shown by a good-natured reference in his journal for February 28, 1786, and by the laughter he excited on one occasion at college, in the journal for March 24, 1786. He mentions his sword in his journal on September 15, 1785. (APM 13) That he had his hair dressed while abroad is shown in *Letters of Mrs. Adams,* pp. 185, 221. The imitation of his father's mannerisms (as demonstrated by Reverend Mr. Wiberd) is mentioned in ES to AA, November 6, 1785, APM 366. Some observers generously thought that he resembled both parents, but the weight of evidence favors his mother, at least on the part of *her* correspondents! A Frenchman once told her that if she had been dressed in her son's clothes, he would have mistaken her for him, *Letters of Mrs. Adams,* p. 309. For her part she thought that he bore a strong resemblance to his father! *Ibid.,* p. 186.
12. The change occurred after his mother had reproached his

brother, Thomas Boylston, for so addressing her in 1795.
Letters of Mrs. Adams, p. 367. Apparently JQA then took the
hint!

13. His deep interest in literature and his pride in American
cultural achievements was to run throughout his life. See
JQA to JA, May 21, 1786, APM 368, and his references to the
Americans, Belknap, Dwight, West, *et al.*, as important cultural figures. His own literary efforts were to be considerable,
beginning with the journal itself in 1785. Many years later
he wrote that he would have devoted his entire life to literary activity had he been able to choose his own fortune.
Shortly after his death a small volume of his compositions
was published, *Poems of Religion and Society*. Other of his
early writings will appear in the course of this work, especially in Chapter Six.

14. "The weather is much warmer than I have for many years
been accustomed to: yet I hear everybody say that there has
been no hot weather this year." He also spoke of the "dog
days." JQA to AA2, July 17-29, 1785, APM 365. AA wrote
JA, December 29, 1792, APM 375, "I find the cold creates
as great an irritation upon my nerves producing a tremor, as
the heat does by relaxation." Although this was said at a time
when she was in generally poor health, it would seem to be
significant.

15. Eliza Cranch to AA, July 1, 1786, APM 368.

16. This and the other journal entries following in this chapter
refer, under date, to APM 13.

17. Journal, May 22, 1785.

18. *Writings,* I, 17n.

19. Journal, July 22, 1785.

20. *Writings,* I, 20.

21. JQA to AA2, August 1, 1785, APM 365.

22. On his bringing despatches, and the coincidental problem in
Congress of his reimbursement for having served as a clerk
to Dana in St. Petersburg, see E. C. Burnett, ed., *Letters of
The Members of the Continental Congress* (8 vols., Washington, 1921-36), VIII, 169n. The "problem" was not to be

settled for years, to the mingled amusement and disgust of
the Adamses, who thought that foreign servants were worthy
of their hire.

23. "Your friend Monroe inquired after you the other day and
wished that you would make me a visit which might give
him an opportunity of seeing you in New York." AAS to
JQA, September 28, 1788, APM 371. Rufus King was particularly close to John Adams, who had strongly sympathized
with King's father when he had been the victim of "patriotic" violence before the Revolution. It is also possible that
young King had once been considered a good catch for
Nabby, when he had lived in Newbury, Massachusetts. See
JQA to AA2, October 15, 1785, APM 366.

24. *Writings,* I, 19; R. H. Lee to JA, August 1, 1785, APM 365.

25. JQA to AA2, August 9-16, 1785, APM 365.

26. Journal, August 9, 1785.

27. One of the homes at which he visited was that of William
Constable, one of the newcomers in New York. See my *Busi-
ness Enterprise in the American Revolutionary Era* (New
York, 1938), Chapter Eight.

28. See Chapter Six on "A Vision."

29. JQA to AA2, August 1-6, 1785, APM 365, on the "Receipt,"
and on the agreement he and his sister had made to keep
each other informed, in the course of their correspondence,
about the "characters" they encountered.

30. AA2 to JQA, September 5, 1785, APM 365; also her reproof
to him on April 26, 1786, APM 367.

31. Journal, August 8, 1785. A copy of "Des Fables de Phèdre"
had been compiled in JQA's handwriting in 1781. See APM
218.

32. JQA to AA2, August 1-6 and 27, 1785, APM 365. JA had
known Chaumont's father in France. See *Familiar Letters of
John Adams to His Wife,* p. 330. JQA was to have some con-
tact abroad with young Chaumont years later. The Frenchman's family was to suffer in the French Revolution. Young
Chaumont had meantime become identified with the development of his father's interests around Otsego, New York,
and had married one of the sisters of Tench Coxe, the Phila-

delphia merchant and early political confidant of John
Adams. See JQA to Mr. Le Ray, Amsterdam, November 23,
1794, APM 126.

33. Journal, August 15, 1785.
34. On Wadsworth and his partner, John Barker Church, "alias"
Carter, who together had constituted the great war-contracting firm whose dissolved assets were being represented by
Alexander Hamilton—see the opening paragraph of this chapter—and whose wife was a sister of Mrs. Church, see my *Business Enterprise,* especially Chapter Four. The business proposal of La Fayette, an old friend and patron of Wadsworth,
was to encourage the sale of French manufactures in America
by letting American whale oil into France duty free. It was
a project which both John Adams and Thomas Jefferson had
been interested in promoting, and was considered a sword
to be held over England in an effort to force her to relax
her restrictions on American West Indian commerce. An unsuccessful effort to organize a whale oil company to take advantage of the French offer was attempted by Samuel Breck
of Boston, another war-time agent of France. The economic
significance of the project may be gathered from the letters
of Stephen Higginson to John Adams. See the *Massachusetts
Centinel* for September 14, 1785; also Higginson to JA, August 8, 1785, APM 365, and July, 1786, APM 368. These
letters are a storehouse of information on New England's
trade conditions, and incidentally on the touchy political
situation.
35. In New Haven on August 19.
36. Journal, August 21, 1785. His father actually thought the
American poets inferior only to Milton! JA to JQA, March
19, 1786. The favorable comparison with *Hudibras* was a
"Whig" point of view. See Alexander Cowie, *John Trumbull,
Connecticut Wit* (Chapel Hill, 1936), esp. pp. 185, 211.
37. JQA to AA2, August 16, 1785, APM 365.
38. Journal, August 26, 1785.
39. The *Massachusetts Centinel* on July 30 had noted the news
of JQA's arrival; but the Boston *Gazette* on July 25 ignored
it altogether, although it had carried other news from the

New York papers for July 18, and ordinarily published information on the arrival of French packets there, *e.g.*, on September 5.

40. See footnote 34.

41. A separate volume could be written on the Tyler affair from the Adams family archives. Mrs. Cranch, and apparently her daughters, had come to find him particularly loathsome, and her letters to Abigail Adams in 1785 and 1786 (APM 365, 366, 367) have almost endless references to Tyler, whom she labeled "the windmill." As noted above, the unfortunate Tyler was a roomer at the Cranches. Katherine Metcalf Roof, in her undocumented *Colonel William Smith and Lady,* pp. 33-49, is extremely harsh on the female Cranches in this connection. The incident is important here because of the attitude taken by Nabby's parents, which foreshadowed JQA's romantic troubles in 1790. See Chapter Six. Madam Adams, while implying that Nabby's "l - r" had neglected to write her, loftily said that the decision to cast off Tyler had been entirely Nabby's own. Her parents had been so fair as not even to mention Tyler's name in her presence! Abigail said that Nabby's delay in turning Tyler off had been due to resentment of her father's criticism—he thought him an idle scribbler and "popinjay." Meanwhile, in the summer of 1785, Colonel Smith was delighting her parents because of his "solid," "sensible," and "judicious" qualities. These were Abigail's terms, but she said that her husband was also "very happy" with him. The "solid" Colonel immediately demonstrated his mettle, and accurately prognosticated the future, by neglecting to mail the very first letter that Nabby wrote home to brother John! Dr. Cotton Tufts of Weymouth, a relative of AA by marriage and business manager for the Adamses, was given the unpleasant job of telling Tyler off, and subsequently of buying for the Adamses the house on which Tyler had already made a large down payment. See AA to JQA, August 11 and 23, AA to Cotton Tufts, August 18, and AA2 to JQA, September 5, 1785, APM 365. Mrs. Cranch's letters are too numerous and discursive to mention

—and almost to read. An interesting account of the affair is in Janet Whitney, *Abigail Adams,* pp. 167-171. There is an extraordinary letter of Tyler to JA, October 15, 1785, APM 366, which, among other things, congratulates him because JQA had brought home no "European Frivolity of Manners." This of course was written before Tyler had heard of his dismissal.

42. It was the sarcastic Reverend Mr. Wiberd who had noticed how JQA "aped" his sire. See ES to AA, November 6, 1785, APM 366. On the former's character and pastorate, see Charles Francis Adams, *Three Episodes of Massachusetts History,* II, 641 ff. For the general background in Quincy see Daniel Munro Wilson, *Where American Independence Began. Quincy Its Famous Group of Patriots: Their Deeds, Houses and Descendants* (Boston and New York, 1902).

43. JQA to AA, October 6, 1785, APM 366; but her own deep emotion on learning of his safe arrival in America, is referred to in J. Bridge to JQA, September 28, 1787, APM 370.

44. MC to AA, August 17, September 14, 1785, APM 365. His excessive curiosity was noted by his Aunt Eliza, who contrarily thought that he resembled his father in the latter's early days of marriage before he had asumed the "austerity & dignity of the Statesman"! ES to AA, September 7, November 6, 1785, APM 365, 366.

45. ES to AA, September 17, 1785, APM 365. Actually, her husband had been a little fearful about taking on the responsibility of tutoring JQA for advanced standing, since it called for "unusual preparation." The Shaws were obviously put somewhat "on the spot." JQA wrote his father on April 2, 1786 that he had been as well prepared the previous September as anyone in his class, but had not read "certain" books, which was the way a college operated, he said! APM 367. See also JQA to AA, May 15, 1786, APM 368.

46. Eliza Cranch to AA, September 5, 1785, APM 365.

47. Journal, September 14, 1785.

48. JA to Samuel Adams, April 27, 1785, in John Adams, *Works,* IX, 532.

Chapter Two

1. George Wingate Chase, *Haverhill, Massachusetts* (Haverhill, 1861), p. 436.
2. November 24, 1785, which was Thanksgiving Day in nearby New Hampshire, although the holiday was not until December 15 in Massachusetts that year. This and other journal entries in this chapter, refer, under date, to APM 13.
3. So says Harriet Nelson in her manuscript, "A Former Resident of Haverhill: John Quincy Adams," p. 2. I am indebted for the use of this to the Haverhill Public Library. It is not clear whether Mrs. Shaw was familiarly called Elizabeth or Eliza (apparently Betsey was her girlhood name); she signed letters both ways, although more commonly the latter. I have employed the latter, except for "Aunt Shaw" in more formal address. For example, JQA referred to "Uncle and Aunt Shaw" in a letter to Eliza Cranch, March 23, 1786, Jacob Norton Papers in the Massachusetts Historical Society.
4. She once told Tommy, when he was growing tall and *"thin,"* that he was getting too much like herself. ES to AA, July 23, 1786, APM 368. Her sister Abigail, however, tended to stoutness, like JQA. AA to JQA, January 17, 1787, APM 369.
5. Chase, *Haverhill*, p. 556.
6. Journal, March 5, 1786.
7. See the quote from Fielding in JQA's journal for October 5, 1785. Apparently Uncle Shaw also had a sense of humor. He told the young folks a "curious story" one night, and advised Eliza Cranch to put in her journal that a "roast apple" was the first cause. The reference seems to have puzzled her. See "The Journal of Elizabeth Chanch," in *Collections* of the Essex Historical Institute, Vol. 80, p. 18.
8. Journal, February 4, 1786.
9. Aunt Eliza sympathized with her husband, and wrote AA on March 18, 1786 (APM 387), after JQA had left Haverhill, that he was too decisive and tenacious in his opinions. She had warned him that young people were too apt to be sure that they were always right. In public, however, he had been polite and modest, and she missed him terribly. He had some-

times read to her in leisurely moments in the evening. As already indicated, JQA for his part remained deeply attached to her throughout the rest of her life and, as soon as he became financially independent, even arranged to send her regularly a little money for her son's education. Poor Aunt Eliza, with her romantic temperament, re-married promptly, but poorly, when Reverend Shaw died in 1794. She married the head of an "academy," and then had to help take care of the boys!

10. Journal, March 5, 1786.

11. *Ibid.*

12. *Writings,* I, 20n; also, journal for February 22, 1786, *et passim.*

13. Nelson, "A Former Resident of Haverhill," p. 1. She says, however, that it was a large house, so "crowded" may be too strong a word. Apparently the Shaws sometimes "farmed out" their children to neighbors for their own good (*i.e.,* the children's), as was another old New England custom. ES to AA, July 20, 1786, APM 368,

14. Journal, February 22, 1786, *et passim.*

15. Journal, January 9, 1786; John Thaxter to JA, January 7, MC to AA, February 9, 1786, APM 367. Aunt Eliza said that he was like "clockwork" in his habits.

16. MC to AA, July 10, 1786, APM 368, and ES to MC, April 21, 1793, APM 376, both mention eye trouble.

17. ES to AA, January 2, 1786, APM 367.

18. "The Journal of Elizabeth Cranch," *loc. cit.,* pp. 11, 29.

19. The introduction and footnotes to Elizabeth Cranch's "Journal" give a wealth of biographical detail about some of the local people. The Duncans and Whites were perhaps the most prominent of these. See James Duncan Phillips, "James Duncan and Son, Merchants, Capitalists, and Chain Store Operators," in *Collections* of the Essex Historical Institute, Vol. 89 (1953), pp. 19-56. JQA to Eliza Cranch, March 23, 1786, said to remember him especially to the Whites for their many kindnesses to him in Haverhill. Jacob Norton Papers in the Massachusetts Historical Society.

20. Journal, December 10, 1785; JQA to AA, December 28, 1785,

APM 366. His father had earlier written him not to dwell too much on the gloomy complaints of the times—gloomily adding that he might soon not be able even to provide for himself! JA to JQA, September 9, 1785, APM 365.

21. ES to AA, March 18, 1786, APM 367.
22. Journal, January 17, 1786.
23. Journal, February 25, 28, 1786.
24. He had had a disagreeable headache and was accused of being melancholy, a reproach he had "seldom known," just before leaving Braintree for Haverhill. Journal, September 26, 1785.
25. Henry Adams, *A Catalogue of the Books of John Quincy Adams*, p. 49, speaks of this problem as confronting JQA at this period in Haverhill, but curiously observes that while he drew pictures of characters, "no trace of personal feeling appears." He goes on, however, to mention the absence of imaginative writing by JQA regarding travel, scenery, and so forth, which presumably is what he referred to.
26. See his journal for October 10, 1785, where a word has been blotted out of his original statement about "melancholy."
27. Journal, October 12, December 26, 1785; JQA to AA2, September 9, 1785, APM 365.
28. Journal, October 12, 1785.
29. Journal, November 3, 1785.
30. Journal, November 9, 1785, *et passim. Cf.* "The Journal of Elizabeth Cranch," *loc. cit.,* p. 13.
31. AA to Cotton Tufts, August 1, 1786, APM 368; also *Letters of Mrs. Adams,* p. 147.
32. Journal, December 2, 1785.
33. JQA to AA2, September 7, 1785, APM 365; Journal, September 9, 12, 16, 1785. Her name was Nancy Hazen and she apparently was an orphaned niece of General Moses Hazen of Revolutionary fame. Some information about her may be found in "The Journal of Elizabeth Cranch," *loc. cit.,* p. 4 *et seq.*
34. *Ibid., passim;* E. Cranch to AA, October 9, and JQA to AA, December 28, 1785, APM 366. See also the journal for October 20, 1785.

35. Journal, October 10, 20, 1785; JQA to AA, October 5, 1785, APM 366. He also thought that American ladies were shockingly neglectful of their teeth.
36. Journal, November 3, 1785.
37. Journal, September 24, 1785.
38. Journal, November 12, 1785.
39. On December 13, the day after, he wrote "An Epistle to Delia," a satire on the young lady, portions of which he was later to incorporate into the "Narcissa" portion of "A Vision." The "Epistle" is in APM 233, p. 3.
40. JQA to AA, December 28, 1785, APM 366.
41. Journal, January 7, 1786.
42. The episode is related in detail in ES to AA, May 20, 1787, APM 370. See also the journal for January 7, 1786.
43. Journal, February 9, 1786.
44. See footnote 42.
45. Journal, March 10, 1786.
46. Journal, March 15, 1786; also *Writings*, I, 20n, where he says that he was examined on March 13, obviously an error.
47. Professor Waterhouse, at least, was known for his "quaint wit." See *Life in a New England Town*, p. 125.
48. The address on "The advantages which are derived from a liberal education" was the first he delivered before the "A.B." society (although it was marked "No. 2."). It is in his journal under June 26, 1786. On May 20 he had dryly noted, on the subject of "happiness," that a poem by Colonel David Humphreys, which sister Nabby had sent him, was "somewhat poetical" in describing the happiness that "reigns in this Country."

Chapter Three

1. This is a paraphrase of what he wrote his mother, May 15, 1786, APM 368.
2. Journal, October 19, 1786, APM 14. See also his forensic address on "Immortality" in the journal, May 16, 1786, APM 13. July 1, 1786, divides APM 13 from APM 14, in the journal entries referred to in this chapter.

3. Journal, April 13, 1787. His attitude towards Dr. Johnson was a mixture of admiration and contempt. He once characterized him as a "brute" and a "cynic." Journal, July 15, 1787.

4. MC to AA, October 1, 1786, APM 369, tells of how heartily the boys ate of her cooking during vacations. Her sister Eliza also took great pride in the apple "pyes" she made, especially for Tommy. ES to AA, February 8, 1787, APM 369.

5. Journal, April 1, May 9, 1786; MC to AA, October 22, 1786, APM 369, tells how the boys would pull the bedclothing off JQA in the mornings, during vacations.

6. *Cf.* the remarks by Henry Adams in "Harvard College. 1786, 1787" in his *Historical Essays,* p. 90 (hereafter referred to as "H.C."). JQA's continued feeling about his higher education having been unfortunately delayed may also be inferred from AAS to JQA, August 20, 1788, APM 371.

7. JQA to JA, April 2, 1786, APM 367; and *Writings,* I, 21n. He also resented the amount of time taken up in reciting to the tutors, as well as at prayers. JQA to Eliza Cranch, April 7, 1786, Jacob Norton Papers in the Massachusetts Historical Society.

8. AA to ES, July 14, 1786, APM 368, a reply to ES to AA, March 18, 1786, APM 367.

9. *Cf.* JQA to AAS, January 14, 1787, APM 369, refuting charges that he had satirized the college officers. But his critical attitude is revealed in his journal, May 31, 1786, and in JQA to AA, August 1, 1787, APM 370.

10. ES to AA, May 20, 1787, APM 370; CM to AA, April 22, 1787, APM 369.

11. *Writings,* I, 33n.

12. The essay by Henry Adams on Harvard College ("H.C.") contains an excellent discussion of the curriculum, based on JQA's journal. See also *Writings,* 1, 21-25, and 21n. Also the journal for May 3, 1786; and JQA to AA, May 15, 1786, APM 368.

13. JQA to AAS, January 17, 1787, APM 369. On his smoking, see Morse, *Adams,* p. 223; the journal for July 9, 1787, APM 14; and H. Packard to JQA, October 15, 1787, APM 370.

14. MC to AA, May 7,, 1786, APM 368; journal, July 17, 1786.
15. Journal, December 22, 1786, January 4, 14, 1787; JQA to AAS, January 14, 1787, APM 369.
16. Journal for December, 1786, and January, 1787; also "H.C." p. 96.
17. Journal, September 16, 1786.
18. MC to AA, May 22, 1786; Eliza Cranch to AA, July 1, 1786, APM 368; AA to JQA, January 17, March 20, 1787, APM 369; journal, May 13, 1787.
19. His chamber is described in Richard Cranch to AA, July 5, 1786, APM 368. See also Charles Storer to AA, April 13, 1786, APM 367.
20. Journal, March 24, 1786. But President Willard never cracked a smile!
21. ES to AA, May 20, 1787, APM 370.
22. So thought Henry Adams, in "H.C." p. 89.
23. Journal, May 16, 1786, on "Whether the immortality of the soul be probable from natural reason." All of his orations and forensic debates are copied into his journal.
24. Journal, June 26, 1786. This, I take it, is the substance of his address on "Education." See the conclusion of Chapter Two.
25. Journal, March 5, 1787, on "Whether love or fortune ought to be the chief inducement to marriage."
26. Journal, August 24, 1786, on "Jealousy." He doubted the validity of a character like Iago, doing evil for evil's sake. Years later his dislike for "Othello" worked into his thesis of Desdemona's being a prime example of filial disobedience by having married the Moor, and hence responsible for all of the tragic consequences. See Chapter Six.
27. Journal, June 5, 1787, on "Women."
28. Journal, June 12, 1786, on "Nothing is so difficult but what it may be overcome by industry."
29. Journal, October 10, 1786, on "Whether the diversities of natural character arise chiefly from physical causes"; also the journal for October 3, 1786, where he and Bridge had had a private argument on "sensual appetites" and had appealed to Mr. Burr, the tutor, who had supported JQA's opinion.
30. On Christianity, see the journal comments on February 17,

1786; also his affirmative address on "Whether the introduction of Christianity had been favourable to the temporal interests of mankind," in the journal on April 3, 1787. His early social optimism is evident in the address on "Education" on June 26, 1786.

31. One of his first expressions of suspicion on returning to America was about Baron von Steuben, whom he met at General Knox's in New York in the summer of 1785. JQA to AA2, August 9, 1785, APM 365. Brother Charles was later to call the Baron "almost immortal." See also the journal for July 4, 1787. On JQA's republicanism while in college, see *Writings*, I, 29.

32. Journal, September 7, 1786.

33. Particularly pessimistic views were held by Dr. Cotton Tufts, the Adamses' business agent: *e.g.,* Cotton Tufts to AA, July 6, 1786, APM 368.

34. Cotton Tufts to (AA), January 2, 1787; AA to Cotton Tufts, January 24, 1787, APM 369. However, Tufts had been investing some of the Adams money in government securities even earlier. See Cotton Tufts to JA, October 1, 1785, APM 366; AA to Cotton Tufts, February 21, 1786, APM 367.

35. Samuel Adams to JA, July 21, 1786, Stephen Higginson to JA, July, 1786, APM 368.

36. C. Storer to JA, July 21; to AA, August 15; to AA, September 12; to JA, September 16, 26, 1786, APM 368. The disturbing matters at the commencement must have been such "forensick disputes" as "Whether the happiness of the people consists most in the constitution or in the administration of government?" and "Whether it would be for the advantage of the United States of America to enlarge the power of Congress?"; or perhaps the M.A. oration by Harrison Gray Otis on "National Faith." See the *Massachusetts Centinel*, July 22, 1786.

37. Journal, July 6, 1786.

38. See my "The Massachusetts Conservatives in the Critical Period," in *Era of the American Revolution: Essays Inscribed to Evarts Boutell Greene* (New York, 1939); also Mercy Warren to JA, January 4, 1787, APM 369.

39. ES to AA, July 23, 1786, APM 368; also MC to AA, April 22, 1787, APM 369.
40. *Writings*, I, 32.
41. B. Hichborn to JA, October 24, 1786, January 16, 1787; Samuel Osgood to JA, November 14, 1786, APM 369. On this whole subject consult Louise B. Dunbar, "A study of 'Monarchical Tendencies' in the United States from 1776 to 1801," in University of Illinois, *Studies in the Social Sciences*, X, No. 1, Chapter Four.
42. MC to AA, September 28, 1786, APM 368. JQA's journal for September 26, 1786, gives both parts of the forensic but it is not clear if the second was Billy's. If so, then he, too, agreed that the recent riots were due to false ideas of equality.
43. Journal, February 25, 1787.
44. "H.C." p. 90.
45. *Writings*, I, 29.
46. Journal, April 8, 1787.
47. *Writings*, I, 30; MC to AA, May 27, AAS to JQA, June 10, 1787, APM 370.
48. Journal, April 10, 1787. See also his reference to "Old Honestus" and the attack upon lawyers, in JQA to JA, January 14, 1787, APM 369.
49. ES to AA, May 20, 1787, APM 370. She had shown an exceptionally keen interest in such matters since girlhood.
50. MC to AA, April 22, 1787, APM 369.
51. Journal, March 14-20, 1787. The poem as here quoted is taken from "H.C." pp. 118-121.
52. Journal, May 24, 1786.
53. Journal, May 24, June 8, 20, 29, 1787.
54. Journal, September 30, 1787.
55. Journal, September 29, 1786.
56. Journal, March 10, 1787.
57. Journal, May 21, 1787.
58. See the next chapter.
59. Journal, June 8, 10, 1787.
60. Journal, July 2, 1787.
61. Journal, November 12, 1786.

Chapter Four

1. MC to AA, July 16, 1787, APM 370. By contrast, his cousin, Billy Cranch, was too busy helping with the preparations for the feast to be morose! There is an excellent article bearing on some aspects of the day's affairs, by Lawrence Shaw Mayo, Jeremy Belknap and J. Q. Adams, 1787," in the *Proceedings* of the Massachusetts Historical Society, LIX, 203-210.

2. See Henry Adams, "Harvard College. 1786, 1787," *loc. cit.,* pp. 97, 98, 117 (hereafter referred to as "H.C."). JQA had recorded in his journal, March 30, 1787, APM 14, that a private commencement would be preferable because public distinctions of this kind created envy. "I am much deceived if I have not lately perceived it, with respect to myself."

3. Journal, May 21, 1787, APM 14, saying that he dreaded comparison with Freeman, and that contrasts might be drawn which would reflect disgrace upon him.

4. ES to AA, July 22, Lucy Cranch to AA, August 18, 1787, APM 370.

5. MC to AA, July 14, 1786, APM 368; MC to AA, July 16, 22, and ES to AA, July 22, 1787, APM 370. There were three tenant families housed on the two farms in Braintree. See *Three Episodes of Massachusetts History,* II, 692. The generally festive character of commencement time may be inferred from a poem the year before in the *Massachusetts Centinel,* July 22, 1786, ending:

> Thus the loose crowd forbidden pleasures seek,
> Drink *Harvard* dry, and so conclude the week.

But this part of it apparently was unknown to JQA!

6. Probably the account in the *Centinel* on July 21 is that referred to in the *Memoirs,* I, 22. The expression was that of his Aunt Eliza Shaw. ES to AA, July 22, 1787, APM 370.

7. The Boston *Gazette,* July 23, 1787. On editor Edes and his paper, see Joseph T. Buckingham, *Specimens of Newspaper Literature,* I, 166 ff. This particular slam on the *Defence* seems to have been ignored by the Adamses in their correspondence, although before long JA was being informed by Dr. Tufts about such criticism of his book in America.

8. *Writings,* I, 30.
9. AA to JQA, November 22, 23, 1786, January 17, 1787, APM 369. "The seditions in Massachusetts induced your Poppa to give to the World a Book which at first he designed only for a few friends. . . ."
10. April 23, 1787.
11. The *Massachusetts Centinel,* July 18, 1787.
12. *Ibid.,* August 29, 1787; AA to JQA, March 20, 1787, APM 369. See also Chapter Seven.
13. A good, general account of the proceedings is in the Boston *Independent Chronicle,* July 19, 26, 1787.
14. The "nervous style" was of course the descriptive language employed by the *Centinel* on July 21. JQA's remarkable facial expressions are mentioned in ES to AA, July 22, and MC to AA, July 22, 1787, APM 370. Mrs. Cranch, however, had had her information by hearsay; she did not actually hear the address. Either she was too busy preparing for the feast, or she could not stand hearing her son and nephew "orate." She had previously sat through a similar ordeal when they had both performed, and had doubted whether she could ever do so again! See Chapter Three.
15. *Memoirs,* I, 22. His father, by contrast, had graduated fourteenth in his class, about half-way down. But "rank" played a primary role in those early days.
16. The *Independent Chronicle,* July 26, 1787.
17. On the *Centinel* and its able editor, Major Benjamin Russell, see Buckingham, *Specimens of Newspaper Literature,* II, 1-17. Russell had been an apprentice of Isaiah Thomas, and a Revolutionary soldier. The *Massachusetts Centinel* (later the *Columbian Centinel*), had only been organized in 1784, and was an up-and-coming sheet. Its format had already had to be enlarged.
18. *Cf.* JQA's poor opinion of President Willard as a speaker, in "H.C." p. 103.
19. JQA to AA, August 1, 1787, APM 370.
20. *Ibid.*; Journal, May 21, July 28, APM 14; ES to AA, July 22, 1787, APM 370.
21. *Life in a New England Town,* p. 125n.

22. See Mayo, "Jeremy Belknap and J. Q. Adams, 1787," *loc. cit.*, *passim*.

23. September 15, 1787.

24. Mayo, *op. cit.*, pp. 206, 207, 208; *Writings*, I, 34 ff.; and Jane B. Marcou, *The Life of Jeremy Belknap, D.D., the Historian of New Hampshire* (New York, 1847), p. 157. The long quote follows Mayo on wording and punctuation.

25. See S. E. Morison, *Three Centuries of Harvard*, pp. 175-177.

26. *Ibid.*, p. 179; also the journal comments of JQA in "H.C." pp. 104-116, especially p. 106. One of the tutors, Mr. Reed, seems to have been somewhat more favorably regarded, at least by James Bridge, a close friend of JQA. See Bridge to JQA, September 28, 1787, APM 370.

27. JQA to AA, August 1, 1787, APM 370.

28. "H.C." pp. 97, 98, 117.

29. *Ibid.*, p. 90. See also Chapter Three.

30. Morison, *Three Centuries of Harvard*, p. 174; Albert Mathews, *Harvard Commencement Days*, pp. 363, 364.

31. Mathews, *op. cit.*, pp. 363, 364.

32. *Ibid.*, p. 364. On an earlier "insult" to Hancock, see Morison, *Three Centuries of Harvard*, p. 156.

33. See Josiah Quincy, *Memoir of the Life of John Quincy Adams*, pp. 5, 6, on his popularity with his classmates, and general record at college.

34. The following is quoted and paraphrased from an original copy of the September, 1787, *Columbian Magazine*, in the New York Public Library. In view of the theme of the address, it seems fitting to ask, whether he was aware of how his family had been investing in government securities in recent months. (See Chapter Three) The only answer is, there is no evidence that he was.

35. In his journal, July 27, 1787, APM 14, he says, "In the after-noon I read a novel, which arrived from England by the last vessel. The title is *Louisa*, or the cottage on the moor. It is light and airy like most novels. . . . The story is interesting, and affecting. The incident of Danvers' carrying off Louisa from Dover is theatrical, and related with more circumstances of probability than are usual in Scenes of that kind. . . ."

Chapter Five

1. *Letters of Mrs. Adams,* pp. 327, 341; John Thaxton to JA, January 7, JA to JQA, April 2, 1786, APM 367; MC to AA, May 22, 1786, APM 368; AA to JQA, January 17, 20, 1787, APM 369; Cotton Tufts to JA, June 30, 1787, APM 370.
2. He had once been troubled with headaches and "flushing" in the face, according to AA to JQA, January 17, 1787, APM 369. On his spells of dizziness see *ibid.,* also MC to AA, September 24, 1786, APM 368, and journal for May 13, 1787, APM 14. A prescription of limewater for acid stomach is in AA to JQA, July 18, 1787, APM 370. He had been repeatedly unwell in the fall of 1786, and trouble flared up again the following spring. See journal entries for March 31, April 12, May 13, 28 (when he suffered the "usual consequences" from a lack of exercise), 1787, APM 14.
3. *Life in a New England Town, 1787, 1788. The Diary of John Quincy Adams While a Student in the Office of Theophilus Parsons at Newburyport,* pp. 23, 68, 95, 132. Hereafter referred to as *LNET.*
4. *Ibid.,* pp. 65, 69.
5. See Chapter Four.
6. *Letters of Mrs. Adams,* p. 341.
7. *Cf. LNET* p. 170; also the following chapter.
8. Journal, September 5, 1788, APM 14. There are copies of this address in the Massachusetts Historical Society and in the Harvard College Library.
9. See Chapter Three.
10. See his father's appraisal of Parsons, *LNET,* p. 126n. JQA's feelings of apprehension are found in *ibid.,* p. 14, also in Chapter Three.
11. *LNET,* pp. 42, 46.
12. *Ibid.,* p. 92.
13. JQA to Cotton Tufts, December 9, 1787; also Tufts to AA, September 20, 1787, APM 370.
14. He had felt particularly unwell and depressed in November: *LNET,* pp. 62, 63, 65; but took new resolution in December: *Writings,* I, 37.

15. *LNET*, p. 71.
16. *Ibid.,* pp. 68, 69.
17. *Ibid.,* pp. 92, 93, 95.
18. *Ibid.,* pp. 107, 111.
19. April 5, 1788, *ibid.,* p. 118.
20. May 12, 13, 14, *ibid.,* pp. 134, 135.
21. *Ibid.,* p. 138.
22. *Ibid.,* p. 127.
23. Perhaps it is a fanciful notion that JQA should have been sensitive on this point, but his great admiration for literary genius should be remembered, and Tyler had already scored his brilliant New York success. Anyone interested in the torturous story of the Adamses' acquisition of the Borland (or Vassal) house in Braintree (upon which Tyler may have lost his down payment, although he had sold off some of the land and also had a "claim" that had to be settled) should read the letters of MC and of Cotton Tufts to AA in 1787, especially those of May 26, June 13, and September 20. It had originally been sequestered as Tory property and leased to Richard Cranch—he had been one of the state commissioners in such matters—then returned to the heirs under the terms of the peace treaty of 1783 who in turn had sold it to Tyler. Dr. Thomas Welch of Boston was finally employed to close the deal, so as to keep John Adams' name out of it.
24. *LNET*, p. 161.
25. *Ibid.,* p. 161; AAS to JQA, August 20, 1788, APM 371.
26. *LNET*, p. 165. The remaining entries, September 3—October 14, must have been written up later from the "almanac" diary in which he continued to make brief daily entries despite his indisposition.
27. *Ibid.,* pp. 155, 156. The day after commencement he had ridden to Boston on a hard trotting horse, with the sun blazing in his face.
28. Including Bolingbroke, Buffon, Robertson, Gibbon, Hume, Vattel, and others. See his father's exhortation for him to read works on ethics and morals, and Parson's advice to read "ethic writers." *LNET*, pp. 64, 125n.

29. March 5, 1788, *ibid.,* p. 106.
30. *Writings,* I, 38; *LNET,* p. 32n; Myron O. Allen, *History of Wenham* (Boston, 1860), pp. 145-148.
31. February 7, *LNET,* p. 93.
32. John Forbes to JQA, January 19, W. Cranch to JQA, January 22, AAS to JQA, August 20, 1788, APM 371.
33. *LNET,* pp. 46, 55, 68, 69, 72. On his republican attitude at college, see *Writings,* I, 29; also Chapter Three.
34. February 10, *LNET,* p. 95.
35. *Ibid.,* p. 96.
36. *Ibid.,* p. 153 and note.
37. April 7, *ibid.,* p. 119.
38. *Ibid.,* pp. 125, 150.
39. *I.e.,* Volume one of the *Defence of the Constitutions of Government of the United States of America* (London, 1787), included in John Adams, *Works,* Vol. IV. See also Chapter Four.
40. AAS to JQA, September 28, 1788, APM 371.
41. *LNET,* p. 109.
42. *Ibid.,* pp. 78, 132.
43. *Cf.* "H.C." p. 90; journal, July 26, 1786, APM 13; *LNET,* p. 72.
44. *LNET,* p. 88.
45. See Chapter Two.
46. January 25, 1788, *LNET,* p. 88. On the "Receipt," see Chapter One.
47. *Poems of Religion and Society,* p. 111 ff. See also the next chapter.
48. *Letters of Mrs. Adams,* p. 115.
49. APM 16.
50. *LNET,* p. 43.
51. *Ibid.,* pp. 99, 159.
52. On Mary Frazier, see the following chapter.
53. *LNET,* pp. 105, 161.
54. *Ibid.,* p. 105.
55. *Ibid.,* pp. 159, 161, 162.
56. *Ibid.,* pp. 45, 61.

57. *Ibid.,* pp. 159, 165.
58. He had been reading the *Notes on Virginia* on August 30, 1787. *Ibid.,* p. 23.
59. ES to AA, September 21, 1788, APM 371. JQA also wrote his mother the next day about his condition.
60. ES to AA, October 3, 1788, APM 371.

Chapter Six

1. *Life in a New England Town,* p. 168, and on Gibbon, p. 112; diary entries for October and November, 1788, APM 16.
2. His diary gives no reason, but presumably this was the case. He had discontinued his elaborate journal in September, 1788, and the "almanac" diaries (*i.e.,* daily entries on the blank leaves of his yearly Fleet almanac) give much less information.
3. APM 16. Another interesting quotation, in French, refers to men so vile as to purchase love, etc.
4. APM 17. Such colorful expressions were apparently much savored by the lads. A year later his friend, James Bridge, referred to one of the local favorites as "the hot wench." Bridge to JQA, September 28, 1790, APM 374. This young lady was duly satirized by JQA in "A Vision." The quotation itself is from "King Henry IV, Part I."
5. See Chapter Two.
6. Bridge to JQA, October 10, 1788, APM 371.
7. Cranch to JQA, June 10, 1790, APM 373. Cranch refers to the poem as "The Vision," but I have employed the earlier title, "A Vision," throughout this work. JQA labeled it so in his "Fugitive Pieces in Verse," APM 223.
8. James Bridge so described it in a letter to JQA, June 28, 1790, APM 373. For a contemporary description of a "club," see the amusing article in the *Massachusetts Magazine* for April, 1789, p. 219.
9. References to fatigue and drowsiness are in the dairy, April 3, May 12, June 20, 1789, APM 17. He slept poorly on May 12, following an evening, presumably social, at Dr. Swett's. On April 17 he wrote his mother (APM 372) that his health

was better than at any time since the previous September,
and that "scarcely anything of my complaints remains, except the Spasms, which are not frequent, nor very troublesome." Perhaps this referred to stomach cramps—medical
terms were used loosely in those days—since he had suffered
earlier from stomach and perhaps bowel trouble. See Chapter Five, especially footnotes 2 and 3. See also the letter to
his father in June, 1789, about his ability to study having
exceeded his expectations (*Writings,* I, 40); and to his mother
on December 5, 1789, (*LNET,* p. 178), about his ancient quarrel with drowsiness threatening to break out again—daytime
drowsiness resulting from insomnia?—and to "a few nervous
twitches" hinting of his need for exercise. Could "twitches"
also have been connected with stomach cramps?

10. See Clifford K. Shipton, *Isaiah Thomas, Printer, Patriot and
Philanthropist, 1749-1831* (Rochester, 1948), pp. 43, 48. The
old literary *Boston Magazine,* with which JQA had been acquainted while at Harvard, had expired with the November-
December, 1786, issue.

11. Shipton, *Thomas,* p. 48. Also Richard Walser, "More About
the First American Novel," in *American Literature,* XXIV,
No. 3, 1952.

12. *E.g.,* "Gyges" in the *Columbian Centinel* for January 17,
February 11, 14, 25, 1789, replied to by "Bon Ton" on January 24, "Mentor" on February 21, and "Aspasia" on February 25, 1789. A popular risqué poem was "The Penance,"
reprinted in the *Herald of Freedom* on February 10, 1789.
Brown's novel is occasionally referred to, as by "Mr. Civil
Spy" in the *Centinel* on February 18, 1789.

13. In May, 1789, on Mary Frazier, signed "Alcander," submitted by a friend who called himself "Septimus," with the
solution in the August number; in June, on Mary Newhall,
and unsigned; in September, on Harriet Bradbury, signed
"Corydon," and the solution in the December number by
"Thyrsis." In the same September issue there also appeared
by "Corydon," a "Pastoral Ode" on "Emma: Or, the Rose,"
undoubtedly also by JQA. Could "Emma" have been the
young lady who, together with "Julia," had contributed to

the *Massachusetts Magazine* for February, 1789, and therefore have been one of those ladies whom he had earlier criticized under the pen name of "Celadon"? See below, especially footnotes 33 and 34.

14. The *Herald of Freedom,* March 10, 1789.

15. He mentioned "Mirror *Leluna*" in his diary on April 29,
    APM 17. It presumably was a satirical character analysis of
    one of the local young ladies. The simple diary entry sug-
    gests that JQA was the author, for such apparently was his
    habit in noting his publications. Unfortunately—most unfor-
    tunately—no copy of this important April 29, 1789, issue of
    the *Essex Journal and New-Hampshire Packet* appears to
    exist.

16. He also mentioned the "Enig: List" in his diary on April 29.
    This, of course, was in the *Essex Journal* for that day. He
    presumably had had a hand in its compilation, although not
    necessarily for publication. Could the characters have been
    related to those in his "Vision"? An "Enigmatical List of
    Young Ladies in Boston," submitted by "Cardenio," had
    appeared in the *Massachusetts Magazine* for March, 1789, p.
    181, so it was quite a fashionable thing to do.

17. The *Essex Journal,* May 6, 1789. He mentions *"Lelius"* in
    his diary that day. Undoubtedly it was he who used this same
    signature in a political article in the Boston *American
    Apollo,* March 29, 1793. See Chapter Eight. In the Boston
    Herald of Freedom, March 20, 1789, there was an anti-Han-
    cockian article signed "Lelius," although there is no reason
    to think that JQA was the author.

18. The manuscript journal of Alice Tucker, 1784-1791, under
    November 14, 1789, and January 30, 1790. I am indebted for
    the privilege of reading this journal to Mr. Gordon Hutchins
    of Punkatasset Farm, Concord, Massachusetts.

19. The quotation is from the communication by "Eugenio" in
    the *Essex Journal* for May 6. There was still another article
    on the subject, entitled "Remarks on the Fair Sex." The
    same issue included a laudatory ode on the arrival in New
    York of the Vice President of the United States, John Adams,
    contributed by "Mr. F****."

20. The satire thus appears in *LNET*, p. 120. It may also be found in any printed version of "A Vision," *e.g.*, in *Poems of Religion and Society* (1850 ed.), or in John J. Currier, *Newburyport*, II, 540 ff. The original of "A Vision" is in his book of "Fugitive Pieces in Verse," APM 223.

21. The "Epistle" and its date of composition are given in his book of "Fugitive Pieces," p. 3. Twelve lines of that production were subsequently transferred to his treatment of "Narcissa" in "A Vision."

22. See *LNET*, p. 125.

23. "Fugitive Pieces," p. 8, APM 223.

24. The Boston *Herald of Freedom*, December 11, 1788, February 27, 1789.

25. AA to Cotton Tufts, January 1, 1788, APM 371.

26. The *Massachusetts Magazine* in 1789 and 1790 has many contributions by a certain "Belinda," who possibly was the young lady who had written in the *Herald*. However, such stock names had wide current usage. For JQA's satire, see above and footnote 20.

27. This verse was widely reprinted. I first ran across it in the Poughkeepsie, New York, *Journal*, May 26, 1791. Who the author was, does not appear.

28. See above, footnote 13.

29. Also in the "Fugitive Pieces," p. 6, APM 223.

30. "Scipio Africanus" is mentioned in the diary, together with a reference to the *Herald*, under that date. APM 17. Here, again, simple entry in the diary suggests his own authorship, while its parodying of "Clara," together with the rhyming couplet at the end, clearly identifies it with his "Vision." The only possible other explanation of its authorship, and one quite far-fetched, would be that someone had secured a copy of the completed "Vision"—if indeed it already was completed—and was playing a joke on him. There was a reply to "Scipio Africanus" by "Toby" in the *Herald* on March 6.

31. If his authorship of this is also doubted on grounds that it shows "prejudice" unnatural to him, see his second "Elegy to Miranda" in his "Fugitive Pieces," APM 223. In that later, unpublished satire of 1792, he laments his ability to fall in

love with any woman, regardless among other things of the color of her skin. See Chapter Eight. His critical opinion of the improbability of "Othello" has already been noted in Chapter Three, an opinion he expanded many years later in a serious essay. See Rufus Wilmot Griswold, *Prose Writers of America* (Philadelphia, 1847), pp. 103, 104. An article by S. Swett, a son of JQA's old doctor, in the Newburyport *Daily Herald,* September 22, 1864, says that JQA had a reputation of having once published in a Boston paper a "pasquinade on Jefferson's Black Sal," which possibly referred to an old political smear, but may be what is acknowledged in the *Memoirs,* VIII, 339. Similar charges may be found in Samuel D. Ingraham, *An Exposition of the Political Character and Principles of John Quincy Adams* (Washington: Printed by Duff Green, 1827). Other "prejudices" of his may be gleaned from George Lipsky, *John Quincy Adams: His Theory and Ideas.*

32. Diary, March 10, 11, 1789, APM 17. "Celadon" was a minor figure slain by Perseus in the war over Andromeda.

33. *Herald of Freedom,* March 10, 1789. Here again the name of the article and the newspaper in which it appeared, are simply mentioned in the diary. However, his authorship is obviously conceded in JQA to John Phillips, January 27, 1790, in the Phillips Papers in the Massachusetts Historical Society. One of the "rebuses" that had attracted his attention, and which seemed to have had some peculiar significance since he mentions it in the "Celadon" article, was in the *Herald* for February 24; but I have been unable to decipher it except that the first name appears to be "DIAN."

34. The *Herald of Freedom,* March 13, 20, 31, April 3, 1789. The *Massachusetts Magazine* for March, 1789, p. 130, expressed the hope that "Emma and Julia" would not be discouraged from sending further communications because of the "illnatured, illjudged, ungallant irony of a coxcomical newspaper scribbler." In its September issue, p. 532, this magazine in its comments on contributors speaks of "*Celadon's* Ode and Rebus—ingenious, spirited, chaste," which refers to contributions by JQA under the signature of "Corydon" in

the same issue. Thus the identification of "Celadon" with "Corydon" would seem to be unmistakable.

35. In JQA's letter to Phillips, January 27, 1790, referred to above, he disclaimed responsibility for the satirizing of married persons, in which the new "Celadon" was indulging. An example of the latter's writing is in the *Massachusetts Magazine*, December, 1789, p. 764. JQA also plainly admits in this letter of his once having written under the signature of "Alcander." See above, footnote 13. His ballad to "Phyllida" in his "Fugitive Pieces" (APM 223), published in this magazine in November, 1789, was also signed "Alcander." It tells how his love persists even though "Phyllida" makes nature lose her charms by comparison.

36. W. Cranch to JQA, June 10, 1790, APM 373.

37. It is not apparent what significance the name of "Clara" must have had for JQA. However, it is interesting to note a poem in the *Boston Magazine* for February, 1786, entitled "A Dutch Proverb," which includes the line, "A slave I am to Clara's eyes." JQA, of course, had a special knowledge of all things Dutch. Could he possibly have been the author?

38. See his "Fugitive Pieces in Verse," APM 223, also footnote 13 above, and JQA to TBA, April 2, 1791, APM 374.

39. W. Cranch to JQA, June 10, 1790, APM 373.

40. Bridge to JQA, September 28, 1790, APM 374.

41. *LNET*, p. 125; "Fugitive Pieces," p. 5, APM 223. A principal point of contention is whether Catherine Jones had any claims to being "Clara" in "A Vision," or whether she was in fact the loathsome "Almira." Although the problem of identifying the originals of the characters in "A Vision" is most interesting, it is subject to exaggeration since JQA was also illustrating various types of young ladies. Nevertheless, various "keys" to the characters got into circulation in Newburyport, perhaps stimulated by the "Enigmatical list" in the *Essex Journal* on April 29, 1789, (of which no copy appears to exist).

There were nine such characters in "A Vision": unfeeling Lucinda, loud-voiced Belinda, disdainful Narcissa, talkative Vanessa, silly, kissable Corinna, novel-reading Nerea, old and sneering Statira (omitted from the 1850 edition of his poems), prideful and masculine Almira, and—finally—the lovely, lovely Clara. The uproar his poem must have caused when it got into private circulation may well be imagined!

There are three principal authorities about these characters: John J. Currier, *Newburyport,* II, 540 ff.; the "Recollections" of James Morss, in the Newburyport *Daily Herald,* June 30, July 15, 1864 (the first reprinting of a letter said to have been written by JQA from Washington, D.C., January 7, 1840); and the article by "S[amuel] Swett" in the *Herald* for September 22, 1864, which defends Catherine Jones on the recollection of what Swett's parents had told him. There was a reply to Swett by Mrs. James Morss, whose husband had meantime died, in the paper on October 15, 1864. The *Herald* had published a copy of "A Vision" years before, on December 27, 1839—after it had first appeared in a New York paper—contributed by James Morss.

An article about JQA in the *Herald* on August 17, 1864, refers to several visits JQA is said to have made there in his old age, one of which is surely apocryphal. The Appendix to his *An Oration Delivered Before the Inhabitants of the Town of Newburyport, at Their Request, on . . . July 4th, 1837* (Printed by Morss and Brewster, Newburyport *Herald* Office), is also worth noting. See also *LNET,* p. 169, for Charles Francis Adams, Jr.'s reaction to all the publicity in 1864 about his grandfather's love affair.

42. Bridge to JQA, February 28, 1789, APM 372.
43. J. Putnam to JQA, October 3, 1789, APM 373.
44. *Ibid.,* saying, "for however phlegmatic you may think yourself you are as capable of as strong attachts as any person I know." James Bridge to JQA, June 28, had said, "This I used to impute to the want of passion on your side—what you would by no means allow, you may remember." APM 373.
45. JQA to TBA, April 2, 1791, APM 374. For statements about his publications made years later, see *Memoirs,* VIII, 125, 339.
46. *LNET,* pp. 170-178.
47. *Ibid.,* pp. 123, 178, 179. The Address to Washington is in *Writings,* I, 43, 44, also in the *Essex Journal,* November 4,

1789. Identification of the "Cough" and the "late rage" of
influenza with Washington's visit, is called "antifederal" in
an amusing anecdote in the *Essex Journal,* February 17, 1790.
48. Diary entries, APM 17.
49. JQA to John Phillips, January 27, 1790, has a mock lamentation, saying that "We can indeed no longer boast, that 'each
nymph is kind'." Phillips Papers in the Massachusetts Historical Society.
50. *Writings,* I, 46.
51. *Ibid.,* I, 61, and note.
52. Diary entries, under date, APM 17.
53. For a description of Mary Frazier (born March 9, 1774), written long afterwards, see *The Recollections of Samuel Breck
with Passages from His Note-Books, 1771-1862.* Edited by
H. E. Scudder (Philadelphia, 1877), pp. 120, 121. See also
John H. Sheppard, *Reminiscences of Lucius Manlius Sargent*
(Boston, 1871), Appendix, p. 31. Most of the latter material
is also in the New England Historical Society *Register,* Vol.
25, p. 210, giving genealogical information about Mary Frazier and her husband, Daniel Sargent, Jr. They had been
married less than two years before Mary's death in 1804.
Sargent had once been a boon companion of JQA. See Chap-
ters Eight and Nine of this work. The Fraziers had been
immigrants to Newbury, Massachusetts, in 1685; a branch
of the family became established in Boston where Nathan
Frazier was a merchant at the time of the Revolution. His
son, Nathan Frazier, Jr., was another close companion of
young Adams, as also mentioned below. See Josiah G. Leach,
Some Account of Captain John Frazier and His Descendants
(Philadelphia, 1910), p. 6. These lines from "A Vision" are
taken from Currier, *Newburyport,* II, pp. 546, 547, except
that I have substituted "Virtue" for "Nature" in one place,
and "and yet" for "when they" in another, which are the
most important variations from the copy in APM 223.
54. See S. E. Morison, *Harrison Gray Otis,* I, 34.
55. *E.g.,* AA to JQA, February 19, July 11, 1790, APM 373, and
JA to JQA, September 13, 1790, APM 374; also JQA to JA,
August 9, 1790, APM 374, about "envy" and "malice."

56. AAS to JQA, August 20, 1788, APM 371; and April 18, July 11, 1790, APM 373 and 374.

57. JQA to JA, August 9, and JQA to AA, October 17, 1790, APM 374.

58. JA to JQA, April 16, 1790, APM 373, had admitted that, despite criticism of the new national government, it had had "all the Influence on public Property that could be expected." See Chapter Three on the Adamses' early acquisition of public securities. JA to JQA, September 13, 1790, APM 374, mentions his estates, apparently in an effort to take up the young man's attention.

59. AA to JQA, August 20, and his reply, August 29, 1790; also AA to JQA, September 9, 1790, APM 374. The "rich girl" was his cousin, Nancy Quincy, who had recently married. JQA had once thought her too fat, as well as a prude!

60. ES to AA, September 28, 1790, APM 374.

61. JA to JQA, September, 1790. He reassured him that industry and honor would overcome malice and envy, as AA had also written him on July 11, 1790. APM 374. His parents seem to have been concerned lest he try for early success in undesirable ways. Could this fear have been related to the news of his infatuation?

62. JQA to AA, August 29, 1790, APM 374.

63. AA to JQA, September 22, 1790, APM 374.

64. JQA to AA, November 20, December 14, 1790, APM 374.

65. Bridge to JQA, September 28, 1790, APM 374.

66. JQA to AA, November 7, 1795, APM 380, and her reply, February 29, 1796, APM 381.

67. ES to JQA, June 9, 1794, APM 377.

68. AAS to JQA, April 18, June 6, 1790, APM 373. In the first she quotes what he had written about her reason and prudence, and in the latter she acknowledges his letter of reassurance as to his discretion, prudence, and caution!

69. *Writings*, I, 58.

70. AA to JQA, May 20, and JQA to AA, July 25, 1796, APM 381 and 382. The "chaos" of his thoughts while undergoing the ordeal of visiting Newburyport in 1837 is referred to in the *Memoirs*, IX, 357-360.

71. According to James Morss' account. See *LNET*, p. 169. Surely one of the "friends" had been Catherine Jones!
72. Bridge to JQA, August 30, 1790, APM 374, about Betsy Frazier's being succeeded by her sister, Mary, as a visitor for the winter at Medford.
73. April 4, 1791, during his brief effort to revive his journal. APM 20.
74. Diary, April 9, 1791, APM 19.
75. Diary, December 13, 1790, APM 18. I have been unable to locate this particular writing for certain. However, the *Massachusetts Magazine* for November, 1790, p. 695, has a poem by "Lysander" entitled "FANCY Unrestrained By JUDGMENT; Or, ANTICIPATION Greater Than REAL ENJOYMENT," which in a treatment strangely similar to JQA's old "Vision" tells how a blue-eyed golden-haired nymph had appeared before the author when he fell asleep. The poem concludes

> I look'd and wish'd, and look'd and wish'd again,
> I sought her love and soon the boon attained,
> Then asked her hand, her hand was quickly gained.
> To crown my bliss, for marriage joys I sigh'd,
> To give me these, the nuptial knot was ty'd;
> I thought 'twas joy, but though it strange may seem,
> I wak'd to pain, and found it all a DREAM.

Comparison of the entire poem with the theme and some of the expressions in "A Vision," suggests that JQA may have been the author. If so, one must suppose that the magazine had been published very late to include a poem written near a month after the termination of the affair with Mary Frazier. There is also a "rebus" by "Lysander" in this issue which I have been unable to decipher. So far as I know, JQA had never previously written under this signature, and its significance is not clear except in the usage of "A Midsummer-Night's Dream." However, JQA's father had employed it as a young man.
76. *New Letters of Abigail Adams*, p. 69.
77. *Ibid.*, p. 70.

78. Diary, March 13, 1791, APM 19. His last, sarcastic use of the sentimental expression, "Celadon," probably was that in JQA to TBA, June 23, 1793, APM 376. See also Chapter Nine.

Chapter Seven

1. *The Education of Henry Adams,* p. 7.
2. "Letters of Publicola II," in *Writings,* I, 73.
3. *LNET,* pp. 119, 120n.
4. See Chapter Six.
5. *Letters of Mrs. Adams,* p. 111.
6. Including Shenstone's "Judgment of Hercules," copied into the blank leaves of his diary, APM 19.
7. APM 20 has a few entries for April 1-10, 1791.
8. Diary, May 6, 1791, APM 19. During his futile attempts to renew his journal (APM 20), he says, under April 7, that he has little pleasure in reflection although "much leisure" on his hands, and that whenever he journalizes, "I soon grow disgusted with my own egotism."
9. Diary, April 10, 1791, APM 20.
10. JQA to TBA, April 2, 20, 1791, APM 374.
11. AAS to JQA, September 28, 1788, APM 371.
12. James Bridge to JQA, July 28, 1791, APM 375. As usual, Bridge's letter was written on the 28th day of the month!
13. AA to JQA, April 18, 1791, APM 374. He was to get twenty-five pounds a quarter. On June 1, his father also gave him power of attorney for handling his Boston estates. APM 375.
14. On this whole matter, see *Writings,* I, 65n; also John Adams, *Works,* I, 454, and Jefferson, *Writings* (Ford), V, 354. On Adams' immediate dislike of *The Rights of Man,* Tobias Lear to Washington, in Washington, *Writings* (Ford), XII, 39n. Jefferson's explanation to Washington, May 8, 1791, is in Jefferson, *Writings,* V, 328 ff.; and to James Madison, May 9, in *ibid.,* V, 331. Jefferson and Madison took a convenient political excursion away from Philadelphia, May 16-June 20, visiting lakes George and Champlain and returning by way of the Connecticut River. On June 28, Jefferson wrote Madison (Jefferson, *Writings,* V, 346), "Nobody doubts here who

is the author of Publicola, any more than of Davila. He is very indecently attacked in Brown's & Bache's papers." Jefferson's explanations to John Adams on July 17 and August 30 are in Jefferson, *Writings*, V, 353 ff., 380 ff.; and John Adams' to Jefferson, July 29, in Adams, *Works*, VIII, 506 ff. Incidentally, JQA had once had luncheon with Tom Paine, in New York, August 10, 1785. JQA to AA2, under date, APM 365.

15. JA to Tench Coxe, July 14, 1791, APM 375. With the increase in the credit and property of the country he thought that America had never been so "happy," and that she would continue so if the French "delirium" should not turn American heads. JA to Colonel Smith, June 19, 1791, *ibid.* JQA noted in his diary, April 1, 1791, that the first interest was paid at the "Loan Office." APM 19. On the family's earlier interest in government securities, see Chapter Three.

16. See Charles D. Hazen, *Contemporary American Opinion of the French Revolution, passim.*

17. *Writings,* I, 64.

18. See Chapter Four, especially the reference to the *Centinel* for July 18, 1787, reprinting a story from Philadelphia commenting on Adams' *Defence* and incidentally defending a different version of one of Dr. Franklin's illustrations pertaining to "divisions" in government.

19. See JA to Jefferson, July 29, 1791, *Works*, VIII, 506 ff, commenting on his political enemies in Massachusetts and Pennsylvania. See also his remarks in the *Defence* on the ideas held by some people in every state at the beginning of the Revolution, for getting rid of senates and governors (*Works*, IV, 299, 300); on Franklin's influence on Turgot, in popularizing the idea of a single assembly as in the Pennsylvania Constitution of 1776 (*ibid.*, IV, 389); and in "Davila" and later remarks thereon, other references to Pennsylvania's single assembly and to Franklin, and the evil consequences of such ideas in France (*ibid.*, VI, 274 and note). The "Stone House" faction in Massachusetts—named after Hancock's residence in Boston—is also mentioned in Amory, *James Sullivan*, I, 248.

20. See John Adams, *Works,* VI, 411, 415, 427, 431 *et passim.* He even went so far as to suggest that the Boston town meetings and Harvard College had had something to do with bringing on hopes of a millenium, and setting the "universe in motion"!

21. See *Works,* VI, 323n; also Zoltan Haraszti, *John Adams and the Prophets of Progress* (Cambridge, 1952), *passim;* but he had on at least one earlier occasion expressed admiration for the "virtuous" Rousseau. See *Familiar Letters of John Adams and His Wife,* p. 349.

22. It should be noted, however, that in the *Defence* John Adams had defended the division of powers in American state constitutions not so much because it was the English system, as because such a division had always existed in America, and was founded in "nature and reason." *Works,* IV, 300.

23. *New Letters of Abigail Adams,* p. 26, and 24n, 25n. She did subsequently attend plays in Philadelphia, however, in company with the Washingtons. See Chapter Eight.

24. *The Columbian Centinel,* August 26, 1789. In the same issue there is a communication by "An American," however, who says that Americans of all ranks favor some titles, such as "Honourable," etc.

25. *The Gazette of the United States,* June 18, 1791.

26. The story, reprinted in the *Columbian Centinel,* June 18, 1791, was "From a Late Connecticut Paper" which I have been unable to locate; but it was based upon an article originally appearing in the recently founded (and soon to expire) New Haven *Gazette* of May 18, 1791. Henry Knox had noticed the article in both New York and Connecticut papers, and had written John Adams about it on June 10. Adams' denunciation of the "Lye" is in his reply to Knox, June 19, 1791, APM 375.

27. Madison, *Writings* (Hunt), VI, 56n, as quoted in JQA *Writings,* I, 66n.   ....

28. "Publicola I," in *Writings,* I, 65 ff.

29. *The Independent Chronicle,* June 23, 1791.

30. *E.g., Writings,* I, 69, 78, 80, 103.

31. *Ibid.,* p. 101.

32. *Ibid.*, pp. 70, 71.
33. *Ibid.*, p. 74.
34. The Boston *Independent Chronicle,* June 23, 1791.
35. *Writings,* I, 87, also 75. Thomas Jefferson had had somewhat similar ideas about the "origin" of English government!
36. *Ibid.*, p. 99; *LNET,* p. 23.
37. *Writings,* I, 73. The question was about Great Britain, whose government according to Paine was a "usurpation." See also *ibid.*, p. 105, on the difficulties of making peace treaties with a nation organized on the French principles of having everything openly debated in the Assembly.
38. *Ibid.*, pp. 79, 98.
39. Quoted in *ibid.*, 66n.
40. Diary, under dates, APM 19.
41. Jefferson, *Writings* (Ford), V, 380 ff.
42. JA to Tench Coxe, September 13, 1791, and AAS to JQA, July 3, 1792, APM 375.

Chapter Eight

1. *Letters of Mrs. Adams,* p. 352.
2. John Verlin Godwin to JA, April 17, 1792, APM 375. So was "Paradise Lost" at that tender age.
3. *Henry Adams, A Catalogue of the Books of John Quincy Adams,* p. 68; Morse, *Adams,* pp. 222, 223.
4. "Journal A," December 9-14, 1779, APM 4.
5. Journals and diaries, 1779-1785, especially APM 11.
6. *Letters of Mrs. Adams,* p. 234.
7. See Chapter One, especially footnote 41.
8. Bobbé, *Mr. and Mrs. John Quincy Adams,* p. 32; also Bemis, *John Quincy Adams and the Foundations of American Foreign Policy,* p. 18.
9. James Bridge to JQA, July 28, 1791, APM 375, quoting a letter of JQA who had attributed his "apostacy" to his "situation and connexions."
10. *Writings,* I, 126.
11. APM 25.
12. *Writings,* I, 125, 126.

13. See Chapter Six.
14. JA to JQA, September 13, 1790, APM 374; *Writings*, I, 56, 57.
15. See *Writings*, I, 124, and the *Chronicle* for December 13. Actually, Sullivan had been trying to be neutral on the subject. See the excellent biography by T. C. Amory, *The Life of James Sullivan*, especially Vol. I, 270-274, on the theater question. At the time of Sullivan's death, years later, JQA was to deliver an impressive, official eulogy! *Ibid.*, II, 320-325.
16. December 19, 1792. He had earlier noted, however, that Sullivan's attitude had been circumspect. *Writings*, I, 121.
17. August 12, 1789.
18. For the general story of the theater problem in Boston, see Mary C. Crawford, *The Romance of the American Theater*, pp. 107-113; George O. Seilhamer, *The History of the American Theater*, III, 13-20; and Morison, *Otis*, I, 37.
19. *Writings*, I, 116.
20. "The Echo No. V," as quoted in Seilhamer, *American Theater*, III, 16. John Adams gleefully quoted "The Echo No. IX," the part relating to Hancock, in a letter to JQA, January 27, 1793, APM 376. See also JQA's reply, in *Writings*, I, 134.
21. See Amory, *Sullivan*, I, 270, 271.
22. *New Letters of Abigail Adams*, p. 38n.
23. October 31, 1791. On Englishmen invading the American state, see Seilhamer, *American Theatre*, II, 353, 354.
24. Amory, *Sullivan*, I, 267. "Board-Alley" was renamed "Hawley Street" that year.
25. Diary, September 21, 1792, APM 21; Seilhamer, *American Theater*, III, 18.
26. October 8, 1792.
27. Amory, *Sullivan*, I, 270-273. The *Centinel* had meantime run a series of articles, beginning November 10, 1792, on behalf of a "virtuous" theater.
28. Diary, APM 21.
29. *Ibid., passim.* See also below for his readings.
30. December 19, 1792.
31. AA to JA, December 23, JA to JQA, December 26, and JA

to AA, December 28, 1792, APM 375. The letter to JQA was a reply to his letter of December 16, in *Writings,* I, 123.

32. The third, unnumbered "Menander" is in the *Columbian Centinel* for December 26, 1792.

33. December 24, 1792. The language is reminiscent of Sullivan's retorts to "Laco," in 1789. See Amory, *Sullivan,* I, 244.

34. However, he wrote his father on December 22, that all of the "other party" had absented themselves from the town meeting, knowing that they would be outvoted. *Writings,* I, 131.

35. AA to JA, January 7, 1793, APM 376.

36. *Writings,* I, 125.

37. Diary, December 18, 1792, APM 21.

38. JQA to TBA, October 28, 1791, APM 375.

39. *Lectures on Rhetoric and Oratory, Delivered to the Classes of Senior and Junior Sophisters in Harvard University.* By John Quincy Adams, Late Boylston Professor of Rhetoric and Oratory. (2 vols., Cambridge, 1810).

40. JQA to TBA, October 28, 1791, APM 375.

41. *Writings,* I, 110 ff.

42. *Ibid.,* also p. 115 ff.

43. "Lelius" in the Boston *American Apollo,* March 29, 1793. The article was mentioned in his diary that day (APM 22), and the implication, as well as the signature (which he probably had previously employed) and style, clearly suggest that it was his own composition. The article was dated March 28, and on the day previous his diary recorded that he "wrote diligently this evening," and on March 26, that he "read" and "wrote" to little purpose. He had been reading "Junius," no doubt for style, as he did for his "Columbus" articles at the end of the year.

44. Diary, especially January 11, 1792, APM 21.

45. *Writings,* I, 134; JA to JQA, January 27, February 19, 1793, APM 376.

46. He lost the case on April 12, and was "very unwell" all next day. Diary, APM 21. The journal that he started on that day of illness, April 13, was continued less than a week, then skipped to a few May entries. APM 20.

47. Journal, May 16, 1792, APM 20; also quoted in Seward, *Adams,* pp. 55, 56.

48. Journal, May 4, 1792, APM 20.

49. Diary, 1792, *passim,* APM 21.

50. Daniel Sargent, Jr., to JQA, July 20, 1795, APM 380.

51. He referred to the club by that name in letters he wrote after going abroad in 1794: *e.g.,* JQA to Nathan Frazier, Jr., March 25, and JQA to T.S. and Daniel Sargent, Jr., May 24, 1795, APM 128. The "raffish" talk may be deduced from the remarks he made in these clever but vulgar letters to his friends. Many of the references are Shakespearean and too esoteric to decipher, but even so it is astonishing that he should have carefully kept copies of such letters. Perhaps he was more egotistic than sensuous! The talk is called "unnatural" here because of his subsequent repudiation of the rakish role which he said he had performed with "little grace or enjoyment," and which he attributed to the "damnable attractions" of some of his Boston associates. See JQA to John Gardner, July 15, 1795, APM 128.

52. John Gardner to JQA, September 26, 1795, APM 380, saying that the hours he had spent in his company had been "the most pleasant and certainly the most profitable that I can recollect in my life."

53. Diary, February 23, 28, March 20, May 24, 1792, *et passim,* APM 21.

54. Diary, November 8, 15, 1792, APM 21.

55. On June 12, he had escorted "R. & M. Frazier home" from Colonel Colman's. Diary, under dates, APM 21. On the flyleaf of this diary the name Frazier is written three times, but the initial of the first name is hard to decipher. It looks like an "N", although one would like to think it an "M"!

56. *E.g.,* January 30, 1793, APM 22.

57. APM 223. These elegies are at the end of the volume, with no page numbers. The second is dated September 16, 1792, although the diary would suggest September 20.

58. Diary, September 2, 1792, APM 21.

59. See the plan of Boston made by Lieut. Page for the British troops in 1775, in the *Memorial History of Boston* (4 vols.,

Boston, 1881), III, iv. The Beacon Street, or "new" mall, was not formally developed until 1815, but this map indicates that two rows of trees were already planted there in 1775, although it does not label these a "mall." See also Nathaniel B. Shurtleff, *A Topographical and Historical Description of Boston* (3rd edition, Boston, 1891), pp. 326, 368-372.

60. Diary, August 27, September 3, 7, October 3, 1792, APM 21.
61. Diary, October 15, 20, 1792, APM 21.
62. Alexander Hamilton to JA, June 25, September 9, JA to AA, November 24, December 2, 3, 9, JA to JQA, December 5, 9, 1792, APM 375; also JA to AA, January 9, 14, 1793, in *Letters of John Adams, Addressed to His Wife,* II, 117, 119.
63. *Writings,* I, 115.
64. *Ibid.,* p. 123.

Chapter Nine

1. *Memoirs,* I, 31, 32, 51, 52. This material is also in APM 23.
2. He was bled on June 18. Diary, June and July entries, APM 25. One reason for the delay was because of Secretary Hamilton's temporary absence from office when JQA went to Philadelphia. It also proved difficult to get sailing accommodations from Boston.
3. JA to JQA, May 29, 1794, APM 377.
4. *Writings,* I, 193 ff.; diary, June 29, 1794, APM 25.
5. See "Isabella" to "Mr. Cabot," January 8, and Cabot to AA, January 17, 30, 1794, APM 377.
6. See Chapter Eight.
7. JA to JQA, January 27, 1793, APM 376. His father called him a "Faneuil Hall orator."
8. Diary, April 26, 1793, APM 22.
9. JA to AA, December 30, 1793, January 9, 1794, APM 376, 377.
10. Bemis, *John Quincy Adams and the Foundations of American Foreign Policy,* p. 40n; *Memoirs,* I, 27.
11. Diary, December 31, 1793, APM 22.
12. Diary, May 13, 20, 21, 22, 23, 31, 1794, APM 25.
13. June 14, 1794, *ibid.*
14. *Memoirs,* I, 7.

238   John Quincy Adams: *The Critical Years*

15. JQA to TBA, November 20, 1793, APM 376.
16. JQA to AA, November 7, 1795, APM 380. This was written from a little Dutch seaport where he had been "cooped up" for three weeks, waiting for wind and weather. His father's letter, saying that he wished JQA could come home in several years and get married, is under August 25, 1795, APM 380.
17. Diary, May 6, 1791, APM 19.
18. Kindly Charles Adams never seemed to have much luck in companions. Even his "chum" at college was "rusticated" for stealing, and he himself was once seriously involved with some college rioters. Later in New York City he became an adulator of General Von Steuben. There is a good deal about him in Janet Whitney, *Abigail Adams*. William Smith, brother of Abigail Adams, and father of a "little tribe" of girls in Lincoln, Massachusetts, not only deserted his family but seems to have been tried on charges of counterfeiting in New York State in 1785. See Catherine L. Smith to AA, October 26, and MC to AA, December 10, 1785, and MC to AA, March 22, 1786, APM 366, 367. On John Adams' drinking of hard cider and his dislike of tippling houses, see *Three Episodes of Massachusetts History*, II, 686, 789.
19. JQA to John Gardner, The Hague, July 15, 1795, APM 128.
20. See *Writings*, I, 158.
21. Diary, APM 22.
22. This was pointed out long ago by the editor of the *Memoirs*, I, 27.
23. He had told his Aunt Eliza of the "cold apathy" that had taken possession of his breast. ES to JQA, June 9, 1794, APM 377. See also JQA to AA, November 7, 1795, APM 380, about his "blunted sensations." Of course these are references to the frigidity of his romantic feelings, but one wonders if such a condition may not have tempered his feelings in general.
24. Dairy, March 30, April 2, 4, 1793, APM 22.
25. Diary, June 19, 20, 1793, *ibid.*
26. April 23, May 14, 15, 16, 27, 28, June 4, 1793, *ibid.*
27. June 28, July 5, 12, 1793, *ibid.*
28. November 26, 28, 1793, *ibid.*
29. December 1, 2, 3, 1793, *ibid.*

30. Diary, March 1, 4, 1794, APM 25.

31. February 6 (when he also escaped "one bad adventure" while out walking after dining at Hall's), March 26, 29, 31, April 1, 6, 22, 1794, *ibid.*

32. May 26, 1794, *ibid.*

33. *Memoirs*, I, 28. Perhaps this is what John Adams referred to, in his letter to AA, January 9, 1794, APM 377.

34. She had said that he would be "destitute of his Father's ambition" if he did not become a great man. MC to AA, August 17, 1785, APM 365.

35. *Writings*, I, 149, 178; diary, November 22, 1793, APM 22; "Americanus No. I," the Boston *Independent Chronicle*, December 19, 1793.

36. *Writings*, I, 135 ff. It appears from his diary (APM 22) that he had begun to write as early as April 8, having been in his father's company several days before, as was invariably the case before he would begin to "write." He was reading Vattel on April 11, and making as much headway as possible despite many interruptions. Curiously, he did not mention "Marcellus No. I" in his diary when it appeared in the *Centinel* on April 24, nor "Marcellus No. II" on May 4, but he did record "No. III" on May 11. Washington's proclamation was not published in the *Chronicle* until May 2.

37. *Life in a New England Town*, pp. 33, 37. His identification of private and public morality went back at least to his commencement speech of 1787. See Chapter Four.

38. *Writings*, I, 7n; *Letters of Mrs. Adams*, p. 343.

39. The *Independent Chronicle*, May 9, 1793. There was also an interesting comment on "Marcellus" by "A Neuter" in the *Centinel* on May 18. Articles which appeared in the *Massachusetts Mercury* on May 22 and 31 were called "infamous" and "scandalous" by JQA in his diary (APM 22). However, it is difficult to identify them, unless they are heavily disguised lampoons of John Adams, as "Beef-loving Jack."

40. The Boston *Chronicle*, April 25, 1793; the Boston *Gazette*, May 13, June 10, 1793.

41. He received a visit and request from the selectmen on April 30. The address was published as *An Oration Pronounced*

76. JQA wrote in his diary, January 3, 1784, APM 25, "Tired of always getting the victory. And to how little purpose!" On the town meeting, see *Writings,* I, 183n. Brother Charles wrote, "You must be your father's own son. . . ."

77. JA to JQA, January 3, JA to AA, January 6, April 7, 27, 1794, APM 377.

78. JA to AA, January 6, TBA to AA, January 22, 1784, APM 377.

79. JA to AA, May 27, in *Letters of John Adams, Addressed to His Wife,* II, 163; JA to JQA, May 29, ES to JQA, June 9, Martha Washington to AA, July 19, 1794, APM 377.

80. JA to JQA, May 26, 1794.

81. There is no record of how his mother felt, however. One wonders. She wanted both JQA and TBA to have miniatures painted of themselves, with locks of hair enclosed, before they left. She said she would pay whatever might be the expense. AA to JQA, July 20, 1794, APM 377.

82. JQA to John Gardner, July 15, 1795, APM 128.

83. His father must have been more affluent than in 1790! It was an order on Dutch bankers for 5000 guilders. JQA to CA, November 20, 1794, APM 126. One of the first things JQA did was to arrange to have a little money paid regularly to his Aunt Eliza to assist in the education of her son. He also turned over his little fortune in 1795 for his brother Charles to invest, at a handsome commission, soon after hearing the news of Charles' marriage to Sally Smith. One can only assume that this was still another act of kindness on JQA's part, revealing a side to his character that was usually concealed. As might have been anticipated, all the money was lost within a few years.

INDEX